# ALDOUS HUXLEY

*Books by the same Author*

THE ART OF ERNEST HEMINGWAY

ARTHUR KOESTLER

TOMORROW REVEALED : A HISTORY OF THE FUTURE

# ALDOUS HUXLEY

*A Literary Study by*

JOHN ATKINS

———

*New and Revised Edition*

**THE ORION PRESS**

NEW YORK

PRINTED IN GREAT BRITAIN
BY PHOTOLITHOGRAPHY
UNWIN BROTHERS LIMITED
WOKING AND LONDON

# CONTENTS

# ACKNOWLEDGMENTS

To Mr. Aldous Huxley, who advised on material and answered some questions.

To John Murray (Publishers) Ltd., for permission to quote " The Inheritor " by Leonard Huxley from his book *Anniversaries and Other Poems*.

THE Memorial Gathering for Aldous Huxley at Friends' House on 17th December 1963 was the occasion for spoken tributes by David Cecil, Kenneth Clark, Stephen Spender and his brother Julian. A more lasting result was the preparation and publication of a Memorial Volume bearing the simple title of *Aldous Huxley 1894–1963*, which appeared in 1965. Twenty-seven prominent people from a wide variety of walks of life contributed. It is in the nature of memorial volumes that they should praise their subject, and this one was no exception. But it is of special note that what most contributors wished to praise was not Huxley's significance as a writer—in fact, they were not all agreed on that—but on his personal qualities. Nearly all of them seemed at pains to stress that the popular image of Huxley as an immensely intellectual but essentially cold man was entirely false; that the quality that impressed itself most deeply on his friends was his human warmth, his capacity for pity and his abiding charity. (I myself can attest to this. A friend of mine, a writer, who was living in great poverty in Paris before the last war, desperately wrote begging letters to all the important and successful writers he could think of. Among the few who responded was Aldous Huxley.)

But if he is to be remembered it will be for his literary qualities and these, in their range if not their depth, were unique for his time. He had a capacity for assimilation of material and deduction from it that seemed almost miraculous. Kenneth Clark said it was extraordinary how much he contrived to know about artists, often fairly minor ones. " I have spent many years of my life studying Alberti and Piero ", he writes, " and in the end I seem to know far less than Aldous had learnt in a few weeks, by some miraculous combination of intellect and intuition. " That was the quality he seemed to have in abundance: intuition. It was this which surprised so many of his readers, that a man who seemed to be the supreme product of intellectual discipline was in fact closer to nature than most of them, for what is intuition if not a direct perception of life's processes? And it wasn't only his mind that seemed attuned, it was also his senses, despite the fact that on the surface he was half blind—and yet he would see something in a painting or glimpse something in a landscape that his keener-sighted but possibly more distracted (shall we say attached?) friends usually missed. And behind the senses and the intuition lay " an incredibly well furnished intelligence ", as one of his friends put it. Late in his life his house burned down, and he lost his complete library, assembled over a lifetime. In the midst of their commiseration, his friends noticed two things. One was that Huxley was able to accept this blow with superb equanimity, merely remarking to one of them: " You are looking at a man without a past ". And the other was the negation of this, the fact that Huxley's past was stored in his mind and that death alone could destroy it. By some rare alchemy feeling and knowledge had been digested into a harmonious whole, and the resultant seemed to have a life of its own.

Huxley was, to use his own terminology, a very successful amphibian. He was able to live creatively in a number of worlds in a way that has been denied most men since knowledge proliferated during the nineteenth century. Isaiah Berlin suggests that no-one since Spinoza " has believed so passionately or coherently or fully in the principle that knowledge alone liberates, not merely knowledge of physics or history or physiology or psychology, but an altogether wider panorama of possible knowledge which embraced forces, open and occult, which this infinitely retentive and omnivorous reader was constantly discovering with alternate horrors and hope." And then Berlin tells us, what all his friends tell us, that contrary to common belief, he was not a walking encyclopaedia. He had a charm and a dignity totally at variance with the popular image. In fact, the best of Huxley was possibly not exhibited by his writings. The fact that so many people thought of him as a cold-blooded sermoniser does suggest that an important part of his personality did not come through the printed word. There was, indeed, a mechanical and derivative element in his writing, and this unfortunately tended to catch the eye—or the mind—of the reader. One of his Central European admirers, Dennis Gabor, says that his Hungarian readers, for instance, lost touch with him (or he lost touch with them) during the period 1931–37. I believe, and I shall revert to this later, that this period was in fact central to his development and that it is a grave misunderstanding to regard it as a temporary departure from the true path. It was not always possible to follow Huxley along the paths he indicated, and it was particularly difficult to persuade a European that a policy that succeeded against a jaded and guilty British imperialism might have equal success against a mad Nazism. Nor would it have done. But Huxley needed to go through this kind of belief, this simplification " that a child could grasp but only an angel could follow ", before he could reach the supreme sanity of his later years. Again, it is possible that the message did not always come through as clearly as he wished. But there were other times when he picked out, perhaps from the work of another artist, truths that were still only dimly felt by his contemporaries. In describing the *Prisons* of Piranesi he refers to " pure and terrible states of spiritual confusion ", and Jacob Zeitlin was prompted to see in this a hint of autobiography. Critics were too apt to dismiss Huxley *because* of his polymorphism. But it was this quality that sometimes caused him to recede, not from sanity, but from normal human blindness. And that was where people lost sight of him.

*

There has been one other book on Aldous Huxley since the first edition of this one. This appeared in 1962 under the title of *Aldous Huxley: A Cynical Salvationist*, and it was by an Indian author, Sisirkumar Ghose. Indian scholars have certain advantages over the rest of us in assessing Huxley, particularly the middle and later Huxley. There is no need to take offence at the word " cynical " for Huxley himself advised a protective coating of cynicism for modern man, providing he knew when and where to stop. But it is clear that Professor Ghose is judging the writer and not the man, as he has every right to do. " The central flaw in Huxley is ", he says, " perhaps not so much intellectual as emotional, it is, briefly, his lack of charity." Few people found intellectual flaws in him, except those who doubted his depth. And many, perhaps most, of his readers sensed the emotional disability, but it was this fault that all his friends were at pains to disavow. Ghose says that most of Huxley's errors are caused by " want of love ". But Ghose's study only goes up to *After Many a Summer*, 1939. It is not enough to base a judgment on. To find the spirit of charity in the early fiction—and it is in the creative work that we should look for it—would be a mug's game. But there are glimmerings, if awkward, in *After Many a Summer*. And in his last novel, *Island*, there is possibly a bit too much attempted charity in the wrong places.

Professor Ghose is convinced that Huxley is not interested in any man as a man. This is another statement of the same point. But it is a dubious point. Huxley was not a born novelist though a brilliant self-made one. It is objected that he is incapable of drawing living characters, though here again the assertion is too sweeping. Both Mrs Viveash and Lucy Tantamount, to mention only two early ones from a vast gallery, are as lively portraits of the living death-wish as one could hope to find. His characters merely express viewpoints. Most of them, yes. But it is not a fair inference to say that he therefore lacks charity or does not care for the humanity of any man. How many of us would pass the test of charity if it were made dependent on one's ability to create character? Ghose quotes Kettle as saying that in Huxley " there is no respect for life ". Worse and worse. This is superficial criticism, instant criticism, and one does not need to turn to his friends to know that it is untrue. Why the later pre-occupation with social problems and the disasters facing mankind if he did not care? After all, he was not a post-graduate student seeking a Ph.D. He was not a newspaper sensationalist. He cared greatly, and if this care was not clearly reflected in his fiction it was because fiction reflects a world which appears to be galloping to perdition with gay abandon. In *Island* his concern rose to the top, yet *Island* is not a very good novel. It's an odd world we live in.

\*

One of the oddest things about Aldous Huxley is that in 1920 he was a leader of the moderns and in 1960, without having become a reactionary or a fuddy-duddy, he had become an upholder of traditional values. We are accustomed to the rebel who becomes a blimp but this was not Huxley. The people he had mocked in 1920 would still have been mocked in 1960 if they had still existed—but they didn't. This was the explanation of his strange and rather lonely position in his later life. The world was still crazy but it was crazy in a different way from what it had been. Inside the young Huxley the " eternal values " of Western civilisation had not really been touched. Later he unwrapped them. In a hundred years time he will be regarded as a rather eccentric spokesman for the true Establishment of our time, not the bogus one that masquerades in the press.

*Adonis and the Alphabet*, 1956, was his triumph as an essayist. In addition to the old urbanity there is a far more serious sense of purpose. They are in effect essays on education, the education of the human race as well as its children, and one inevitably compares them with *Proper Studies*, greatly to the disadvantage of the latter. The difference is simply that in the period between the two publications Huxley had worked out a valid conception of man, and therefore knew what he was dealing with. In the earlier volume he is merely, often awkwardly, feeling his way. The later essays lie in the shadow of *Ends and Means* and *The Perennial Philosophy* and benefit enormously.

And it is the traditional values of our culture that are offered to us, but they have been carefully examined and refurbished in places where they had become seedy.

There was one pitfall into which many of our modern mystics and Zen-addicts have fallen headlong and which Huxley managed to avoid. This was the belief that to quote knowledge was to understand it. It had always been a virtue of his to realise that you cannot transmit understanding. You feel it, even grow it, like an extra skin. There is an academic pleasure to be gained from repeating the wisdom of the medieval and Buddhist mystics but it is fruitless to imagine that repetition of another's wisdom will make you one whit the wiser. One can even fault Huxley for over-quoting in *The Perennial Philosophy*—and perhaps in this respect this noble and well-intentioned book may have the status of a delightful *objet d'art*, like a Ming vase. But he came to re-cognise the fault. In the essay " Knowledge and Under-standing " he said we ought to know all we can about the understanding of the past, but we should not take it too seriously. " We must know all about them, while remaining acutely aware that such knowledge is not the same as under-standing and that understanding will come to us only when we have substracted what we know and made ourselves void and virgin, free as we were when we were not."

That man is his own worst enemy is a long recognised truth but Huxley brought a new dimension to it from his studies in the perennial philosophy. It is our human selves that frame the ideologies and engineer the collective suicides that disgrace our culture. He was optimistic enough to believe that life is invincible and that in man's being there is a " non-human otherness " (which Wordsworth had described as " something far more deeply interfused ") which represents our part of the godhead and will be largely instrumental in saving us. Or helping us to save ourselves. Huxley was immensely excited by the " do-it-yourself " movement, and there are few ways in which he could have demonstrated his strong contact with everyday life so clearly. It is a safe bet that most thinkers and philosophers of his background and erudition would be mildly contemptuous of such a movement, which was essentially amateur and could never hope to produce work of real excellence. But never mind, warns Huxley. It is the critic who is wrong to judge by such standards. The modern Jack of All Trades may produce horrible hashes and medleys which might offend even the least-formed taste—except, of course, that they don't, but that's another matter. The significance of this movement is not aesthetic, nor was it ever meant to be. It is therapeutic, a guarantee against boredom and an antidote to TV and other passive forms of entertainment. " Altogether admirable ", says Huxley (" Liberty, Quality, Machinery ").

In his later years Huxley was largely exercised by the insane squandering of resources that characterises our society. We live like " drunken sailors ", " the irresponsible heirs of a millionaire uncle ". Again and again he returns to the charge. " How long can this spending spree go on?" (" Tomorrow and Tomorrow "). Very soon man will have to learn to live on his income. Not everyone agrees that man will learn the lesson in time. The pundits are pessimistic. Sir Charles Darwin does not believe that man will succeed in stabilising his population. Harrison Brown also has his doubts and in addition is not convinced that man will be able to make the transition to new and less concentrated sources of energy and raw materials, or abolish war. But if man can avoid regression to a simple agrarian existence it will probably be by the adoption of a completely controlled and collectivised industrial organisation. In other words the nightmare of Brave New World was on the horizon, certainly much closer than Huxley had imagined in the 1930's. (He had really started to write it as a joke, a parody of H. G. Wells.) During his last years he seemed almost obsessed by this vision he had conjured up, and returned to it again and again. But there was also another vision, one of complete breakdown and return to savagery, and he expressed it in *Ape and Essence*. It was not one on which he liked to dwell. But if it came it would be the direct consequence of a problem that at times seems insoluble; the tremendous rate of growth of population in underdeveloped countries. Not even a vast international Marshall Plan providing subsidies in grain, money, machinery and trained manpower will save us. Huxley's mind oscillated unhappily between the two alternatives. In " Usually Destroyed " he makes a few " reasonable guesses " about the sum of human misery we can look forward to. More people will be hungrier and malnutrition will be more widespread. Birth control measures will, by and large, fail. Improvements in agriculture will be unable to catch up with the expanding population. The processes of erosion and deforestation will be speeded up. There will be increasing political and social unrest, culminating in wars, revolutions and counter-revolutions. The power of the central governments will increase and individual liberty will diminish. If we go on fighting wars the future must be totalitarian. That is, if we don't destroy ourselves altogether.

In the end these essays become rather tedious. They are all good essays but suffer from being read in quick succession. (It is never fair to read essays in this way. Even the most erudite writer will tend to repeat himself.) There is a central theme and a lot of marginal themes, but they are not developed. Each piece of writing is a new beginning. One feels that the author is performing a rather dignified dance around half a dozen fixed points, and after a while we realise that the pattern is merely being repeated. In fact, our major criticism of Huxley, who regarded himself as a serious critic of his culture, was that, with the single exception of *Ends and Means*, he never got down to a penetrative critique of the society he appeared to understand so well. He kept starting and stopping. And he was too liable to lose himself in those by-ways of culture he enjoyed observing so greatly. There is a good example in this collection, " Hyperion to a Satyr ", which is, quite frankly, a wallowing in dirt. Dirt is his subject and it is not one we are surprised to find him choosing. He has always been seen, even reprimanded, as Swift's successor in the field of disgust, and like Swift he chose his subject. The dirt is not metaphorical, as sex is described by some perverts, but dirt *per se*. This purports to be an essay on the Natural History of Personal and Social Dirt but in fact it is an excuse for the full unleashing of Huxley's disgust for all that festers, stinks and breeds. And this is his Achilles heel, for where there is breeding there is stench. Breeding *en masse* is mankind's most dangerous activity. The whole thing stinks to high heaven.

\*

I observed in the first edition of this book that Huxley felt that the modern artist had succumbed to a sense of boredom which he tried to eliminate by the endless pursuit of novelty. If this was true during the first part of his life, how much more true is it today! The development of art today, through *tachisme* and action painting to pop art and op art, reflects neuroticism rather than sensibility. As I have said, the ultra-modern Huxley was really a traditionalist at heart. Living in a jazzy society, he felt the jazz rhythms, but underneath he was as susceptible to life's little ironies as Thomas Hardy himself. His novels were sexy, but he quickly developed a distaste for sex which later rationalised itself into a fear of sex at large as man's greatest enemy. In recent literature boredom with sex has been expressed partly through a cynical distaste, partly through scenes of violence which symbolically show the dragon mastered. But what did Huxley do? In *Adonis and the Alphabet* he advocated a mode of sex activity called *karezza*, according to which the man does not allow himself to have an orgasm. I think three comments may be made on this recommendation. First of all, it harmonises admirably with Huxley's demand for some measure of birth control; secondly, it does away with the orgasm which I imagine Huxley regarded as a deplorable aspect of man's ungovernable, animal nature; and thirdly, and most cogently, I feel certain that no healthy young man would be capable of practising *karezza*. It belongs to an old man's philosophy.

Huxley lived through some of the most revolutionary changes in man's history and, after a kind of hypnotised fascination, he withdrew. Ultimately hardly any of the new things were going to improve man's lot: neither communism nor behaviorism, sexual freedom nor technological advance, educational reform nor new movements in art. In the future loomed the end of the individual, as he knew him and admired him. In a sense, he acted out the bewilderment of the refined, highly educated product of the Enlightenment. He was a sort of diplodocus, carrying more knowledge than his cranium could bear. Aircraft, action painting and slogan politics all pointed in the same direction, and it was one that had no place for him. He himself would die and his type could not survive. The Brave New World which he had not invented but merely foreseen could not accommodate his free and roving intelligence. He was the last of the polymaths, still tackling human problems in every sphere in which they operated. No other writer who has emerged since the first war attempted anything on the same scale. The modern tendency, encouraged by our universities, is the restriction of spheres of thought to the smallest possible areas. One wonders how communication will be effected when the final division of labour takes place.

What ought a modern man to do? is a question he tries to answer in *Literature and Science*, 1963. The book begins with a pertinent question: " Snow or Leavis?", and he proceeds to demolish the two learned asses. A man should make the best of all possible worlds—and it had always been an article of faith with Huxley that we live in many worlds simultaneously. " My own belief is that he should try to make the best of all the worlds in which, willy-nilly, he has to live—the world of stars and the world of astro-physics, the world of crowded halls and the world of silence, the worlds of grey theory, green life and many-coloured poetry." Our job is to breach the spiritual Iron Curtain. There is growing recognition of the inescapable fact that men and women are multiple amphibians inhabiting half a dozen disparate universes at the same time. The partial approach to his world is doomed if man hopes to solve his problems. He must advance on all fronts: the chemical and the psychological, the verbal and the non-verbal, the individual, the cultural and the genetic. It is quite clear that not even the most brilliant individual can even approach such a task today. Huxley was referring to the coordination of man's labours, and he gave as an example of the way ahead the correlation of Freud's work with that of other researchers, not only in psychology (this is obvious) but also in other disciplines. The next, and perhaps the final, revolution will be the psychological one. We are now gathering our forces, enlisting pure and applied psychology, neurology, bio-chemistry and pharmacology, for a massed assault on the secret corners of the mind. The Victorians knew nothing about the human mind. By the twenty-first century we will know everything. But imagine the danger! How exciting to think that knowledge of the mind will be pushed to its furthest reaches in the foreseeable future—but how appalling to think of the power that will be wielded by Psychic Energy Commissions, " operating huge secret laboratories dedicated, not to our hopelessly old-fashioned ideals of mass murder and collective suicide, but to the more constructive task of man's definite domestication and total enslavement." The religious, political, economic, industrial and nationalistic revolutions have come and gone. In comparison with the coming psychological revolution they were but ripples in the ocean of conservatism. Just wait for *that* one!

*

The art of abstraction was a necessary faculty in the building of civilisation. But abstraction carried with it its own built-in danger, the stultifying effect of prejudice. Having learnt how to abstract and to generalise, man had to rediscover the art of looking at the world plain and simple. But it hasn't been easy.
*Brave New World Revisited*, 1965, reviews the various ways in which the New World can be and is being brought into existence. This is no place to review a review—it is a model piece of writing in so far as it is expressed in simple and direct language, with none of the ambiguity or density that sometimes spoils such work. In general, Huxley claims that we are moving towards Brave New World much more rapidly than he

had originally expected, and that his own vision of a possible future is more probable than 1984. In simple terms, it is more likely that the lust for power will be satisfied by providing pleasure than by providing pain. It is far more sensible and far more likely to succeed.

Man can be prepared for this new world and will accept it far more willingly if he can be taught to see not reality but a substitute for reality. Substitutes for reality are abstractions, symbols and verbalisations, and it is by the production of these three types of experience and knowing, already far advanced, that the tyrants of the future will effect the control of their subjects' minds. Irrational propaganda, which is what they will supply, depends for its effectiveness on a general failure to understand the nature of symbols, says Huxley. Simple-minded people tend to equate the symbol with what it stands for, as advertisers well know. In the commercial world men do not buy oranges, they buy vitality; they do not buy a car, but prestige. And the same process operates in the political world. Men do not support a leader, they ensure security; they do not kill Jews, they improve their standard of living. The real danger is that education of children, already affected by this trend, shall be swamped by it. Education for freedom must be, among other things, an education in the proper use of language. A great deal of research has been done in recent years on the relationship between words and sentences with the things they represent. The materials and the resources exist but whether they will be used and exploited in the interests of individual men rather than collectivities is still extremely doubtful.

In this line of attack Huxley was only returning to a field where he had long been active. Several essays in *Adonis and the Alphabet*, for instance, were concerned with the obscurantist effect of the verbalised symbol. In " Mother " he urged the value of direct experience. Whenever we are dealing with mystery, the verbalised concept is less satisfactory as a means of presentation than the pictorial or diagrammatic symbol. This is to admit the potency of symbols (which no-one denies) and to deplore the insufficiency of our religious symbols. The Hindu religion has been more successful in symbolising Nature and the processes of continuous creation and destruction than the western religions. Nature has been monopolised by science. We must learn how to express the reality of both worlds—the world of clear conceptual knowledge and the world of obscure understanding, " the world of verbal analysis and the world of comprehensive symbols, the world of science and the world of religion and metaphysics." The title essay in this volume, " Adonis and the Alphabet ", urges us not to take language too seriously. Nature presents us with a complex of *Gestalts* to which words and sentences, however rich, can only approximate. Language is serious as an instrument, but it is a crude interpreter of direct experience.

As a logical result of this approach to language and reality, Huxley became increasingly interested in the possibilities of non-verbal education in his later years. There are really two points to concern us here: first, that we should not regard symbols, any symbols, as being interchangeable with reality; and secondly, that it is unbalanced to rely too uncritically on verbal symbols, for there are others which are equally potent and in some cases more closely aligned with direct experience. The two innovations which Huxley felt held out most hope for the human race in their present unhappy condition were mind-improving drugs and non-verbal education. Psychotherapy and mescalin might, between them, help us to use more than the ten per cent of our capacities that we do in fact use at present. According to Isherwood, he actually planned a novel which " explores the problem of the meaning of words and the utter inadequacy of all existing language."

*

Serious people today urge commitment, not non-attachment, the Huxleyan ideal. Of course, the two are not mutually exclusive, for non-attachment means non-attachment to sensual life and urges spiritual commitment. But the kind of political commitment urged by contemporary writers is anchored deep in consumer goods and satisfactions.

In the thirties and again today, Huxley suggests the visitor from another planet. He sees salvation in ways that have little appeal for his fellow-men. Since the last war we have seen a rise of interest in Zen but it has not been metaphysical. With some it is a hard-headed experiment in a different technique of living, with others it is a phase in the search for novelty —the last thing Huxley would have recommended. And in both cases we can attribute the interest to the failures and unsatisfied demands of contemporary life. The reaction has been automatic, not (as with Huxley) a step in a determined programme of enlightenment.

The first edition of this book culminated in *Brave New World*. It seemed to me at the time that this was the peak of his achievement. It is certainly his best known work and, if we are to judge by dozens of University and College Courses in Mod. Lit., it is his major achievement. Its inventiveness is tremendous, and its vast progeny should not obscure the fact that at the time of publication it was highly original. It is also a fact that, during the later years of his life, Huxley returned again and again to his vision of the Brave New World. He devoted one book to a revisitation, and in his essays he continually reverted to the ideas and the techniques of that earlier vision. It fascinated him and frightened him. And yet, now his work is complete and we can look at the full cycle, I feel that Brave New World is not really the crux of his thought. The watershed, the moment to which all before led and all after departed from, is *Ends and Means*. After 1937, but particularly after the war that followed, the future, whether hypothetical or prophetic, was seen through spectacles coloured by the perennial philosophy. Huxley's thought had been permanently influenced and his remedies and solutions for a sick world were all envisaged in the light of " otherness ". So let's take another look at *Ends and Means*.

I hope a personal note will not be out of place here. Before I read *Ends and Means* I was a fairly conventional

Marxist, although I had never quite felt sufficient identity between Marxism and Communism to join the Communist Party. But Strachey's *The Coming Struggle for Power* was a persuasive document. I suppose I must have felt certain intellectual qualms and insufficiencies to have even opened *Ends and Means*—it was not the kind of reading most Left-wingers indulged in. But by the time I had finished reading I knew that it had raised certain questions that neither Marx nor Strachey nor Shelvankar (author of *Ends Are Means*)[1] had answered or, I was afraid, considered worth answering. And they seemed to me to be very important questions indeed. I suppose, apart from the cogent argument contained in the book, there were two factors which compelled me (and thousands of others) to take this book seriously. One was that a leading and extremely intelligent but previously uncommitted writer had taken up a positive position. Secondly, although every thinking person knew that a catastrophic war was on the way, the collective will seemed strangely paralysed. Marxism, for all its economic value, showed no way out of that dilemma. Huxley at least indicated a possible solution. Nothing was very hopeful at that late stage, but what he offered was better than nothing.

How does *Ends and Means* stand up to examination in the light of the thirty years that have passed since publication? I doubt if the general thesis has been invalidated, but some of the emphases have been proved wrong. In his first chapter ("The Contemporary Starting Point") he declared that the non-attached man is the ideal man. A sense of urgency ran through the book, suggesting that if man did not put aside his inordinate attachments to bodily sensations and lusts, his craving for power and possessions, his anger and his hatred, his exclusive loves, his wealth, his fame and social position, then he would rapidly bring about his own destruction. Today it is quite clear that man has not progressed in this respect and

---

[1] Shelvankar's book came after Huxley's, of course, but pretty hotfoot. I suppose the Comrades were worried. Huxley had raised issues which were better left buried.

that he is even further removed from non-attachment than he was at the time Huxley wrote. The restraints and inhibitions which used to control the behaviour of men and women before the war have been swept away over large areas of the world, and a freedom of conduct uncontrolled by any code of morality flourishes today as it has not flourished for at least seventeen centuries. Yet man still survives, though it is true he often seems to be perilously close to the precipice. It is quite normal for prophets to foresee doom as being imminent when in fact it is little more than a cloud on the horizon. It some-times seems that we have an unconscious wisdom which guides us, despite our blunders and follies, so that, without any conscious planning, we do in fact reject the particular acts which would plunge us all to perdition. We play about agonisingly with hydrogen bombs but we don't actually drop them on populations. Over a hundred pompous nationalisms scream abuse at each other, and even slaughter each other, but without quite going to the extreme point of no return. It is part of man's history that he should test many different types of (for example) government, and go to war over them, and finally agree to let them all exist contemporaneously. In our bad-tempered world the United States of America, Great Britain, Sweden, Spain, the Soviet Union, the Chinese People's Republic, Yugoslavia, two Congo Republics, the Union of South Africa and Saudi Arabia all manage to exist together, swearing eternal enmity and managing to survive.

In the same chapter Huxley claimed that the world is in regression. Technological advance is rapid but without progress in charity this is useless. Is it possible that we are in fact progressing in charity, without it being visible? Move-ments of charity are not easy to see. It is true, we don't give the appearance of being a particularly charitable species, yet the fact that we do manage to rub along even when the dice appear to be completely loaded against us suggests that perhaps we have a little more sense, which may mean a little more capacity for charity, than appears on the surface. On the whole, it is a common fault of intellectuals, who can see cracks

in the structure invisible to others, to imagine that the danger
is greater than it actually is and to discount the ability to take
counter-measures.

In his chapter on " The Planned Society " Huxley exhibited
this weakness in a way that it is possible to check.   " ' The
defence of democracy against Fascism ' ", he wrote (using
quotation marks to stress the popularity of the phrase), " entails inevitably the transformation of democracy into Fascism."
This is demonstrably untrue.  During the war Britain was
compelled to restrict civil liberties, but most of these have been
regained, and those that have not are not beyond recall, nor
were they essentially victims of the war against Fascism.
There is never complete agreement about whether a society is
becoming more or less free, but all we are concerned with now
is whether Huxley was justified in the use of such terms as
" inevitably " and " transformation ".  The answer is surely
that he was not.

But in other respects Huxley was extremely far-sighted.
It is always more satisfactory to test a writer's prophecies in
the field of fact rather than opinion, because opinion is rarely
measurable.  Those critics and thinkers who have insight
are capable of foreseeing events and situations which are
hidden from the practical men.  D. H. Lawrence was fully
aware that a catastrophic war was on the way when the experts
and practical politicians were convinced that another war was
unthinkable, and were messing about with such extraordinary
documents as the Kellogg Pact.  Huxley's declaration in his
chapter on " War " that " within a couple of generations from
now, it is quite possible that China will be an aggressive im-
perialist power ", was exceptionally percipient.  In the climate
of 1937 such things simply weren't envisaged.  In those days
most people could not take even the Soviet Union seriously
as a military power.  It was agreed that she had immense
armaments but most people seemed agreed that they would
not stand the strain of war for long.  Looking back, it seems
strange that the rise of China should not have been foreseen
as a certainty that should be entertained by any serious poli-

tician. But looking forward from 1937 few things seemed less likely.

This chapter on War must be one of the best of its kind by any writer. It is direct, admirably expressed and, to my mind, unanswerable. I can think of nothing that has happened in the past twenty years to invalidate it. The odd thing is that Huxley came within a hair's breadth of seeing just how war will be abolished, if it is ever abolished. Naturally, I don't know if war will be abolished but I do know how it will occur if it is. " Twentieth century armaments are an insurance against small and trivial wars ", he wrote, meaning that they are too costly and devastating. He did not take the extra step of declaring that ultimately the cost and the devastation will be too great even for large and important wars. Aldermaston marches are admirable things and only mental crooks laugh at them. Disarmament conferences are less admirable because more hypocritical, but few people would go so far as to denounce them publicly—I mean, the idea of a conference, not a particular one. But war will not be banned by these methods. This will come about when the governments realise they can no longer afford war production and that any resultant war would not be worth the risk. We are very near that point now. It's strange that Huxley did not see this, although I think he came to see it in later years. Complacency was impossible in 1937 and a degree of complacency is required to believe that mankind will not step over the brink. The notion of " brinkmanship " was unknown in 1937. Now I think it is fair to say that man is so constituted that he cannot overcome a danger without first playing with it.

Some of Huxley's ideas did come perilously close to nonsense (such as his historical revision based on the notion that Robespierre and the other Jacobin leaders were pacifists) but these were usually in the field of theory, not practical politics. They are on much the same level of those letters to the press (especially the *Daily Telegraph*) which assume that if Britain had built two more Dreadnoughts in 1910 there would have been no war, no communist revolution, no Hitler, no Labour government and no miniskirts.  But at one point Huxley classified himself as a " field naturalist ", which may be a strange claim for such a bookish gentleman to make, and yet he justified the claim. He observed facts and recorded them.  Later he was justified in making deductions from them.  His main fault was not of logic but of impatience.  Like all intellectual critics, he expected events to move more quickly than they do, probably because (subconsciously) a person who makes a prophecy likes to know whether it will be realised.

*

I would like to indulge in a minor departure here, though not amounting, I hope, to an irrelevancy.  In his chapter on " Education " Huxley made a brief but furious attack on the dramatic profession.  This, I well remember, roused the ire of St John Ervine in the Sunday papers, and that was no small thing.  " Acting inflames the ego in a way which few other professions do.  For the sake of enjoying regular emotional self-abuse, our societies condemn a considerable class of men and women to a perpetual inability to achieve non-attachment. It seems a high price to pay for our amusements."  " Condemn " is hardly the word.  Far more people clamour to enter the acting profession than ever make a career of it.

In view of this opinion, why did Huxley dramatise his story, " The Gioconda Smile "?  This appeared in the collection, *Mortal Coils*, published in 1922.  His attack on the dramatic profession was made in 1937.  And his play, *The Gioconda Smile*, was produced at the New Theatre, London, on 3rd June 1948.  Was it hypocrisy, or did Huxley feel he expressed something so important in the story it ought to be given maximum circulation?  And as no writer, apart from a megalomaniac dictator, can force his work upon the public, one has to use every possible device to get his message across.

What the query amounts to, is: did the story present the kind of non-attached character Huxley represented as the best type of human being?  One can say quite fairly that the story did not (it was far too early) but an effort was made to project him in the play. In the story the very Huxleyan-type persona, Mr Hutton, gloats over man's mortality. Returned from the funeral, " it pleased him to think that all these people would soon be dead too." But Hutton has pricks of conscience about his self-indulgent life, and it may be that in him we have the first glimpse of non-attachment struggling to be born—and perhaps Huxley felt this, and could not quite forget these intimations of a better life. Hutton felt disgusted with himself and determined to reform: " he would live by reason, he would be industrious, he would curb his appetites, he would devote his life to some good purpose." Naturally he didn't. With the first itch, a sexual one, he surrendered. When the end came, he felt that justice had been done, even if in a circuitous way. " He had been wanton and imbecile and irresponsible. Now Fate was playing as wantonly, as irresponsibly, with him. It was tit for tat, and God existed after all." And here we have another of Huxley's later convictions, that in this life you can never get something for nothing, that ultimately the books balance.

Huxley knew how to construct a play but his weakness in creating character, concealed to some extent in his novels, could not be hidden. There are simply two types: the persona (even the unlikely character of a country G.P. is made to fit into this pattern) and the mindless pleasure-seeker (who is always a woman). The theme, which is unchanged from the story, emphasises the diabolical aspect: a woman deliberately sends the man she loves to the gallows, out of pique. It is handled with great sophistication. Hutton comments that no-one today believes in the Gospel stories of people being possessed by the devil, and yet it is the most plausible explanation for some of the things we do. Why should we so constantly act against our own interests? Here we have the other side of the coin of " otherness ". It is Libbard, the doctor, who suggests that " God in me " can help us and protect us if we will only find him and trust in him. If God is real, so is the Devil, though he may be known under various disguises: Lucifer, Belial, Eros, Priapus. The mention of Belial suggests why Huxley's mind fled back over the years to this unpleasant little story, written a quarter of a century before. In the same year as the play was produced, *Ape and Essence* was published. In it we see Belial triumphant and the notion freely canvassed that men could be possessed. " Not I but trauma in me." But four years later he was to assert that the unfortunate nuns of Loudun had not been possessed but had been victims of mass hysteria, which is different. If there was a case of possession in that story it was of the civil and clerical authorities who hounded an innocent man to a dreadful death.

The discussion between Hutton and Libbard in Act II Scene 1 is *Ends and Means* dramatised. Later, when Hutton is in prison, awaiting the end, he undergoes conversion and explains his new faith to the warder. (One wonders at times if the phonemic similarity of Hutton and Huxley may have been deliberately suggestive.) He tells the warder that the good man is he who concurs with the "living, inspiring spirit of God within him", and the bad man resists it. This explained why Christ thought the scribes and Pharisees were worse than the publicans and sinners. The former were the solid, respectable men who shut themselves off from the spirit of God within them. " They were all so busy doing the proper, conventional things and all so cocksure of being the benefactors of the human race that it was impossible for them even to be aware of the spirit of God within them—much less to concur with it. And when you're in that state, I suppose you're in hell."

This had been added to the story. And so Huxley overcame his repugnance to the stage sufficiently to preach the perennial philosophy through the medium of drama.

*

*Ape and Essence* in the same year. Some people regarded it as a final surrender, even although *The Perennial Philosophy* had appeared only two years earlier. Others thought it was a temporary lapse. The writing and production of *The Gioconda Smile* surely proves it was not. It was a negative expression of his new beliefs. It is felt by some people that any form of negativism (whether imaginative or critical) is wicked, a betrayal of humanity. Concentration on evil will lead eventually to a surrender to evil, but indifference to evil will result in a defeat just as total. *Ape and Essence* begins with a reference to the most famous non-attached person of our age: " it was the day of Gandhi's assassination." The horrible events which are to be described are linked in the mind with one of the most senseless events even in our day. At the same time the saintly Gandhi is contrasted with the fictional Bob Briggs, who is all too much attached to the world's trivia and whose life is a squalid mess. The tone is set and before we have any excuse to put the book down we know the author's sympathies.

The point of this book is that we know that we are committing suicide and do nothing to stop it. The astonishing hypocrisy of our society is suggested by the instruction to send the film script containing the story to the incinerator *because no stamped addressed envelope had been sent for return!* Man always has a cover for his stupidity. Man's only hope is that Belial, or the evil in us, always goes to the limit and defeats itself. And then the Order of Things comes to the surface again—but how much destruction will have taken place in the meantime?

There is a similarity of pattern between *Brave New World* and this alternative vision. (Which is the more hopeless? Huxley does not tell us.) In each there is a non-conformist, one who has not " taken " the conditioning. Loola is the new rebel, and her conditioning is naturally less effective than the scientifically applied conditioning of Brave New World. But it works, just as it works in our own world, although the methods are still hit-or-miss. But they are improving all the time. Conditioning, of course, is a process that cannot be avoided and no-one is immune. Sometimes both the planned and the unplanned societies reach a strange unanimity of purpose. There seems, for instance, no hope for the conception of the mother. It has become a dirty word. In one society she has become unnecessary and her functions are remembered as an unpleasant nuisance; in the other she has not been abolished, because the skill is lacking, but she is deplored as the creator of monsters. The Arch-Vicar is another Mustapha Mond, equally intelligent but unable to call on the same techniques. Each is suave, cynical and well informed, making a virtue of expedience, and each explains his world to a naïve protestant. There is even a parallel of the Savage Reservation—the Hots, the incorrigibles, those who don't or won't fit in, providing an escape valve for those human impulses that have not yet been ironed out of existence.

\*

In the same brief period, while dramatising the perennial philosophy and issuing a fearful warning to those who ignored it, he wrote an essay on a piece of writing which expresses the right way more successfully than any other. This was his introduction to Prabhavananda's and Isherwood's translation of the *Bhagavad-Gita* (*Song of God*), 1947. In both *Ends and Means* and this essay Huxley spoke of the doctrines of the perennial philosophy as proven facts. Their existence could not be demonstrated with the precision of scientific formulae but it was a measure of the narrowness of the human outlook that we demanded this, assuming that there was only one mode of proof. Human progress required the unlimited acceptance of these doctrines. What he calls the third doctrine of the philosophy affirms the double nature of man and he points out that it is fundamental to all the higher religions. In other words, we are not being asked to accept something strange or revolutionary, but a belief that we (perhaps unknowingly) have often parrotted in our creeds and prayers. A spark of divinity illuminates the inner man, but we cannot become aware of it until we have cleared away the folly, evil and ignorance that constitute our personality. By identifying ourselves with this spark we come to unitive knowledge of the Divine Ground. Huxley calls these " empirical facts ". The different religions have rationalised them variously. The existence of direct, super-rational intuition is acknowledged by them all. Modernism has been so fascinated by scientific discoveries and techniques, external circumstances have come to be regarded as more important than states of mind about external circumstances. The end of human life is now regarded as action, not contemplation. Utopia has replaced Eternity. Huxley calls these doctrines " false, aberrant and heretical."

Yet there is one aspect of the *Gita* which Huxley must have found difficult to swallow and which he leaves unresolved. Arjuna appeals to Krishna because he is appalled by the slaughter that will certainly take place if he joins battle with the enemy.

> Krishna, hearing
> The prayers of all men,
> Tell me how can
> We hope to be happy
> Slaying the sons
> Of Dhritarashtra?
> Evil they may be,
> Worst of the wicked,
> Yet if we kill them
> Our sin is greater.

Which is perfectly orthodox pacifist sentiment.

But Krishna's reply is absolutely uncompromising. " Arjuna ", he says, " is this hour of battle the time for scruples and fancies? Are they worthy of you, who seek enlightenment? Any brave man who merely hopes for fame or heaven would despise them. What is this weakness? It is beneath you. Is it for nothing men call you the foe-consumer? Shake off this cowardice, Arjuna. Stand up." Arjuna persists, and Krishna tells him that the Self, the Atman, can never be destroyed. The Body dies but That which possesses the body is eternal. The *Gita* is in fact a celebration of God in man and there are some very difficult passages for the moralist to accept. For example:

> The Lord is everywhere
> And always perfect:
> What does He care for man's sin
> Or the righteousness of man?

asks Krishna. Thus, although at first sight Hindu philosophy, with its concentration on the reality of the Atman, appears to be the ideal antidote to the "false, aberrant and heretical doctrines", it could easily be taken as a support for indifference. Why worry about war? It cannot harm the divinity in man. Why worry about sin in general? It is absolutely extraneous to the Godhead. Did Huxley ever consider these objections to the philosophy? If he did, he never referred to them in his writings. On the other hand, he was certainly attracted by the Hindu (and Buddhist) view that there are many different paths leading to the Truth, or Reality. Perhaps he accepted (as other thinkers have accepted) that one can find one's way through sin and self-indulgence, although he himself would never choose such a path. But it's odd that he never faced this aspect of the *Gita's* message publicly.

*

We come to his last novel, *Island*. Huxley's feelings about this novel are pathetically familiar: they are those of the novelist who is on the downward path, who has lost the intuitive knowledge of what makes a good novel (this is the first to go) and is hoping to replace it by intelligence and good intentions. He wanted desperately for it to be admired, but the critics could not praise it—and in fact it is second-rate and tedious. It is a thesis novel, and the thesis is what you might expect, a Huxleyan hotchpotch of Hinduism, non-attachment, the food-population complex, and a number of other pressing contemporary problems. And if we wish to probe a little deeper to discover why it fails, we might take a tip from his *Literature and Science*, published in the following year, in which he says that while the scientist aims to say one thing, and only one thing, at a time, the literary artist tries to report the multifarious levels of experience which man undergoes simultaneously. Huxley had always failed in this, as I stated in the first edition of this book, but never more disastrously than in *Island*. In fact, one has a kind of schizoid feeling while reading this novel, as though two distinct things are happening in different parts of the mind, instead of several events being entwined and known together. There is a tendency to proceed by epigram—for example, "A people's theology reflects the state of its children's bottoms." A splendid starting point, this, for an essay, and that is why it is so out of place here. And of course the author, reflecting from time to time that he is writing a novel, throws in the odd physical touch ("'Psycho-physical means to a transcendental end', said Vijaya, raising his voice against the grinding screech of the low gear into which he had just shifted.") But the novelist's duty of making a vital selection of experience is not performed. It is casual and arbitrary.

One has always thought of Aldous Huxley as a creative writer in the sense that he compelled his genius by an act of will, and this he did extraordinarily well. Philip Quarles had admitted that he was not a congenital novelist, and one can say the same about Huxley (who probably regarded Quarles as in some respects a self-portrait). Such writers do not create living characters but "monsters" (Quarles's term), although some of these monsters come very close to humanity. Huxley had managed to simulate life sufficiently well to dazzle his reader, if not to convince. But the sparkle has gone out of them in *Island*. Most of his friends seemed to be in agreement on this, judging by the Memorial. Leonard Woolf said that his imagination never broke loose from the reasoning part of his mind, and his novels ultimately suffered. Maurois felt that one reason for their failure was because the ordinary man never figured in them. Chesterton once said that the great novelist must be vulgar because he must be close to people, and people in general are vulgar. This is another way of putting Maurois's point. Huxley had once discussed vulgarity in literature and had particularly singled out Dickens and Balzac. And yet, in a way, there is vulgarity in Huxley, only it is of a rather refined type, if this is not a contradiction in terms. All that preaching—is it not a spiritual vulgarity to be always nagging people on the way they behave? It comes to a head in *Island* and reveals itself in a score of trivial ways: the capitalisations, for instance ("'I mean', she elaborated, 'in the eyes of those

who Truly Understand '. (Capital T, capital U.) ") What
is this but the kind of heavy humour one meets in a club bar—
and of course he wasn't good at it. Or the painful vulgarity
of the names he chooses for most of the characters throughout
his output. We've had Jeremy Pordage. Now we get Joe
Aldehyde.

We have been told that he wanted to write a novel about
the dangers of verbalisation. One might say, a little mali-
ciously and with overtones of philistine satisfaction, that
" this is hardly likely to pull in the Boots subscribers." But
there is a far more serious criticism than that, for Huxley rarely
showed much concern for conformists. It just isn't the way
that a novel gets written. Only critics imagine that novelists
set to work in this way. And yet one has a very strong suspicion
that the genesis of *Island* must have been rather of this type.
There are moments when one feels that it could have been the
" verbalisation " novel, or at least parts of it. And it is in
exactly these sections of the novel that the vulgarity comes
uppermost. Take, for instance, the small green booklet read
by Will Farnaby and quoted in different parts of the novel.
It is called *Notes on What's What, and on What it Might be
Reasonable to Do About What's What*. This is sufficient to
make one squirm, with the sudden fear that G.B.S. himself is
to be foisted on us, in a new, swami-type role. We find the
title is not just an unfortunate mistake for Will says, as he takes
the book, " What an admirable title!" Then we have large
chunks thrown at us. The reader doesn't have to be a philistine
to resent this, but he may very well take the view that the
points made by these extracts could be made much more
effectively through plot and characterisation. " *The more a
man knows about individual objects, the more he knows about
God*. Translating Spinoza's language into ours, we can say:
The more a man knows about himself in relation to every kind
of experience, the greater his chance of suddenly, one fine
morning, realising who in fact he is—or rather Who (capital W)
in Fact (capital F) ' he ' (between quotation marks) Is (capital
I)." Such methods of emphasis are distinctly unpleasant and

make the reader feel he is in some kind of kindergarten. As for the meaning of the passage, we are being told that words frequently serve to obstruct understanding rather than assist it. We are told it again and again. " Abstract materialism— that's what you profess ", lectures Dr Robert. " Whereas we make a point of being materialists concretely—materialistic on the wordless levels of seeing and touching and smelling, of tensed muscles and dirty hands." I am not denying that characters in novels speak to each other, and that through their speech they express their philosophies, but nearly all the speech in *Island* is lecturing. Huxley comes closest to avoiding this kind of tedium when Will Farnaby takes the *moksha*-medicine and we share his new, enhanced state of conscious-ness—for this is something which Huxley does well, as anyone who remembers *Time Must Have a Stop* will know. When Will dropped his eyes to the floorboards and saw his own bare foot lying across the grain of the wood, he got behind words and for a moment helped us to do the same—for, even without *moksha*, we have all experienced those rare moments when common objects take on an extraordinary undiluted reality. " ' Boards ', ' grain ', ' foot '—through the glib explanatory words the mystery stared back at him, impenetrable and yet, paradoxically, understood."

The traditional values (not all of them, and in any case selected from different civilisations) are upheld by the island kingdom of Pala and the author of *Antic Hay*, forty years on. As in *Brave New World* and *Ape and Essence*, there is a dual pattern. Freedom and personal happiness belong to the past and are linked with technological backwardness, even in-efficiency. (In *Ape and Essence* this aspect is blurred, but it is still true.) It must have been the greatest sacrifice of Huxley's life to decide that the good life cannot produce great art. At first this seems confusing, because a similar situation existed in Brave New World. Each society has opted for a type of monism, but the two are worlds apart. It is the monistic nature of society that destroys the art. Art requires conflict— one branch of it, drama, is named conflict—and neither Brave

New World nor Pala encourage conflict. Brave New World, in fact, will not permit it. Pala does everything it can to discourage it. The liberating experiences granted by the *moksha*-medicine are the people's replacements for art. There are Palanese artists but their symbols are probably less moving than those of artists elsewhere, because they are not tragic, they are not compensations for the sufferings caused by war, ignorance and stupidity. *Notes on What's What* puts the situation in a nutshell: " Dualism . . . Without it there can hardly be good literature. With it, there most certainly can be no good life." In Brave New World the mind was cauterised, in Pala it is soothed by understanding. But there is hope for literature, thinks Farnaby cynically. A neighbouring dictator is preparing to take over and he will give Pala all that is necessary for the artistic life: corruption, falsehood, insanity and injustice, crime, insatiable ambition and a load of guilt.

In the failure of *Island* Huxley realised, paradoxically, his greatness as a man. No modern author had shown a more intuitive grasp of artistic truth; everyone who knew him remarked on his sensibility in this respect, and it is apparent to all who take the trouble to read him. At times one had the feeling that if Huxley had two loaves of bread he would exchange them both for daffodils—but not quite, for he never lost his contact with the physical and appetitive side of life. And yet, at the end of his life, he announced that man must be prepared to give up this faculty, and the marvellous heritage that it had created, or at best relegate it to an inferior position such as that now enjoyed by basketwork or embroidery. Through *Ends and Means* and *The Perennial Philosophy* and his readings of Eastern mystics and the Hindu *Gita* he slowly yet remorselessly came to this, for him, appalling conclusion: that the life of great art was inimical to the life of goodness. Ironically, this is why *Island* is a failure. It does not and cannot satisfy our formed, or malformed, taste. There is no drama in Pala, it has to be brought in from Rendang. In Pala, preaching is a substitute for art. The spirit of Pala is too good to allow free play for the passions that art thrives on

Throughout his work Huxley had occasionally expressed the view, hinted at rather than stated explicitly, that man lives in a prison of his own making. In the essay, " Knowledge and Understanding " (*Adonis and the Alphabet*) this conception had for once broken through with exceptional vigour. On the level of knowledge, manners and custom, man can never get very far away from the *persona* created by his family and society. " The culture within which he lives is a prison—but a prison which makes it possible for any prisoner who so desires to achieve freedom, a prison to which, for this and a host of other reasons, its inmates owe an enormous debt of gratitude and loyalty." In fact, so powerful is the sense of gratitude that few prisoners wish to get out. Is this the reason why Huxley wrote an introductory essay for an edition of Piranesi's *Carceri*, with a critical study by Jean Adhemar (undated, but published 1950, with a reissue in a slightly different format)? Piranesi drew no earthly prisons. They were the metaphysical prisons which Huxley located within the mind, " whose walls are made of nightmare and incomprehension, whose chains are anxiety and their racks a sense of personal and even generic guilt." But no matter where they may be, Piranesi always gives the impression that they are co-extensive with the universe. And so they are, for they map " the obscure and terrible states of spiritual confusion and *acedia*."

He returns to the prison metaphor in *Island*. Dr Robert discovered early in his life that history and prisons were closely related. History is man, and prison is his environment. He began to ask himself what kind of people became dangerous delinquents, whether the grand ones of the history books or the little ones of Wormwood Scrubs. Put in another way, who are the people who develop a lust for power, the people who feel a tremendous compulsion to bully? He began to recognise the existence of two types of people who fall into this category, and he named them the Muscle Men and the Peter Pans. In Pala he had learned to spot the Peter Pans early and to nip them in the bud. One year of the appropriate biochemical treatment was sufficient. Jail never was. The moral is that today we know enough to be able to spot the potential criminal before he can do any harm and to cure him. Exactly the same treatment is required for the inmates of the bigger prison, whether we regard it as the mind or the world— for in effect, they are the same. This is the progress that Huxley made during his career as a thinker and a writer. From a bemused fascination with the delinquent Coleman in *Antic Hay*, half admiring, half deploring, he had come to a recognition of the man's essential stupidity, arrogant stupidity, and he had puzzled out exactly what was wrong with the man and how it could be put right. Coleman reappears in *Island*, where he has been renamed Murugan—but there is no doubt about Murugan's status. He is a horrid little pest, whose mere presence irritates the intelligent reader profoundly. Huxley has put him in his place. Unfortunately, we, the fellow-prisoners, have not.

# Chapter 1

### THE PERSONA: LIVING AS A FINE ART

Y O U might meet him anywhere: in the long gallery, with its rows of respectable and rather boring Italian primitives, Chinese sculptures, dateless furniture; in the panelled drawing-room, where the huge chintz-covered arm-chairs were oases of comfort among the flesh-mortifying antiques; in the morning-room, with pale lemon walls, Venetian chairs, rococo tables; in the library, rich in portentous folios; or the dining-room, " solidly, portwinily English ". The moment he saw you he would mark you down as a potential victim—a victim of his marvellous erudition, his restless critical spirit. You would become an audience whose rôle was simple enough. You would be a sympathetic ear for the cascade of witty generalisation that would pour effortlessly and serenely, on whatever subject that presented itself. You might be standing outside the house, admiring its lines and masses—particularly its masses. That would be sufficient. His eye would take it in at a glance and he would comment on its challenge to nature. He would quote Shelley's *Epipsychidion,* and then demolish the quotation. A large part of his discourse would be devoted to the thesis that we grow steadily more imbecile. Our forefathers built for effect (he would return to this theme again and again, in one form or another). We, on the contrary, employ our wealth and know-ledge to belittle man's title to grandeur. Life becomes pro-gressively saddening as an experience.

It might be sex that would stimulate that tireless intelligence, set the facile tongue wagging. Talk, talk, talk—nothing like words to disguise the harshness of reality. Some chance association reminds him of a custom followed in the time of the " amiable Brantôme." He describes it. Part of the collec-

tive ear essays a comment. "Havelock Ellis says—", begins
a young woman. He holds up his hand, "like a policeman
arresting the flow of traffic". She tries again, but it is no
good. Havelock Ellis must wait, wait while he, the all-
knowing, completes his thesis. It is concerned with the transition from secrecy to openness in the discussion of sex. But
the openness was not jovial, in the spirit of Rabelais or
Chaucer. Amour became a terribly serious matter. Young
women, such as the one who had had the temerity to inter-
rupt him, discussed with philosophic calm matters that would
have thrown the youth of the sixties into a delirium of excitement. He sighed. More degeneration.

The place was Crome, the man Scogan. It might have been
the palace of the Cybo Malaspina or a mansion near Florence,
he might have been Cardan or Pordage or Barnack. There had
even been an early Emberlin, but he had not matured as well
as these other vintages. The Persona strides through the
novels, rarely at a loss, shaping the raw material of life to his
own liking. Life does not always treat him kindly. He
always has *some* money, but rarely enough. His needs are
great. He is the natural aristocrat and, as such, is owed
more than a mere competence. As a young man he has to
take work of a distasteful character; he can only deploy his
talents at weekends in the homes of wealthy friends, who may
drop him at a moment's notice. In later life he sponges, on
the same friends or perhaps his family, especially an indulgent
mother. He has to amuse and stimulate tirelessly, it is his
living. At the same time he keeps an eye open for the main
chance, a wealthy marriage (even with an idiot) or a place on
a rich scoundrel's payroll. There are usually a few invest-
ments, for he is not of proletarian birth. (How he despises and
fears the lower classes!) In all probability he comes from
some such family as the Staitheses (*Eyeless in Gaza*), with
their Knight Commander of St Michael and St George, the
Permanent Under-Secretary, the Indian Civil Servant, the
successful stockbroker. But none of this for him. It was too
easy, too boring, it bred mediocrity and complacency, it pro-

vided no challenge to the man of culture. He is an over-sensitive young man, deeply versed in art and literature, who inevitably becomes a cynical old man, relishing his disillusioned wisdom.

His creed is art. During his youth art led him trustingly to nature but now he knows that his feelings for nature were always false. He had merely been an unthinking victim of tradition. His intellect had persuaded him that nature was important to him, that he himself was a natural. But later he saw through this youthful misconception. His way of life had always set him against nature, and if he acquired no other virtue he at least attained to intellectual honesty. Human nature, and especially his own human nature, had passed far beyond the horizon of non-human nature. The primitive links were of the most tenuous character. Scogan confessed to a particular pleasure in what he insisted on calling " Cubismus ", which sounded even more remote from natural forms than Cubism. " I like to see pictures from which nature has been completely banished," he said, "pictures which are exclusively the product of the human mind." Nature disturbed him; it was utterly pointless and incomprehensible.

He was no newcomer to English literature. He had talked all through the novels of Peacock and he had made a brilliant reappearance in *South Wind*. Frank Swinnerton even compared him with the mind that lay behind *Pride and Prejudice*. Elizabeth had said, " I hope I never ridicule what is wise and good. Follies and nonsense, whims and inconsistencies, do divert me, I own, and I laugh at them whenever I can." Aldous Huxley, young or old, through his Persona or from his own ego, was always on the look-out for follies. Swinnerton said he was " as fastidious as a maiden aunt, as bawdy as a highbrow and as unaffected in his amusement as a common man." Whether wisdom or goodness existed were matters of doubt to him in his early years, but folly was always there to be chastised. Yet even at his post-war brightest he wanted to admire the patience and the perseverance of the unfortunate and the suffering, sometimes allowing an alien sentimentality to enter his work. (It was usually confined to his lesser pieces.) And there is the co-lateral fact that he wrote a film script of *Pride and Prejudice* in his middle age.

The Persona was not as irredeemably cynical as his reputation suggests. In some of the novels his appearance is only fragmentary. In *Antic Hay,* for instance, he only partially invests the soul of Gumbril Senior. Gumbril was too single-minded to be a Scogan or Cardan. He was an architect, although his architectural practice was confined to the construction of models, and his view of life was far less comprehensive than that of the thoroughgoing, hundred per cent Persona. He took his stand on the firm belief that an architect must be a man of sense, whereas an excellent musician might be a perfect imbecile. About architecture he could talk endlessly and stimulatingly, but outside it he was almost an average professional man, a little eccentric and very kind-hearted. A Scogan's spiritual stoniness was lacking.

The first full Persona was Emberlin in " Eupompus Gave Splendour to Art by Numbers " (*Limbo*), and he failed to impress. We are told that he " exhaled an atmosphere that combined the fantastic speculativeness of the undergraduate with the more mellowed oddity of incredibly wise and antique dons "—but he never exhaled this atmosphere in sufficient quantity to enforce the reader's admiration. We are told he was " immensely erudite, but in a wholly unencyclopaedic way —a mine of irrelevant information "—but a short story is not the vehicle for the presentation of such erudition. It requires space for a slow and remorseless build-up, which is exactly what we get in the early novels, particularly *Crome Yellow* and *Those Barren Leaves.* And as a result the Persona broods over them and half strangles them. While reading them you are amused, impressed, you even suspend disbelief and accept them as transcripts of life. Then you read one of Huxley's more organic contemporaries, Forster say, and you realise how dry and crackling these novels are. Take Forster's *The Longest Journey,* one of the most profoundly depressing novels in the English language, yet its grasp of life overwhelms you.

4

The characters are rough and inconsistent, like real people are, and the Huxley Persona melts away in their presence like a figure cut out of rice-paper.

I am comparing two types of utterly different novel, which is a dangerous thing to do. If you are looking for life, you will read Forster. But the Huxley novels belong to a different species, and should be approached as such. *Point Counter Point* and *Eyeless in Gaza* in particular are tremendous constructions, where the elements of life are re-combined in a new and exciting way. They have not the freshness of work by a more congenital novelist, but they achieve as much in their way as is humanly possible. They are thought creatively transformed. (Forster is instinct partially transformed.) The Persona would have killed more conventional novels, but these rise triumphantly above the limitations imposed by their own scaffolding. The achievement is real, even if marked by artificiality.

The clearest impression one receives from these novels is of cleverness—at times an almost diabolical cleverness. It is this that sets up the resistance, for in the face of too much cleverness we feel incomplete, inferior. There is a tendency to hate the Persona, after we have got over the first wave of admiration, for we know that he despises us. Elizabeth Bowen perceived very clearly the tension set up by this kind of writing. Huxley is not only a very clever person but at the same time "the stupid person's idea of the clever person." At one time Huxley used to be compared with Noel Coward. They had some superficial qualities in common. They were both sophisticated figures who mocked the bourgeoisie. But the resemblance cannot go much further. There was always the uncomfortable suspicion that Huxley was also mocking the mockers—and this suspicion was well founded. Coward's feeble jokes, lack of intellectual wit, his coyness and slyness, were all parts of an attitude that could be easily acquired by anyone who took the trouble to learn the trick. But Huxley's attitude could not be acquired by "anyone"—it required immense erudition and an essential aloofness that few, very few people possessed. Thousands became efficient Cowardites who never possessed the equipment to become Huxleyans.

The Persona regarded himself as a natural aristocrat and in consequence shuddered at the mere thought of inferior beings. Inferior beings come to resent the shudder, particularly in the twentieth century. Dick Greenow, one of the Persona's earliest and most youthful incarnations, had to admit that he did not like the middle classes, the lower middle classes, the lower classes. The narrator in " Chawdron " (*Brief Candles*) could never resist the shudder when his maid entered the room; her father had owned a shop. Fanning, the novelist in " After the Fireworks " (*Brief Candles*), writhed to think that middle class couples discussed his work, and dismissed it as " extraordinarily brilliant, but . . ." When he was recognised in public he felt humiliated and insulted. The trouble with these people was that they defiled everything they touched, degraded all that was noble. " Their intellectual tradition was all wrong." Dick Greenow even had doubts about being a pacifist when he discovered that most of his fellow-pacifists were of middle class origin. And when one of them praised the poems of Fulke Greville he felt irritated beyond measure. To read is one thing—but could they understand or appreciate ?

In the later novels these low, vulgar people begin to get their own back. The Persona undergoes penance. Thirty years have made a vast difference, the many-headed monster now considers itself as good as its master. Poor Jeremy Pordage (*After Many A Summer*) has a wretched time. The girl in the Western Union office regards him as a poor old chump, he is despised by the wealthy but illiterate Stoyte and almost patronised by the detached, intelligent Propter. A workman addresses him in the language of the gutter.

Such a cross was not made easier to bear by the possession of a social conscience. At first this was thin and fugitive, and was shuffled off on to characters who tended to stand apart from the Persona. Gumbril Junior in *Antic Hay*, for instance, was a man who realised only too keenly how insufficient he was for the part. It was he who was occasionally stabbed by indignation and pity, as when he encountered (in the midst of his revelry) the old man who had walked with his wife and baby from Portsmouth to London in search of work. His friends all the time and himself most of the time were too obsessed with themselves and their personal interests to be concerned with the misfortunes of others. But here and there was a crack in consciousness and social ugliness could not always be excluded. That was in 1923. Sixteen years later, in *After Many a Summer*, the man from Portsmouth is replaced by the transients from Kansas. They are still an ugly reality but the social conscience has grown stronger.

The Persona was an assimilator of culture, and wonderfully dextrous at it. Nor had he any misgivings. That was why Gumbril Junior was not fitted to succeed in the role, and why Huxley himself was capable of redemption and able later to bury the monster with full rites and obsequies. They knew that assimilation was not enough. It was amusing and temporarily satisfying to view life through a barrage of literary similes ("her long ear-rings swung and rattled—corpses hanging in chains" —how agreeable!) but it led nowhere. There was a feeling of emptiness when people tried to tell you of their happiness; happiness transcended these sterile cultural values, and emphasised their own aridity. Gumbril felt this keenly when he met the business man, Boldero. He felt himself infinitely superior to this common little philistine, until he realised that Boldero was flinging back at him his own words and ideas. Boldero had picked up a little artistic jargon from Gumbril and now considered himself an expert. Wasn't this exactly what Gumbril himself did, only more tactfully and elegantly? But to know this was at least a sign of grace. Scogan would never have admitted he was a reflector of other men's ideas.

The young man is never a fully-formed Persona. He is an apprentice, and can still worry about his integrity. He is still aware of the gap between what ought to be and what is. He persuades himself that he doesn't care, but not until persuasion is unnecessary will he become a full member of the brotherhood. His fingers creep over the girl's thorax, she whispers, " Was there ever such passion as ours?"—and he is calculating how much he will spend on his lunches in a year. Or he may remember the French pun about love: *sentiments-centimètres,* and is appalled, humiliated—but hastens to assure himself that it is " only humiliating because we choose to think it so, arbitrarily." Does he care, should he care, does man or nature order him to care ?

> " Jenny, adorable—" (what draws the line
> At the mere word ' love '?) " has anyone the right
> To look so lovely as you look tonight,
> To have such eyes, such a helmet of bright hair?"
> But candidly, he wondered, do I care?

The situation is summed up at the evening party where the singer with the " broad Flemish back " holds her listeners in " frozen rapture ". He alone is unable to freeze. He laughs. There is ptomaine in the treacle.

It is a very delicate situation. He has to gain a reputation for profound learning and exquisite taste, persuade the world that they are genuine and at the same time not be carried away by his own mischievous eloquence. The first part is easy. Instead of quoting Virgil you chant Sidonius Apollinaris. If someone mentions Raphael, restrain your vomit with difficulty and announce that the Raphael Mengses at Petersburg are the only tolerable paintings. Huxley sets the aspirant on the right path in his essay " Conxolus " (*Along the Road*). The patron saint of the Huxleyan Persona Brotherhood is Paul Morand. He has a " wonderfully airy, easy way of implying that he has looked into everything—absolutely everything, from God and the Quantum Theory to the slums of Baku (the world's most classy slums—didn't you know it?), from the Vanderbilt family and all the Ritz hotels to the unpublished poetry of Father Hopkins. Just the quick passing implication of know-ledge, just the right word in each particular case, the absolutely correct, esoteric formula—that is all" (*Vulgarity in Literature*). Although it was impossible for a fool to succeed, he could go a long way by the application of the technique. Even a semi-imbecile like Sidney Quarles in *Point Counter Point* was able to maintain a wonderfully impressive façade, which foxed those who didn't know him. He was incapable of becoming a Scogan, of course, but he tried hard.

The Persona never bothered his head about social utility but if challenged he would have been ready with an answer. One of Cardan's gratuitous lectures was on the importance of display in the life of the State. Treat the people to a procession or some similarly spectacular function every now and again and they would keep quiet. Huxley said the same in " A Night at Pietramala " (*Along the Road*). Shows and masquerades were symptoms of bad government. They keep the oppressed in good humour. And what was the Persona but the incarnation of display, for the benefit of the rather superior rabble that congregated in country houses at weekends? Francis Chelifer knew that his own dabblings in art were utterly unimportant. They provided a more personal and private form of display against the time when, the old Adam overcome and his spiritual cravings quenched, he could settle down in tranquillity to the life of refinement. Meanwhile, his pen ran riot, and he apologised to himself.

Cardan and Chelifer represent the Persona at different points of development, the one complete, the other in a state of becoming. (It is largely a question of age and experience.) Sentiment must be rigorously excluded, there must be an unsleeping concentration on self-interest, but the outward performance must always be perfect. Chelifer remarks shrewdly that there must be " a fixture of the attention upon the relevant ". He is referring to his art, but the dictum applied equally to his life. Superficially, conversation seemed to leap from one irrelevancy to another, but the guiding intellect of the Persona restrained it in the interests of a long-term policy. Cardan knew that violent gestures were the stock-in-trade of comedy, however we may associate them with tragedy. The quiet, controlled voice purred on. " Passion must never be allowed to dissipate itself in wild splashings and boilings over. It must be shut up, so to speak, and compressed and moulded by the intellect." And the Persona must never allow itself to become comic. (Poor Jeremy Pordage's failing!) Except in the hands of genius (and no Scogan or Cardan would ever succumb to such self-delusion, it was one of the things they grew out of, one of the things that distinguished them from the youthful apprentice, such as Denis in *Crome Yellow*), except for genius, the baroque or the romantic too easily became ludicrous. The Persona did not deal in Gargantuan comedy, although it professed to appreciate it in other (but lesser) mortals.

No, the Persona lived in its own reality-tight world, divorced from either Comedy or Tragedy. (When one or other of these intruded, the Persona burst like a bubble.) "The world of Platonic Ideas," Huxley wrote in *Texts and Pretexts,* "is the most comfortable and sanitary of dug-outs." It was the world inhabited by the Persona, and by Huxley himself, until the Perennial Philosophy routed him out with the violence of high explosive—and then the world of the Persona began to crumble too. We see the collapse in its most humiliating form in the career of Jeremy Pordage, but it is also clearly overwhelming Eustace Barnack in *Time Must Have A Stop.* Eustace is as self-confident and complacent as ever Scogan was, but his creator has forsaken him. Eustace has been set up, with superb skill, only to be knocked down—not crudely by circumstances but by the pity and distaste of the reader. His sister Alice is shocked by his appearance. "The face was like a loose rubber mask sagging from the bones, flabby and soft and unwholesomely blotched." The mouth, so amusing and touching in boyhood, was now damp and shapeless. Eustace had become a combination of senility and babyishness, " of the infantile with the epicurean ". This was the net result of treating life as a fine art, as Eustace himself proudly expressed it. " Live and let live " was the motto of such people. They harmed nobody and were dismissed as idlers and wasters. They were fascinated by the magic of triviality. " How frightfully intense it is ! Trifles for trifles' sake." And yet the alternative appeared to be killing and maiming others on behalf of some fierce principle.

It sounded attractive, yet the results were disappointing. One might welcome the harmlessness of triviality, yet it deposited the practitioner in a Waste Land where nothing really mattered. And Huxley had a steadily growing conviction that some things do matter, and matter very much, though it is not necessary to kill to prove it. Mr Propter was no longer attracted by the charm of even the most erudite bosh. He was barbarous enough to prefer sense. But Jeremy wanted only cosiness, the cosiness represented by his mother's home, a non-exacting but well-paid job, an absence of spiritual challenge and most of all, an attitude that admitted the existence of no solutions. It gave him enormous pleasure to go round and round, like Fabre's caterpillars. Paradoxically he found that the vulgar, garish castle of the American millionaire Stoyte was his spiritual home. It was "the embodiment of an imbecile's no-track mind." Round and round he went, "like caterpillars inside the mind of an imbecile; round and round in an infinite cosiness of issueless thoughts and feelings and actions, of hermetically bottled art and learning, of culture for its own sake, of self-sufficient little decencies and indecencies, of impassable dilemmas and moral questions sufficiently answered by the circumambient idiocy".

The *coup de grâce* is given in *The Perennial Philosophy*: "The difference between the mortified but still proud and self-centred stoic and the unmortified hedonist consists in this: the latter, being flabby, shiftless and at heart rather ashamed of himself, lacks the energy and the motive to do much harm except to his own body, mind and spirit; the former, because he has all the secondary virtues and looks down on those who are not like himself, is morally equipped to wish and to be able to do harm on the very largest scale and with a perfectly untroubled conscience." Emberlin, Scogan, Cardan, Pordage and Barnack pass in review, and are found wanting—but who will take their place? Coleman? Webley? Dr. Obispo? Sebastian Barnack? But first of all a consideration of Huxley's own development will be helpful.

11

## Chapter 2

### ETON TO THE MOHAVE

ALDOUS LEONARD HUXLEY was born in 1894, the son of Leonard Huxley, editor of the *Cornhill Magazine,* and the grandson of Professor T. H. Huxley and, through his mother, great-grandson of Dr Arnold of Rugby. Julian Huxley is his brother, Matthew Arnold was his great-uncle, Mrs Humphrey Ward his aunt. I am leaving a more detailed consideration of this impressive heredity to the next chapter when it should be easier to determine how much he owes to it. All I will say at this point is that H. G. Wells, who was T. H. Huxley's pupil, noticed a strong facial resemblance between grandfather and grandson. Aldous once referred to his social background as " that impecunious but dignified section of the upper-middle class which is in the habit of putting on dress clothes to eat—with the most studied decorum and out of porcelain and burnished silver—a dinner of dishwater and codfish, mock duck and cabbage " (*Jesting Pilate*).

Ideas of impecuniosity vary considerably. Young Aldous was sent to Eton and graduated to Balliol. For a little while he maintained family tradition (especially Arnold tradition) by teaching at Eton. But, like Gumbril Junior, he didn't stick it long. There are hardly any references to his own schooling in his writings, although there are boarding-school passages in *Eyeless in Gaza.* We know, however, that Dick Greenow considered the most precious gift of Aesop College, for those who knew how to use it, was " ample leisure ". (" Farcical History of Richard Greenow ", *Limbo.*) This sounds like Eton.

Frank Swinnerton said Aldous was the tallest English author he had ever met. When he lived in Hampstead little boys used to call out to him, " Cole up there, guv'nor?" just as they did to Gumbril when he became the Complete Man. This, in conjunction with his long intellectual, bespectacled features, gave people the impression of hauteur. Expecting conscious superiority in him they naturally found it and accused him of an excessively lofty manner. In fact, he loved conversation and was usually full of high spirits. He revelled in long words but not because they were long—they came naturally to him. Swinnerton noted the constant use of the words " fantastic " and " incredible " in Huxley's conversation, particularly his narrative. He seemed to have an enviable knack of meeting odd people and seeing odd sights.

With his great gifts he found entrance to the literary world comparatively easy. He contributed to *Wheels,* the Sitwell rival to *Georgian Poetry,* published his own volume of verse, *The Burning Wheel,* in 1916 and was one of the editors of *Oxford Poetry* in 1917. He contributed essays under the pseudonym Autolycus to *The Athenaeum* under Middleton Murry's editorship, and some of these appeared in his first volume of essays, *On The Margin.* In those days he kept good literary company. In the first number of *Art and Letters,* for instance, we find him alongside Richard Aldington, Siegfried Sassoon, Wyndham Lewis and Gaudier-Brezska. In 1917, at a poetry reading organised on behalf of charity, with Edmund Gosse in the chair, he read with Robert Graves, Siegfried Sassoon and the Sitwells. He used to attend Sickert's breakfast parties with Nina Hamnett and W. H. Davies, Sitwell dinners with Nevinson and Roger Fry, and listen to Violet Gordon Woodhouse playing the clavichord with Eliot, Arthur Waley, Graves and Sassoon. In January 1920 we read of him attending the Olympia Victory Circus with Arnold Bennett, whom he watched drive off in a brougham-full of balloons. By this time Aldous was married to Maria Nys.

In *Laughter in the Next Room* Sir Osbert Sitwell gives a characteristic portrait of Aldous visiting him in hospital just after the war. He looked " interestedly disinterested, aloof," and was a study of Nonchalance in trousers. He could already talk fluently about everything under the sun, particularly modern theories of science, politics, painting, literature and psychology, but—what was peculiarly Huxleyan—at the same time did not despise the ordinary gossip of the day, although he treated it as a philosopher, with detachment and an utter want of prejudice.

> But he preferred to discourse of more erudite and impersonal scandals, such as the incestuous mating of melons, the elaborate love-making of lepidoptera, or the curious amorous habits of cuttlefish. He would speak with obvious enjoyment, in a voice of great charm, unhurried, clear without being loud,[1] and utterly indifferent to any sensation he was making. Thus the most surprising statements would hover languidly in air heavy with hospital disinfectants. "From his novel conduct", I remember his announcing on one occasion, one must assume that Every Octopus has read Ovid on Love.

And then, having made his point, Aldous would fall to silence again, "drooping into a trance-like state of meditation."

He wanted to be a doctor, yet became a sub-editor on *Vogue*. This in itself reflects the post-war dilettantism of the period, and is in turn reflected in his earlier work: observations on fashion-plates (as in "The Bookshop", *Limbo*), the essay on "Beauty in 1920" (*On The Margin*) and his close attention to women's clothes, evident in most of the stories and novels. But it was part of his comprehensive approach to his environment, his refusal to treat anything as being beneath his notice.

Yet it was certainly not a leaning towards the fashionable life that frustrated his desire to be a doctor. At the age of sixteen he had a violent attack of an eye disease called *keratitis punctata*, which seemed likely to destroy any possibility of an active career. For eighteen months he was nearly blind, and had to depend on Braille for reading and a guide for walking. Even when the condition had improved he was left with one eye just capable of light perception and the other with enough vision to permit him to read the two-hundred foot letter on the Snellen Chart at ten feet. At first he read with the aid of a magnifying glass, then was promoted to spectacles. But at the best he suffered from continual strain and fatigue, and was

---

[1] Even after ten years in America Huxley made the second syllable of "petrol" ring like a bell, according to Cyril Connolly.

sometimes overcome by a sense of complete physical and mental exhaustion.

We get some idea of his courage when we realise that all the early work was written against this background of physical difficulty and spiritual depression. The high spirits seem the more remarkable, the moods of pessimism the more forgivable. Yet there are no direct references to his condition, save for a few in a light and bantering vein, certainly no traces of self-pity. The only occasions on which his private sorrow obtruded, and then not at all starkly, were in some of his poems, written as a young man when the disaster was fresh and appeared irredeemable. For instance, in " The Cicadas ":

> I hear them sing, who in the double night
> Of clouds and branches fancied that I went
> Through my own spirit's dark discouragement,
> Deprived of inward as of outward sight:
> Who, seeking, even as here in the wild wood,
> A lamp to beckon through my tangled fate,
> Found only darkness and, disconsolate,
> Mourned the lost purpose and the vanished good.

But, for the rest, he was matter-of-fact, even cheerful. When he went on his travels he tells us he always carried a plentiful supply of " optical glass ". A pair of spectacles for reading, a pair for long range and a couple of monocles in reserve went with him everywhere. But in addition he carried three pairs of coloured glasses—two of lighter and darker shades of green, and one black. By these means he tempered the illumination of the world to his exact requirements. Sometimes he even felt thankful for his deficiency, for at a distance of more than four or five yards he was " blissfully unaware of the full horror of the average human countenance ". Yet these countenances were clearly and often cruelly delineated in the novels.

In 1939 not even his greatly strengthened glasses were sufficient. Reading became increasingly difficult and fatiguing, and it became obvious that his sight was rapidly failing. It was then that he heard of the Bates method of visual re-education and of a teacher who had had several successes with the method. He decided to take the plunge. Within two months he was reading without spectacles and without strain or fatigue. Today, although his vision is far from normal, it is about twice as good as it was when he wore spectacles. By this time he was in California and found that the strong and constant sunlight was an important factor in his recovery. Out of gratitude, and perhaps wonder and a desire to help others who had suffered from the same disability as himself, he took time off from fiction and *belles lettres* and biography to write *The Art of Seeing*.

But I have gone too far ahead. Long before Huxley gained relief from his eye-strain he was astonishing, delighting and (in some cases) shocking the reading public with his early novels, *Crome Yellow*, *Antic Hay* and *Those Barren Leaves*. The War to End War was over, the Bright Young Things had emerged, sex was blowing its lid off, discipline was being regarded as an offence against humanity, and the middle-class was becoming a collective laughing-stock for the emancipated. It was natural that, at the time, Huxley should have been compared with two other rebels, Noel Coward and Richard Aldington. All three chose as their target what Coward called the " massed illiteracy " of the now socially dominant bourgeois. The comparison seems strained now, the differences appear greater and more significant than the similarities. In fact, from Huxley's point of view Coward might well have been one of the " massed illiterates ". Swinnerton said Huxley had the mental capacity to distinguish the good from the pseudo-good and the unco' guid; unlike the others, he was not morally indignant but aesthetically appalled. Coward's rebellion seemed amusing and refreshing on first acquaintance, but on reflection it seemed as strident as its target was dreary. The Coward-Aldington response was entirely emotional, and provided no solid replacement. This was Calamy's criticism of Chelifer, who told Calamy he had no right to retire from " real " life. " You're just the common variety of sentimentalist reversed. The ordinary kind pretends that so-called real life is more rosy than it actually is. The reversed sentimentalist gloats over its horrors " (*Those Barren Leaves*). Coward did this, and at the same time Huxley appeared to be doing likewise. But later it became clear that something more productive than gloating informed his attitude.

Because these novels were set in a world where familiar and traditional values had been shattered, it was commonly assumed that their characters were keenly aware of their own insecurity. But this is a good example of reading into fiction something that is not even implicit. The insecurity existed in the society of the time but made little impact on the novels themselves. There is no hint of it in *Crome Yellow*, none in *Those Barren Leaves* and only a slight intrusion in *Antic Hay*. The atmosphere of these works, of the country houses and the night life of London, betrays neither fear nor doubt. In this society, whatever was happening in the society of which it was a reflection, most things were still taken for granted. Insecurity means fear of the future, and there is no trace of a future in these books, with the single exception noted. Nor does it really make its appearance until the publication of *Point Counter Point*. This generalisation does not always apply to the Persona, of course. Living on his wits, as he often is, the future is more than an abstraction for him. But then the Persona was not as other men.

Like most intelligent young men, who have imbibed more knowledge than they can effectively digest, Huxley believed he had a systematised grasp of life; in a few words, it was meaningless. If you cared to treat anything as important or significant, it was something you selected arbitrarily. But it was Huxley's merit that, on encountering facts and situations that could not be dismissed quite so lightly, he at first stretched his system to accommodate them and then abandoned it altogether. One of the first discoveries of this nature that he made was that pain, however ludicrous it may appear to the spectator, is always real. The person may be laughable, but his pain is as hard to bear as yours or mine. He expressed this troublesome conviction several times, but mainly in the lesser-known stories, and it has always remained with him. For instance, Peddley's astonishment (in " Two or Three Graces ") at his wife's infidelity was laughable to those who knew him and her, but he was genuinely hurt. In " After the Fireworks " Fanning discovered that you could be as desperately unhappy when you were robbed of your crazy desire as when you were robbed of love. " A *porco* suffers as much as a Dante." Even when Pamela was behaving like " a character in fiction ", he knew that her suffering was none the less real. In *Grey Eminence* he noted, discussing Callot's etchings, that in art sincerity depends on talent. If a man expresses himself feebly it does not thereby follow that his feelings are inferior or the less intense. Grandier's letter from prison to the bishop was mannered and laboured—but there is no reason to doubt the genuineness of his belief that afflic- tion had brought him nearer to God (*The Devils of Loudun*). And so on, right up to *The Genius and the Goddess,* where Rivers observes that the cuckold experiences anguish, even if for others it is material for a farce.

It is a short step from this to the experience of vicarious suffering. Gumbril Junior knew it, and it is evident that Huxley himself knew it keenly. The narrator in "Two or Three Graces ", trying to console Grace in her misery, was filled with a pity that was almost remorse. " I felt that it was somehow my fault; that it was heartless and insensitive of me not to be as unhappy as she was. I felt, as I have often felt in the presence of the sick, the miserably and hopelessly poor, that I owed her an apology. . . . Has one a right to be happy in the presence of the unfortunate, to exult in life before those who desire to die? Has one a right? " It was not the kind of emotion one easily confessed to, in that society at that time, and it was one of the things that set Huxley apart from many of his contemporaries, although at first its expression was rare and fitful. But it emerged again in India, where the poverty and animalism of the population moved him to pro- test. He imagined the response of the owners of motor-cars, the eaters of five meals a day: " Ah, but they feel less than we do.

They're really quite happy." He agreed, they knew no better, they were incredibly resigned, and he added significantly: " All the more shame to the men and to the system that have reduced them to such an existence and kept them from knowing anything better " (*Jesting Pilate*).

It has often been remarked that the bohemianism of the post-war era was really a new form of provincialism. The province may have extended, geographically, to France and Italy, but emotionally it was no less narrow than suburbia. One of the first signs that Huxley was breaking out of it is to be found in the record of his journey round the world in *Jesting Pilate*. Before that he had travelled extensively on the continent, but his itinerary tended to be from art gallery to museum—and when he was not in an art gallery he was discussing it. For a time, he admits, travelling was a vice, like reading. He read " promiscuously, omnivorously and without purpose." Later he realised that reading can easily become an addiction, like cigarette smoking. And at this period he was able to indulge both vices simultaneously. His brother Julian told Swinnerton that he had a special packing-case made for his *Encyclopaedia Britannica* when setting out on his journey to the Far East and America. On shorter journeys he was content to carry one volume only—any of the thirty-two would do. " It takes up very little room (eight and a half inches by six and a half by one is not excessive), it contains about a thousand pages and an almost countless number of curious and improbable facts. It can be dipped into anywhere, its component chapters are complete in themselves and not too long " (" Books for the Journey ", *Along the Road*). The absorption of " curious and improbable facts " was possibly the only purpose in Huxley's life at this stage, before his conscience was aroused.

Most of his continental travels were done in a ten horse-power Citroën. He became a motoring fanatic. All was grist to his mill. In addition to the art galleries and encyclopaedia he pored over motoring papers, studying the news from the racing tracks and coming to terms with a new technology. Nothing was beneath his interest. And after all, technology was applied science. Unlike so many of his literary contemporaries he did not despise science. "There is no credit in not knowing what can be known ", he wrote in " The Traveller's-Eye View " (*Along the Road*). " Some literary men, for example, positively pride themselves on their ignorance of science; they are fools and arrogant at that ". Arthur Koestler, from his continental standpoint, once told me how striking this peculiarity of the English literati is to an outsider. E. M. Forster even regards Huxley as a scientific populariser, ranking him with Voltaire, Charles Kingsley, Samuel Butler and Gerald Heard in this respect. Huxley was aware of the difficulties encountered by a poet in his attempt to use scientific terms and ideas in an expression that must be rooted in his passions, but such difficulty did not justify pride in ignorance. " Chaucer would have regarded such persons with pity and contempt " (" Chaucer ", *On the Margin*).

In fact, if he could have been born again and could have chosen his vocation, he would have been a scientist—" not accidentally but by nature, inevitably a man of science." He would rather have been Faraday[1] than Shakespeare, despite the latter's posthumous reputation. His reasons for this choice are extremely significant; the scientist works in a non-human world, his work is not concerned with personal relationships and emotional reactions. " We are all subdued to what we work in; and I personally would rather be subdued to intellectual contemplation than to emotion, would rather use my soul professionally for knowing than for feeling " (" A Night at Pietramala ", *Along the Road*). A secondary reason for this choice was that the scientist enjoyed much smaller social prestige than the artist and was therefore more immune from the intrusion of frivolous bores !

Huxley's literary tastes at this time were fully in accord with his scientific leanings. He most of all appreciated the rational, the pragmatic, the common-sensical, the worldly and earthly. High flights of fancy, ecstasy, decoration, mannerism and

---

[1]By the time he wrote *Ape and Essence* he may have changed his mind, for Faraday was then being led round by apes on a chain.

verbosity were not to his liking. Good maxims and aphorisms —" and they must be very good indeed; for there is nothing more dismal than a Great Thought enunciated by an author who has not himself the elements of greatness "—are the best reading. Hence he always carried with him a small sexto-decimo of La Rochefoucauld's *Maximes*. At the other extreme was Ruskin, whom he detested. Again and again he returned to the attack; Ruskin's influence ruined travel and guide books, he bullied the Italians unmercifully, he flew into passions of moral indignation, he prevented Huxley from seeing the beauties of St. Paul's Cathedral before he had learnt to think for himself. Against Ruskin he would set Chaucer, his most abiding love among the English poets, " so beautifully objective and unemphatic and free of verbiage ", living through the forty disastrous years after the Black Death and making only one reference (a comic one!) to the troubles in the whole of his work, being a diplomat and not considering it worth a single mention. Whereas Dante rushed into party politics and spent the rest of his life in rage and self-pity! On the whole, poets should have something sensible to say. Spenser's art of saying nothing, at interminable length, in rhyme and rumbling metre, left him cold.

Yet the most frequently quoted passages in Huxley's work are not from Chaucer nor from La Rochefoucauld or any other aphorist; they are from Wordsworth and Baudelaire, and they provide keys to the extension of his working mind. Wordsworth expressed for him his preoccupation with the place of science in artistic production :

> The remotest discoveries of the chemist, the botanist or mineralogist, will be as proper objects of the poet's art as any upon which he is now employed, if the time should ever come when these things shall be familiar to us, and the relations under which they are contemplated shall be manifestly and palpably material to us as enjoying and suffering beings,

Wordsworth had written in the Preface to *Lyrical Ballads*. Huxley wanted to believe this was true; it would represent an important advance in man's instinctive grasp of nature; but he had to admit that there were few signs of realisation. The

Baudelaire, on the other hand, expressed for him his horrified fascination with physical corruption, which I shall refer to later at length:

> Une nuit que j'étais près d'une affreuse juive,
> Comme au long d'un cadavre un cadavre étendu
> Je me pris à songer près de ce corps vendu
> A la triste beauté dont mon désir se prive.

Another clue to the cast of Huxley's mind is to be found in the frequent use of certain words. The best example is " stanchless ". Its frequency is, it is true, largely relative; we notice it because it is unusual. There are a hundred other adjectives he uses more often, but none that draws the attention more. It often appears in the adverbial form, ugly, difficult to say, but obviously expressing some deep emotion in the writer's mind. It is always used metaphorically—a "stanchless wound" in the world's side, or a "stanchless flux." It is used over too long a period to be dismissed as a mere verbal fashion. It stands for an abiding impression in Huxley's imagination of the universe, society, mankind, even the human spirit, wasting away, the victims of a chronic hemorrhage, a ruinous expense of vitality, which can be illustrated from every field of human activity, whether it be man's proneness to emotional outpouring, his lavish production of spermatozoa or his cutting down of forests and massacre of agricultural resources. The Waste Land is replaced by the Wasting Planet. There is a continuous seeping and nothing can (or nothing does) hold it.

Although Huxley was always regarded as absolutely contemporary (as he was) and, from that, ultra-modern (which he wasn't), his literary favourites belonged to the past. He did not share, for instance, in the fashionable denigration of Wordsworth, although he was aware of his deficiencies. In Huxley's view the modern artist had succumbed to a sense of boredom, a feeling that unless something novel and exciting appeared in his works they would be nothing more than inferior copies of their predecessors. They had a terror of the obvious and, in their search for an outlet, adopted the assumption that human nature had changed radically in modern times. The result was a topsy-turvy romanticism, which exalted the machine, the crowd, the merely muscular body, and despised the soul and solitude and nature. " Almost all that is most daring in contemporary art is thus seen to be the fruit of terror—the terror, in an age of unprecedented vulgarity, of the obvious. The spectacle of so much fear-inspired boldness is one which I find rather depressing. If young artists really desire to offer proof of their courage they should attack the monster of obviousness and try to conquer it, try to reduce it to a state of artistic domestication, not timorously run away from it." (" Art and the Obvious ", *Music at Night*.) In Huxley's view, the greater part of psycho-analytic literature, "the music of Schreker", most expressionist painting and *Ulysses* were all " obscene and certainly non-sensical ".

Huxley had no sympathy with the modern fashion of admiring the composition in art and ignoring the drama. Formal relations had become the be-all and end-all of con-temporary art. " Every germ of drama or meaning is disinfected out of them; only the composition is admired. The process is analogous to reading Latin verses without under-standing them—simply for the sake of the rhythmical rumbling of the hexameters " (" Breughel ", *Along the Road*). People managed to look at Giotto, for instance, without what was represented, despite its obvious significance to the master, engaging their attention in the slightest. As for Giotto him-self, he knew no better. In *Do What You Will* (1929) Huxley complained of the impoverishment of art. Painters insisted on subjecting the outer world to their abstracting and geometrising intellects, even when their work was representational.

Huxley wrote that he was old-fashioned enough to believe in the higher and the lower—the kind of statement that sur-prised the cursory reader of his early novels. He was convinced that an absolute standard of artistic merit did exist, and that in the last resort it was a moral one. It may sound paradoxical when we read the author of *Antic Hay* declaring his faith in moral principles, but these principles were not those of suburbia. Many a good artist behaved badly towards his fellow-men, many a good man was a bad artist. What was important was that he should show honesty towards himself. Bad art was of two kinds: the dull, stupid and incompetent, negatively bad; and the positively bad, which was a lie and a sham. Too many contemporary artists produced work of the second kind, denying themselves in the service of a narrow abstract theory.

But the art was only the reflection of behaviour. The behaviour of the post-war world (or rather, of that sector in which Huxley moved) was in angry rebellion against the society which had gone before. The world was in such a mess, everything that had been done before 1914 must be wrong— that was the easy logic. In " Two or Three Graces " the narrator enters a room in which a party is being held in time to hear a young man say in a loud, truculent voice: " We're absolutely modern, we are. Anybody can have my wife, so far as I'm concerned. I don't care. She's free. And I'm free. That's what I call modern."

" I could not help wondering why he should call it modern," the newcomer reflects. " To me it seemed rather primeval— almost pre-human. Love, after all, is the new invention; promiscuous lust geologically old-fashioned."

It was the young women, the Mrs Viveashes and the Lucy Tantamounts, who illustrated this outlook most garishly. Lucy said she came out of her chrysalis during the war, when the bottom had been knocked out of everything. She didn't believe that even old age could make her believe in God or morals. In conversation with Spandrell she confessed that she was fed up with " the ordinary conventional kinds of liveliness ". It was true, people had fornicated and cheated and murdered in the past, but in such a dreary way, always pretending there were good reasons for it, always seeking justification. The new kind of liveliness was distinguished from the old by its bitchiness. When Spandrell asked her why she wished to do what was forbidden, seeing that in her view right and wrong did not exist, she replied that it amused her. She shrugged her shoulders. "Curiosity. One's bored."

During this period one gets the impression that Huxley realised perfectly well the shallowness of the social round yet could not resist the temptation to participate. Although he knew it was a waste of time there was always the fear that, on just this one occasion, he might be missing something. He was ruefully aware that his objection to parties, fornication and idle chatter were only theoretical. In "The Monocle" (*Two or Three Graces*) Gregory asks himself why he still goes to parties, after so many disappointments—but he still goes. On the way to India Huxley was assured that he would have a "very good time" there. He knew what that meant: races bridge, cocktails, dancing till four in the morning, talking about nothing. "And meanwhile the beautiful, the incredible world in which we live awaits our exploration, and life is short, and time flows stanchlessly, like blood from a mortal wound. And there is all knowledge, all art" (*Jesting Pilate*). A frequently quoted proverb in Huxley's writing is *Video meliora proboque; deteriora sequor*. I know what I ought to do, but continue to do what I know I oughtn't to do. Both Philip Quarles and Anthony Beavis laboured under the same curse. Hugh Ledwidge (*Eyeless in Gaza*) was another: "Why on earth did one ever go to these idiotic parties? Kept on going, what was more, again and again, when one knew it was utterly pointless and boring . . ." In a later book we find the philosopher Maine de Biran asking himself the same question: "There are two reasons for going into society. Either to amuse oneself by participating in the fun, or to observe and be instructed. I do neither." Yet he dined out constantly and would go to as many as three receptions in a single evening. As Huxley asks, why, why? (*Themes and Variations*).

It was Huxley's first visit to America that finally impressed on him the imbecility of the search after a "good time". This was before the slump, when American society as a whole was intent on the search, and genuinely believed that it had discovered the Grail. But Huxley was horrified. He realised instinctively that the spiritual emptiness would have to be paid for. (That you can never get anything for nothing has become one of his firmest convictions.) The moral conscience had been abolished and "amuse yourself" had become the sole categorical imperative. "The theories of Freud were received in intellectual circles with acclaim; to explain every higher activity of the human mind in terms of incest and coprophily came to be regarded not only as truly scientific, but also as somehow virile and courageous. Freudism became the *realpolitik* of psychology and philosophy. Those who denied values felt themselves to be rather heroic; instinctively they were appealing to the standards which they were trying, intellectually, to destroy" (*Jesting Pilate*). On his first contact with Californian society he was immediately reminded of Rabelais: food in Gargantuan profusion, barbarous music throbbing unceasingly, flappers and young men wrestling amorously between each satiating course. But he knew something was lacking, a necessity of the Good Life that the Good Time did not provide. Rabelais would have missed the conversation and the learning, which serve as the accompaniment and justification of pleasure. In the Californian City of Dreadful Joy Pantagruel would soon have died of fatigue and boredom.

The world trip was a chastening experience. Besides the Good Time of California he had tasted the squalor and misery of the East. Soho and Mayfair fell into their true perspective, small and, on the world-scale, provincial. When he set out on his travels he had known all the answers: how men should live, how they should be governed, how educated and what they should believe. He returned without any of these " pleasing certainties ". He discovered that his previous knowledge had been rather like that of the man who, asked how the electric light works, replied: "You just press the button". But he had acquired two important new convictions: that it takes all sorts to make a world, and that the established spiritual values are fundamentally correct and should be maintained. There was nothing new or breath-taking about these convictions, but "there is all the difference in the world between believing academically, with the intellect, and believing personally, intimately, with the whole living self".

In 1929 he wrote that whereas he would once have felt ashamed of not being up-to-date, he had now lost his fears. The goals of Modernity and Sophistication were bright but elusive. "I simply avoid most of the manifestations of that so-called 'life' which my contemporaries seem to be so unaccountably anxious to 'see'; I keep out of range of the 'art' they think it so vitally necessary to 'keep up with'; I flee from those 'good times', in the 'having' of which they are prepared to spend so lavishly of their energy and cash" ("Silence is Golden", *Do What You Will*). The youngest generation seemed to be interested in nothing outside its own psychology—but this he knew to be a dead end. Amusement, rather than money-making or power-seeking, consumed their energies. And how desperately bored they were! Among the lights, the alcohol, the hideous jazz noises and the incessant movement he felt a growing despondency overtaking him. By comparison with a night-club a church was positively gay. Feelings and moods were justified by an appeal to the "right to happiness", the "right to self-expression". But it was a poor, insufficient rationalisation. Man became his own end. He was claiming to do what he liked, not because it was in harmony with some supposed absolute good but because it was good in itself.

Conduct, which Huxley had dealt with so airily in the early days, was now replacing aesthetics at the centre of his thought. In the relationship between man and the external world, something more realistic than the obscurantist egotism of Lucy Tantamount was required. He approached the problem in a brilliant essay entitled "Francis and Grigory" (*Do What You Will*). St Francis was for him the supreme example of a man who subdued "things", including his own body and instincts, to his self. But Grigory Rasputin, despite his evil reputation, deserved credit for choosing the opposite rôle, the abasement

27

of the spirit before the flesh, the will before the instinct, the intellect before the passions. It was a necessary correction to orthodox Christendom and contemporary Businessdom. In practice it might lead to the behaviour of a Tantamount, but it was not the product of despair and it did have a positive aim. Huxley liked to believe that Rasputin's self-indulgence was a means to an end, not an end in itself. In this re-orientation of his thought we can discern the influence of D. H. Lawrence, who had just died and with whom Huxley was on very intimate terms just before his death. The solution to the artist's (and others) quandary lay in the reconciliation of Francis and Grigory: subjugation of things to self and self to things.

This idea receives expression in three books of the middle period: *Point Counter Point, Do What You Will* and *Brief Candles*. In his essay on Pascal he names the artists who attained most successfully the " ideal of completeness, of moderation in terms of balanced excess ": Burns, Mozart, Blake, Rubens, Shakespeare, Tolstoy (" before he deliberately perverted himself to death-worshipping consistency "), " the adorable Chaucer ", Rabelais and Montaigne. These men are the life-worshippers—more, the saints of the life-worshippers. Most people, whether they are running after pleasure like Lucy Tantamount, or mortifying themselves like Pascal and the later Tolstoy, or " existing dimly in the semi-coma of mechanised labour and mechanised leisure ", like the majority, are as much afraid of living as they are of dying. Their idea of felicity is to putrefy gradually. Unfortunately they infect others.

But artists are dangerous models. Art is a talent, the individual artist may belong to any psychological type, advocate any moral system. Readers are influenced by writers, not to think and feel as the writer does, but to become more or less of themselves. They may try to imitate an author or one of his creations (Byron, Keats, Hemingway have all exerted this kind of influence) but in effect they only emphasise one of their own potential roles. In his introduction to D. H. Lawrence's *Letters* Huxley remarked how frequently

Lawrence's doctrine was invoked by people of whom he himself would have passionately disapproved, in defence of behaviour which he would have found deplorable, even revolting. This was one danger. Another lay in the too easy possibility of exchanging good religion for bad art. In his conclusions to *Texts and Pretexts* Huxley asserts that it is impossible to have adequate data for the construction of an attitude towards life. All that the individual reasoner has by way of data is his own individual experience and his own feelings about that experience. Going to others for ready-made opinions is useless. At best, one can derive hints. Religion can only survive as a " consciously accepted system of make-believe ". He ends by stating that every art has its conventions which the artist must accept. The most important of arts is living. In his first serious grapple with religion Huxley retreats into the Persona's cosy study.

One of the major complications of life comes from our capacity to gain pleasure from the bad as well as the good. (It is necessary to assume the existence of " good " and " bad ", even if we are unable to define them. Our choices are usually instinctive.) The cult of the amusing, to which reference has been made, blinds its votaries most effectively. " In the end Erasmus Darwin comes to be preferred to Wordsworth, Longhi to Giotto." Huxley himself admits to this very human weakness. He loved the stucco that mimicked marble, the washstands in the form of harpsichords, the biscuit boxes looking like Shakespeare's Complete Works tied together with embroidered ribbon. The contemporary · atmosphere is favourable to pastiche. When adapting Mrs Francis Sheridan's *The Discovery* for the modern stage he consoled himself with the thought that, even if the result were not a work of art, it might at least be " odd, unexpected and amusing ". In *Little Mexican* he declared that Salzburg was " in the movement ". Everything was exquisitely " amusing ", without being really good. If the city lacked in taste, its magnificent tunnel at least provided scope for one's feelings of sentimental awe.

But a far greater danger lay in the pursuit of art for art's sake. Despite the ridicule that has been levelled at this notion, a large amount, possibly the greater part, of modern art is of this kind. It is almost inevitable that this should have happened. From being the handmaid of religion the arts are now independently cultivated for their own sake. But " where beauty is worshipped for beauty's sake as a goddess, independent of and superior to morality and philosophy, the most horrible putrefaction is apt to set in. The lives of the aesthetes are the far from edifying commentary on the religion of beauty " (*Proper Studies*). Cardan and Pordage immediately spring to mind. Incidentally, Huxley could not appreciate the Taj Mahal because it seemed to be related to nothing beyond itself. It is generally admired for its expensiveness and picturesqueness, neither of which qualities appealed to him.

One important development that was taking place in Huxley's mind in this period was the growth of a more human, more intimate approach to other people. At first, as he confessed in *Along the Road,* he could only tolerate them at a distance. (" Neighbours whom one never sees at close quarters are the ideal and perfect neighbours ", he was to write later in *Little Mexican.*) He did not want to be more closely involved with people than he would be with a work of art. When set apart, another person seemed wonderful, charming, a real slice of life—but get to know him and the fascination changed to repugnance. He once shared a *pension* with six other people, and delighted to watch and eavesdrop on them. When the landlady offered to introduce him he declined. " From wonderful and mysterious beings they would have degenerated into six rather dull and pathetic little employees." Anthony Beavis summed it up in his diary: " One can work hard, as I've always done, and yet wallow in sloth; be industrious about one's job, but scandalously lazy about all that isn't the job. Because, of course, the job is fun. Whereas the non-job—personal relations, in my case—is disagreeable and laborious " (*Eyeless in Gaza*). This attitude was partly the result of his phlegmatic nature, which makes it difficult for him to enter into the experiences of those whose emotions are

easily and violently aroused. It also causes him to feel
bewildered by such works of art as *Werther, Women in Love*
and the *Prophetic Books* of Blake. Huxley is not a congenital
novelist, as has frequently been remarked, and there are large
areas of feeling he cannot enter into with sympathy.

There is a great gulf between those writers who live with
their creations, such as Dostoievsky and Tolstoy, and those
who can only look at them from a distance, like Conrad and
Huxley himself. To know, says Huxley, one must be an
actor as well as a spectator. But by this he does not mean
what one might expect—a plunge into society. That is not
action but the most elementary form of spectatorism, according to which one is constantly in the company of people one
never gets to know more than superficially. " One must dine
at home as well as in restaurants, must give up the amusing
game of peeping in at unknown windows to live quietly, flatly,
unexcitingly indoors " (" The Traveller's-Eye View ", *Along
the Road*). Action is not ceaseless, purposeless movement.

Nor does the Christian ideal of superhumanness help the
author, or indeed the ordinary man. At the root of the aspiration to be more than human in knowledge and behaviour is a
kind of cowardice, a refusal to cope with the difficult, complicated facts of life. " Harmonious living is a matter of tact
and sensitiveness, of judgment and balance and incessant
adjustment, of being well bred and aristocratically moral by
habit and instinct " (" Spinoza's Worm ", *Do What You Will*).
To aspire to be superhuman is an admission that you have
neither the guts, the wit nor the judgment to do this. Super-
humanity is as bad as subhumanity, said Tilney in "Chawdron"
(*Brief Candles*).

It was all self-criticism, finding its way out deviously, attached
to others before the full realisation that it applied with equal
force to himself made itself known. The simplicity of the
rational inner world was such a relief after the complexity of
the shapeless, unmanageable outer world. Gregory felt it
keenly (" The Monocle ", *Two or Three Graces*) when he
strolled through Cambridge Circus with Spiller, who was

droning complacently about the " main function of art ", while three ravishing tarts hooted and giggled at them. Spiller was so wrapped up in his monologue he didn't even notice them, but Gregory felt two worlds had met that could never be reconciled. In despair, his solution was a head-on attack: " For God's sake ", he shouted, " shut up ! How can you go on talking and talking away like this?" Spiller was mildly astonished.

It was a necessary struggle. Until the dilemma had been resolved he could not move on to the next stage in his spiritual Odyssey. To live, the soul had to be in intimate contact with the world, had to assimilate it through all the channels of sense and desire, thought and feeling, which nature had provided. Anything that obstructed the channels poisoned the soul, whether it was deadening routine, dull unawareness, exclusive monomania, excessive vice or excessive virtue. Dead souls stink. Calvin's Geneva, De Nerciat's Paris, Podsnap's London, Babbitt's Zenith, were all open sewers. It was like a warning of doom when a French Professor of English told him that advanced students treated him as a leading member of the Neo-Classic school. He did not wish to be a classic of any kind, for it implied escape from the author's true work, the adequate rendering of actual reality. Anything else was a retreat into the comfortable Wombland of the mind.

Huxley called himself a moderate extravert, and could therefore understand the activities of the extravert when he ventured on the introvert's domain better than he could understand the introvert's activities among external facts. (Lawrence told him this was *bunk;* he was an extravert by inheritance far more than *in esse.* He'd have been a much better introvert if he'd been allowed !) The novels are those of a more than moderate extravert; even the diary-extracts in which *Point Counter Point* and *Eyeless in Gaza* abound are by no means exclusively introspective. And he had no desire to encourage his introversial tendencies—he saw, like Maine de Biran, where they were likely to lead: the transformation of the active conscience into a merely speculative conscience. The man who spends his time trying, introspectively, to " know himself " discovers less than anyone else. " Self-limited, his sole experience a kind of spiritual onanism, he only partially exists " (" One and Many ", *Do What You Will*). The soul needs the direct, physical experience of diversity.

Huxley was finding his way by a process of elimination. Examining himself, he discovered his personal graces and failings, set out to use to the fullest extent the capacities he had and to alleviate, if possible, the lack of those he had not. As a young man he enjoyed flux and change. In 1927 he could write that he felt no need of an Absolute which he regarded as " the introvert's subjective compensation for the multifariousness of strange and hostile objects " (*Proper Studies*). He had suggested the same thing in *Jesting Pilate* and in the following year he was to let Philip Quarles make a similar entry in his notebook (*Point Counter Point*).

The most faithful self-portrait of this middle period is in fact to be found in Quarles. His notebook gives us the current equivalent of a *Do What You Will* or *Proper Studies*. In one place he writes how much easier it is to know a lot about art and philosophy than about people. The real charm of the intellectual life lies in its easiness. " Living's much more difficult than Sanskrit or chemistry or economics." People try to drown their realisation of the difficulties of living properly in some kind of absorption: alcohol, fornication, dancing, movies, lectures, scientific hobbies—in his case, dilettantism. Under the heading Search for Truth it sounded noble and disinterested, but Quarles had discovered that the Search for Truth was just an amusement like any other—refined and elaborate, it is true, but still a substitute for living; and Truth-Searchers became just as silly, infantile and corrupt in their way as the boozers, the business men and the Good-Timers. The influence of Lawrence is again discernible; he had told Huxley that every man should be an artist in life, must create his own moral form. But the artist is in a peculiarly difficult position to follow this precept. He is compelled to cut himself off from society, to repress his " societal instinct ", which Lawrence considered even stronger than the sex instinct. And familiarity with ideas, such as Huxley possessed, gave him and others the false notion that he understood all about personal relationships, because he was an " excellent psychologist ". What he was beginning to discover was that he was only at home with *ideas* about personal relationships.

Obviously Huxley was passing through a mental crisis. The author of *Antic Hay* was dead—or morally transformed. A more realistic attitude was struggling to be born, but the struggle was a long one and, from about 1930 to 1936, it made only occasional appearances in his work. For the struggle was with himself, and this familiar phrase possessed for him more than its normal everyday meaning. He was literally seeking for his self, trying to uncover it from the mass of attitudes and ideas that he had previously mistaken for his interior essence. There is little reflection of what was going on in the work of the early thirties. *Brave New World,* for instance, still represented the intelligence turned outward. The great step forward was taken when he realised, not merely intellectually but through his own participation in the life of his time, that there was no real gulf between the inner man and the outer world, his internal psychology and his external actions. There must be some medium in which all moved, some principle which connected every aspect of a man's life. The multitudinous diversity of his past life, the flux and the change, were all appearances masking a reality that he felt impelled to discover. Then everything seemed to happen at once. *Eyeless in Gaza* (1936) indicated the way he had chosen, he became a pacifist (the inevitable outer response to the inner revelation), and in 1937 he cut loose from the familiar surroundings that had given birth to *Antic Hay* and *Two or Three Graces,* and went to live in the Mohave Desert. His choice was influenced by his wife's ill-health and by his own need for clear, strong sunlight, and also the presence there of excellent teachers of the Bates method of visual re-education. The remainder of Huxley's progress, which is a spiritual one, will be followed in later chapters, and also some of the particular paths he followed. The latter is a misleading phrase because Huxley is a far more integrated writer than most, and the paths all coalesce into one broad one. The same mind that struggled to a conception of the unitive life with God also considered man in his animal and human aspects, and never ceased to concern itself with political and social problems. But the exigencies of a study such as this demand a certain amount of compartmentalisation. In the article on Goya in *Themes and Variations* he traced the artist's progress from " light-hearted eighteenth century art, hardly at all unconventional in subject-matter or in handling, through fashionable brilliancy and increasing virtuosity to something quite timeless both in technique and spirit." We can follow the same stages in Huxley's work: the light-hearted *Crome Yellow,* the brilliancy and virtuosity of *Point Counter Point* and at least the attempt at timeless art in *Time Must Have A Stop* and *The Genius and the Goddess.* One of Goya's pictures showed an ancient man tottering along under the burden of years, with the accompanying caption: " I'm still learning ". It was Goya himself. His greatest work was done during the second forty years of his life. One is reminded of Michelangelo's *Imparo ancora* (" I am learning still ") and even of Professor T. H. Huxley's " I have always been, am, and propose to remain a mere scholar ". The test of Aldous Huxley is that we always look forward with excitement to his next book. We know that it will not be a mere re-trampling of the same ground as was covered in previous ones, in the manner of Bertrand Russell.

In *After Many A Summer* Mr. Propter complains that most literature accepts the conventional scale of virtues and treats them too deferentially. Power and position are respected, success admired, the lunatic preoccupations of statesmen, lovers, business men, social climbers are treated as reasonable activities. (One reason for Chaucer's greatness was his refusal to regard his diplomatic missions as having any intrinsic importance.) Such literature helps perpetuate misery by explicitly or implicitly approving the thoughts, feelings and practices which always produce, and cannot fail to produce, misery. Huxley, as is evident from his later novels, is striving to avoid this kind of treatment. A good satire is much more deeply truthful and more profitable than a good tragedy, says Propter. In his youth Huxley had realised that the highest literary values are moral, and now he is trying to put this realisation into practice.

Mr. Propter felt that an adult mind could only be wearied by the merely descriptive plays and novels that critics expect us to admire. Innumerable anecdotes and romances and character-studies, but no general theory of anecdotes, no explanatory hypothesis of romance or character. " Just a huge collection of facts about lust and greed, fear and ambition, duty and affection; just facts, and imaginary facts at that, with no co-ordinating philosophy superior to common sense and the local system of conventions, no principle of arrangement more rational than simple aesthetic expediency. And then the astonishing nonsense talked by those who undertake to elucidate and explain this hodge-podge of prettily patterned facts and fancies!" The net result is that a satisfying literature becomes much more difficult for the truly enlightened man, who is as much concerned with value as with sensation. Sebastian Barnack realised that adherence to the Perennial Philosophy rendered it practically impossible for many of the most admired works in the European literary canon to retain their significance and charm (*Time Must Have A Stop*). The new crisis presented itself, not as a question as to what should be written but whether it was possible to go on writing at all! In *The Devils of Loudun* Huxley notes how Surin was tempted to equate his total personality with his literary gifts, which were considerable, and to become a professional man of letters. Surin regarded this as a temptation to succumb to the most respectable of " the lusts of the eye."

It was a cruel dilemma. Just at the time when Huxley had reached full maturity as a writer came this challenge, not from outside (in which case it could have been resisted with all the resources of his spirit) but from inside, from his own carefully purged psyche, to abandon all he had lived and work for. A rapid review of his literary progress will help to set the new dilemma in its strongest light. In the early part of his career he had dazzled by the brilliance of his façade rather than by the depth of his thought. The novels were to blame. They gave great scope for all the surface erudition of which he was capable but there was never any need to develop the arguments so attractively presented. There could always be an interruption before the complexities became too tangled. This weakness became most obvious when *Proper Studies* was published (1927). It starts off with a scholarly roll of drums that makes the reader sit up. Here, he thinks, will be a march past to be remembered, a parade of the theories followed by a stupendous slaughter of the prejudices, and homage to the eventual victor. But it fizzles out. There is no victor. It is very much a case of modern war. We are left with bits and pieces, and no coherent system. Somewhere along the road the armoury was exhausted, and the army itself seems to lose confidence in its own powers.

*On The Margin* had not strained the intellectual muscles unduly. It was good on the superior feuilleton level. *Along the Road* was largely a record of sensitive appreciation. Huxley was in command, but the commentary was of no very high intellectual quality. *Jesting Pilate* was travel, and again perceptive recording—but social comment was strengthened. It was in *Do What You Will* that Huxley found the right road for himself, and thereafter he went from critical strength to strength. He had found his true subject, man's spiritual nature. He could now make forays from his central position into the social wilderness and the spiritual landscape, with the latter always bringing the best out of him, giving his talents wider scope. Although it would not be true to say that there was an internal struggle between social commentator and spiritual explorer, for the same entity appeared in both rôles, it was happier and more effective in the latter. It moved on to *Ends and Means, Grey Eminence* and *The Devils of Loudun,* with a grasp of subject and a control of expression that was both magisterial and humble, single-pointed and eclectic.

Huxley had fought and overcome the demon within himself and the enemies that assail and conquer most writers. At the moment of victory the still small voice, the Divine Ground, the god-in-man, put the question: was even such a victory commensurable with unitive knowledge of the Father? This is a question whose answer, which can at this stage be only tentative and uncertain, must be left to a later chapter, as must a consideration of the Perennial Philosophy itself. This chapter has been a panorama. I now intend to select for closer examination certain features of the landscape with a view to elucidating some of the problems that have been posed, and possibly finding some not too evasive solutions.

# Chapter 3

## FAIRY GODFATHERS

Baby mine, how strange to see
　　Other faces blent in thine,
Other greatness touching thee,
　　Baby mine.
Something in a curve or line
　　Here revives thine ancestry:
Each on thee has laid his sign.
And thyself ?　Ah, thou for me
　　Shalt this heritage enshrine;
All I was not, thou shalt be,
　　Baby mine !

WHETHER Leonard Huxley addressed this poem to
Aldous or Julian I am uncertain, but at any rate it
establishes his awareness of the family heritage.　The
importance of ancestry in the bequeathing of mental gifts is
disputed.　All we can say for certain is that consciousness of
paternal or ancestral abilities will act as an influence even if
they are not transmitted.　It is usual, in writing a book of this
sort, to start with a few paragraphs about family circumstances,
careers and attitudes of parents, with a suggestion of inherited
characteristics.　These details tend to exist in a vacuum as no
one really understands the laws of psychological heredity.　The
subject is so vague that almost any fitting together of the pieces
is considered acceptable.　The subject of biography is open-
hearted because his father was or, conversely, because his
father wasn't.　All the same, Aldous Huxley's recent heredity
is so distinguished we can hardly ignore it.

Besides the Big Three (Professor T. H. Huxley, Dr. Thomas
and Matthew Arnold) there was a small galaxy of minor stars:
his father Leonard, his aunt Mrs. Humphrey Ward, and all the
Arnold educators.　Among them I will merely make passing
reference to William, author of *Oakfield, or Fellowship in the*

*East,* a novel of military life in India, who summed up the English task in that country as follows: "physical improvement first, then intellectual, then spiritual; that seems the natural order of things "—an order that reversed the one put into practice by his father at Rugby. Matthew's order was again different and Aldous, who came to share this Arnold preoccupation with classified priorities, adopted yet another.

It is probable that a cast of mind can be handed on from father to son, but not specific ideas. Yet the distinction is not a great one because specific ideas come from the interaction of a particular psychological bent with external reality, and where the latter remains fairly constant the ideas are likely to be similar. Aldous is much further removed, spiritually and intellectually, from the worlds, internal and external, of Dr. Thomas Arnold than from those of the other eminences in his family background. The Doctor was the man with the puzzled frown, in Lytton Strachey's view. This Aldous has never been. He shared the family interest in education, and gave special vent to it in *Proper Studies,* but his priorities were not the doctor's. The latter's views were summarised in his now hackneyed remark, " What we must look for here is, firstly, religious and moral principles; secondly, gentlemanly conduct; thirdly, intellectual ability." After years in the wilderness Aldous believes that men should try to advance at an equal pace on all available fronts. He calls them the animal, the human and the divine.

Moving to the other branch of the family, we find little in common to begin with, except that both the Doctor and the Professor expressed a horror of fanaticism, echoed by their descendant. Perhaps Aldous got his taste for omnivorous reading from the Professor. Although the latter, being a scientist, was necessarily concerned with classification, he did not apply it in the generalised Arnold fashion. (In fact, a major characteristic of the Arnold family has been its admiration for general principles.) The Professor announced that his life-objects had been " to promote the increase of natural knowledge and to forward the application of scientific methods of investigation to all the problems of life to the best of my ability, in the conviction which has grown with my growth and strengthened with my strength, that there is no alleviation for the sufferings of mankind except veracity of thought and of action, and the resolute facing of the world as it is, when the garment of make-belief by which pious hands have hidden its uglier features is stripped off." By utterly different routes the Professor and Aldous reached conclusions that were at least proximate—it is only when we begin to analyse them that we discover differences that are transitory rather than teleological. Each realised, in his own particular sphere, how words mask reality; each came to a similar awareness of the true idolatry of modern times. Their disagreement on the ultimate nature of reality, the Professor's absorption in molecular change and Aldous's conviction of independent spiritual activity, are reflections of scientific and cultural phases rather than of basic antagonisms.

But it is in Matthew Arnold, who was not a direct ancestor, in whom we find the greatest affinities with Aldous Huxley. Despite his apparent modernness, Aldous often reads very like a nineteenth century intelligence in a twentieth century setting. By this I do not mean that he mechanically applies a Victorian attitude to modern problems, but that he reacts as an intelligent and highly educated Victorian scholar might be expected to react if he could revisit the world today. He believes in the rightness of reason and he respects science. This is the reality behind his often repeated statement that he is old-fashioned enough to believe in values. If he is much more tolerant towards the existence of irrational and noumenous phenomena than his paternal grandfather was, it is because his environment and its mental climate insist: grandfather would have behaved similarly in similar circumstances. Where Huxley is not modern is his refusal to be stampeded into an acceptance of panaceas and an enthusiasm for universal curricula that are not based on evidence or, at least, widely held intuitions. (" The moral law, like the laws of physical nature, rests in the long run upon instinctive intuitions ", his grandfather wrote.) Like all artists, Aldous dreams, but like a Victorian artist, he selects carefully among his dreams. As he is a displaced Victorian artist, he has learnt to adapt his standards of assessment. " I still prefer reason and experiment to plain-pathed experience and its wish-fulfilments, to even the most high-class instinct, the most appealing feminine intuition", Huxley wrote in *Texts and Pretexts,* commenting on a sonnet by Drayton and some Higher Unlearning from Mrs. Mabel Dodge Luhan. His grandfather knew where to stop in his pursuit of instinct, and *he* knew where to stop in his pursuit of reason.

Like Matthew Arnold, Aldous was more interested in the thing said than in how it was said, though he had the additional advantage of saying it well. This is why he is not a congenital novelist, for most people, including the raw material of fiction, prefer to drift than to illustrate a thesis. In addition to this talent, he was a much better poet than Matthew was a prose-writer. Had Matthew not been so transparently sincere (a preview of Herbert Read, in this respect) it would be impossible for us to read his ugly, cluttered essays with their amorphous appeal to " general principles ". (It was this typically Arnold characteristic that eventually dominated *Proper Studies* and spoilt it after a good start.) But style apart, in method and content the two have much in common. They classified men as the Professor classified Medusae, and they were both keenly aware of the two currents at work in human aspiration, the Hebraising and the Hellenising in Matthew's terminology. " The governing idea of Hellenism is *spontaneity of consciousness;* that of Hebraism *strictness of conscience*", wrote Arnold. Aldous came near enough to this in *Grey Eminence.*

Matthew Arnold was interested neither in " solving the Universe " like Clough nor " dawdling with its painted shell " like Tennyson. Aldous began by dawdling, then impatiently kicked the painted shell up the backside, and finally seems to have come to rest with a solution, although he would be too fly to boast about it. No man can, these days; it was a peculiarly Victorian exercise. Matthew believed that his own particular talent lay in fusing the poetical sentiment of a Tennyson with the intellectual vigour of a Browning, and Aldous may claim to have done something of the kind for our own time. Like his contemporary, Aldous's grandfather, Matthew was very much aware how easily consciousness could be overlaid with words, and like the grandson he knew that Utopia would never come at a nod.

In the Preface to the 1853 *Poems* Arnold explained why the poet so often chooses his action from the past. The action must appeal to the " great primary human affections: to those elementary feelings which subsist permanently in the race and are independent of time." It so happens that antiquity can usually provide better examples of great, noble and intense action than modernity. Some such reasoning as this must have swayed Huxley in his choice of the Grey Eminence and the Devils of Loudun as subjects, for in each case he was discussing matters that are as active and relevant today as ever they were, only in different guises. Arnold felt that poets were too much concerned with rhetoric, too eager in search of the fantastic, too lacking in what he called sanity. The early Huxley deserved all these epithets but the later one seemed to drop back into a hereditary mould: he complains of mere anecdote, overdose of fact (for fact is the twentieth century's substitute for Victorian fantasy) and the lack of an explanatory hypothesis.

But Aldous is not a direct reincarnation of Matthew Arnold, even if we allow for the altered pressure of environment. It would be truer to see in Arnold a model for the Persona, though a more high-souled example than any that appear in the Huxley novels. He believed in culture, and spent a large part of his life trying to explain to people like Frederic Harrison and Roebuck·what he meant by culture. He would have liked the average Englishman to. have emulated Scogan, but without Scogan's egoism. Or conversely, if cornered and compelled to declare himself, Scogan would have stated his ideals in an Arnoldesque fashion—with reservations, of course.

for there was the aura of a prig about Arnold which Scogan could not have borne. In *Grey Eminence* Huxley stated that Arnold chose the " mild and respectable road of literary modernism ". The only solution to the kind of dilemma in which Arnold found himself lay through spiritual exercises, and he was inhibited from them by the mental climate in which he lived.

Arnold realised that most people exalted personal or class ideas into what they imagined to be eternal verities. Like his father, he believed he could shatter these chimera by the application of " general principles ". The time had come to Hellenise, to praise knowing, " for we have Hebraised too much, and have over-valued doing." Huxley repeated these ideas but in modern terms—and he also went further. He knew, like Arnold, that there were people who could transcend their own class, Barbarians and Philistines who knew how to Hellenise. What Arnold never managed to discover was that Hellenisation was not enough; that, having Hellenised, it was then necessary to pass beyond it to a new kind of single-pointedness, almost a refined Hebraism, but without the machinery of word and ritual in which Hebraism abounds. Arnold demanded that the " ordinary self " should give way to the " best self ", but Huxley has been unable to express himself in such naïve terms. Reading in Oriental philosophy and Western parapsychological research has revealed to him a much more complex internal world, in which the ego is influenced by a cauldron of dark impulses as well as by the conscious will, the personality is subject to invasion from a hypothetical psychic medium, and the " divine spark " is something more than a poetic trope. Arnold did as much as contemporary psychology allowed him, but he could not go beyond stating a preference for sweetness and light over fire and strength, or transforming the personality according to the " law of perfection ". In consequence, he at times becomes almost as unbelievable for the modern mind as, say, Gregers Werle in *The Wild Duck*.

The normal philistine attitudes of their times were similar

to each other. The *Daily Telegraph* called Arnold a Jeremiah, and doubtless believed it had scored a point. Today the *Daily Express,* which believes that man can only find God through support of the British Empire and destruction of U.N.O., simply cannot understand what Huxley is getting at and, through one of its mouths, Miss Nancy Spain, dismisses Huxley as a chip off the old block. In fact, each writer is concerned with the imbecility of the world in which we live, and in which the press plays a leading part. The difference lies in this: Arnold sought no practical remedy to the world's misery and even denied, as a matter of theory, the possibility of such a remedy existing; Huxley, on the other hand, believes in the cultivation of the mystical approach to God. For people who do not believe in its existence such a remedy cannot exist. Arnold fell short of it. Modern critics reject it.

## Chapter 4

### CHILDHOOD, INNOCENCE AND ADOLESCENCE

IN one respect Huxley's fiction portrays a very limited world. Practically all the action is confined to the upper middle class, and only a section of that: the aesthetic and speculative branch, merging at one extreme with bohemia and at the other with the aristocracy. But it is not the conventional landed aristocracy of English life and letters, the world described and occasionally satirised by Trollope; it is rather a group that has been drawn into an alien sphere of action by the interests and friendships of a literary son or a dilettante wife. Within this group, however, there is a very wide psychological range, taking in respected imbeciles such as Quarles Senior and diabolists such as Spandrell. To borrow jargon familiar to economists, the trustification is vertical rather than horizontal. We rarely venture outside narrow class limits. There is an occasional foray into the ranks of the unemployed and American transients, the odd business man makes his appearance, and there is even an uneasy encounter with a representative of the depressed lower middle class (" Half Holiday ", *Two or Three Graces*). The major interest of " Fard " (*Little Mexican*) is shared between a restless, discontented woman of the world and her worn-out maid—and that is about the sum total of Huxley's excursion outside the select group. Within the group, however, there is intensive exploration.

In this respect Huxley's work is not exceptional. But in another it is. More than any other contemporary novelist he takes in the whole range of the individual's life, from birth to death. The Huxleyan world is not one exclusively of young men or middle-aged men or old men; it is a world of children and adolescents as well as adults. Many novelists find children difficult material. Huxley doesn't. But more than this, he attempts to portray the human being in all his phases, and his children are usually much more than the impedimenta with which life plagues the novelist who would rather ignore them, if they didn't so palpably and noisily exist. One of the most important characters in *Point Counter Point* is a little boy; in *The Genius and the Goddess* a young girl; and in " Fairy Godmother " (*Two or Three Graces*) all the action revolves round a baby. Childless marriages are more common in sophisticated fiction than in life, but not in Huxley's fiction.

Some of the references to childhood are quite conventional —little boys bullying each other at school, or falling in love. This type of treatment, containing very little significance, appears in the early " Farcical History of Richard Greenow " (*Limbo*). Dick was gibed at by his schoolfellows because they thought him girlish—which he was. He felt a violent emotion in the presence of Francis Quarles, " clad in white flannels and the radiance of the sunshine ". But Dick was a very special case, being hermaphrodite, and we will gain nothing from lingering over him. Gumbril Junior could remember a similar emotion overtaking him—but it was all part of the process of growing up in an English public school.

It was in *Jesting Pilate* (1926) that Huxley first remarked upon something more than the nuisance or the nauseating or the amusing, where children were concerned. He referred with unexpected approval to some reflections made by Benjamin Kidd on the " superhuman beauty " of children. He continues: " We are like angels when we are children— candid, innocently passionate, disinterestedly intelligent. The angelic qualities of our minds express themselves in our faces ". Not a very profound remark, perhaps, but interesting coming from Huxley. Then he continued in a more recognisably Huxleyan vein: " as middle-age advances we become less and less human, increasingly simian ". (If we live long enough we will become completely simian, seems to be the message of *After Many A Summer*.) A few years later, in *Vulgarity in Literature*, he wrote: " Children are remarkable for their intelligence and ardour, for their curiosity, their intolerance of shams, the clarity and ruthlessness of their vision." In "Uncle Spencer" (*Little Mexican*), however, he had decried the famous wisdom of babes, and stated that those who study the souls of children in hopes of finding out something about the souls of men will be disappointed.

This difference between child and adult, between innocence and falsity, seems to have made a deep impression on Huxley. Added to this was the fact that each child was a population of strangers. Mrs Quarles, worrying about her little Phil, could see in him not only herself and her husband but her deplorable father-in-law. And how many hundreds of others? His name "was an abstraction, a title arbitrarily given, like ' France ' or ' England ', to a collection, never long the same, of many individuals, who were born, lived and died within him, as the inhabitants of a country appear and disappear, but keep alive in their passage the identity of the nation to which they belong " (*Point Counter Point*). Opinions held in childhood often persist into manhood and are linked with others, acquired later, with which they are quite incompatible. " I shall go down to my grace," he wrote in " Uncle Spencer ", " making certain judgments, holding certain opinions, regarding certain things and actions in a certain way—and the way, the opinions, the judgments will not be mine, but my Uncle Spencer's; and the obscure chambers of my mind will to the end be haunted by his bright, erratic, restless ghost."

No wonder it was so difficult to establish contact with a child ! In some ways he had not yet fused into a whole. For an unimaginative man like Anthony's father (*Eyeless in Gaza*) it was really impossible. When Anthony's mother died Mr Beavis hoped that common grief, common memories would draw them together—he could never understand that the way to a child's mind did not lie through adult ritual. Rivers, in *The Genius and the Goddess,* realised much more clearly the kind of imaginative effort necessary for the success of such a venture. The child's sensations are preternaturally acute, far beyond those of the normal adult's. " When you're a child your mind is a kind of saturated solution of feeling, a suspension of all the thrills—but in a latent state, in a condition of indeterminacy." The dim, half-alive rationalisations of the adult mind cannot quicken him. He needs everything to be presented in the form of a thrill, else he will not come to terms with it. Death is not a quiet sob and cow-like eyes, but guts and corruption. These can be understood.

In general there is a wall of misunderstanding between child and adult, illustrated in novel and story alike. Barbara in " Green Tunnels " (*Mortal Coils*), although seventeen, is still a child—indeed, she is rather backward for her age, considering her creator's tastes. Her dilemma is simple but insoluble: the world is full of wonderful things but Mr Topes has an unerring faculty for making them appear dull. What was obviously gold turned to lead at his touch. He took the reality from things by referring them to art, just as Huxley himself was inclined to do as a young man. " Why do you always talk about art?" said Barbara. " You bring these dead people into everything. What do I know about Canova or whoever it is?"

What every Huxleyan parent learnt was that their children unaccountably fail to follow parental interests. Mr Porteous discovered that they were only interested in behaving like apes. While he had sat up most of the night reading Latin texts, his son " sits up—or rather stands, reels, trots up—dancing and drinking " (*Antic Hay*). Mrs. Chelifer had been saddened by her son's failure to follow in his father's footsteps at the college. " The child, I thought, grows up to forget that he is of the same flesh with his parents; but they do not forget " (*Those Barren Leaves*). Rampion, in his forthright way, generalised on the tendency of children to spite their parents. " Not on purpose, of course, but unconsciously because they can't help it, because the parents have probably gone too far in one direction and nature's reacting, trying to get back to the state of equilibrium " (*Point Counter Point*).

In Huxley's view of childhood, therefore, we have two

dominant elements to consider: the familiar notion of innocence, plus reaction against the parent, what Rampion called spite. It is possibly the inevitable destruction of innocence that calls up the spite as a form of retaliation. In Huxley's fiction it is possible to trace the various stages of this conflict.

What we normally understand by " the innocent eye " in literature is almost entirely absent from Huxley's work, even the earliest poems. At a very early age he seems to have adopted the habit of seeing things in relation to ideas, like Mr Topes. He starts one poem, for instance:

> Fine on the dust of plumy fountains blowing
> Across the lanterns of a revelling night,
> The tiny leaves of April's earliest growing
> Powder the trees—

but a few lines later the trees seem " things beatified, Come from the world of thought which was their home ". The world of thought dominated Huxley's perceptions, and it is not till much later that we discover that he had in fact enjoyed the direct vision of a child. Increasingly as he grows older a sense of inescapable destiny overwhelms him. In " Seasons " (*The Cicadas,* 1931) "time stanchlessly flows"; he acts, but not to his design; " winter has set its muddy sign/Without me and within ". Spring can act as a restorative (" The doors are down and I can run,/Can laugh, for destiny is dead ") but such incursions are more and more rare. Huxley's youthful work, poetry as well as prose, turns away from direct experience and direct emotion to secondary rationalisation. But somewhere inside him was a sense of guilt, a recognition that by turning away from nature he was abusing his own gifts. This feeling expressed itself in his admiration for Chaucer, the only great poet who consistently accepted the " law of kind ". All other poets, except in moments of illumination, protested against the law. He was another. He told himself that nature is inevitably material, not a symbol, and then acted upon the opposite intuition.

Being young and rather foolish, even if extremely intelligent, he did not understand the real significance of this innate respect for Chaucer for many years. Meanwhile, he was able to introduce innocence into his novels as a rather amusing quality possessed by the immature. Mary Bracegirdle's innocence was "moon-like", her face "shone pink and childish", despite her twenty-three years (*Crome Yellow*). She simply couldn't understand why Denis found everything so complicated. "Why can't you just take things for granted and as they come?" she asks him. "That's all very well," he replies, "but you've got to learn the lesson gradually." "I've always taken things as they come," she replies. "It seems so obvious. One enjoys the pleasant things, avoids the nasty ones. There's nothing more to be said." Lucy Tantamount might have said the same, but it would have come out of a dark cellar of knowing bitchiness. And of course Denis was only making a desperate attempt to cover up his own inadequacy. There were times when his eyes suddenly became innocent, childlike, unprejudiced, and he saw people for what they were. But the real pain, on such occasions, lay in knowing what *he* was too.

In *Antic Hay* there is a much more sympathetic account of simplicity and innocence. For a while Gumbril Junior is fascinated by Emily. They sit on a bank and he gazes at her. "She had taken off her hat; there was a stir of wind in those childish curls, and at the nape, at the temples, where the hair had sleeved out thin and fine, the sunlight made little misty haloes of gold. Her hands clasped round her knees, she sat quite still, looking out across the green expanses, at the trees, at the white clouds on the horizon. There was quiet in her mind, he thought. She was native to that crystal world; for her, the steps came comfortingly through the silence and the lovely thing brought with it no terrors. It was all so easy for her and simple." She also thought he made everything unnecessarily complicated. She once told him her idea of perfect happiness: driving together in a trap to her cottage, having tea, going for a walk, sitting under the trees, going home to a supper ready prepared. But how did all this fit into a world ruled by Mrs Viveash? Gumbril could only think how simple it would be to destroy this simplicity, " to puddle clear waters and unpetal every flower . . . How simple to spit on the floors of churches!" And he proceeded to break her heart.

All this struggling out of childhood, turning away from innocence because it is the mark of childhood, is part of the turbulence we call adolescence. And just as the children suffer from repression in Huxley's fiction, so the adolescents are tortured by their inability to take decisive action. Telling the world and especially themselves that they are really men and women, even if lamentably young ones, they are nevertheless aware that the world does not take them at their face value. Pretension and bravado rule their lives. Humming and hawing about things that don't really matter, they suddenly behave outrageously in a field where things do matter; they mean to prove their worth and only prove their inconsequence.

The poem "Soles Occidere et Redere Possunt" tries to set forth the quandary of the adolescent. The subject of the poem, John Ridley, was killed in 1918. He was an adolescent and Huxley says he " suffered from that instability of mind ' produced by the mental conflict forced upon man by his sensitiveness to herd suggestion on the one hand and to experience on the other ' " (the quotation is from Trotter's work on the Herd Instinct). Here are a few moments from the life of John Ridley, Adolescent :

> Action, action ! First of all
> He spent three pounds he couldn't afford
> In buying a book he didn't want,
> For the mere sake of having been
> Irrevocably extravagant.
> Then feeling very bold, he pressed
> The bell of a chance house; it might
> Disclose some New Arabian Night
> Behind its grimy husk, who knows ?
> The seconds passed; all was dead.
> Arrogantly he rang once more.
> His heart thumped on sheer silence; but at last
> There was a shuffling; something behind the door
> Became approaching panic and he fled.

The most famous adolescent in Huxley's fiction is Denis, in *Crome Yellow*. I have already referred to his desperate attempt to confuse the universe inextricably; or, in other words, to annihilate his childhood. Denis feels it is his duty to reduce the world to order, his own kind of chaotic order. He is always starting odes and throwing them away. We meet him one morning after making an unsuccessful effort to write " something about nothing in particular ". His head is always full of poetic tags, other people's ideas. He is liable to start a conversation with a love-hungry young girl in this fashion: " The individual is not a self-supporting universe. There are times when he comes into contact with other individuals, when he is forced to take cognisance of the existence of other universes beside himself." (Collapse of love-hungry girl, as the *Punch* of an earlier day would have had it.) As for taking effective action, he was miserably incompetent. When, with an effort, he managed to do it, everything went wrong.

Scogan had no patience with adolescents and said so. They *would* write about their own mentalities, and who could expect the adult reader to be interested in such a subject? It was just possible that a professional anthropologist might concern himself with the philosophical preoccupations of undergraduates, as a relief from those of Blackfellows, but you could not expect anyone else to do so for pleasure. Twenty-four years after Bruno Rontini remarked that the adolescent can be quite as inept as the old. There wasn't so much to choose between early Shelley and late Wordsworth (*Time Must Have A Stop*).

In *Do What You Will* Huxley says that the majority of chronological adults never emerge from adolescence. They spend a great deal of their time trying to justify their compensatory imaginations intellectually. This was the main preoccupation of Shelley and Denis, while the Emilys of this world had never reached this stage and never would. And beyond either class were the Propters and Bruno Rontinis, who had discovered the imbecility of trying to prove that something was other than it was, just because its true nature didn't suit man's pretensions. " The newly conscious and the newly rational ", writes Huxley, " have all the defects of the newly rich; they make a vulgar parade of their possessions, they swaggeringly advertise their powers. . . . The childish fancies are inspired directly by life. The adolescent noumena are abstractions from life, flights from diversity into disembodied oneness."

One of the convictions Huxley came to in later life was that we ought to acquire the habit of accepting nature in its own right—the Chaucerian attitude, in fact. The painfully won habit of abstraction and rationalisation may be jettisoned, for it only sets up a wall between ourselves and reality. *The Genius and the Goddess* is an attempt to give this conviction expression. Rivers praises experience, but it must be pure experience, unsteeped " in the tripe and hogwash dished out by the moulders of public opinion ". If you can make this effort you will then discover that it is possible to recapture lost innocence. Age is no barrier. Man starts his career as a lump of protoplasm, a machine for eating and excreting; he becomes something almost supernaturally pure and beautiful; then come pimples and puberty, followed by Praxiteles; and finally the horrible descent into gorillahood. And only a new effort of innocence can save him from the latter fate.

## Chapter 5

### ART—AND THEN NATURE

THERE is a strong pastoral element in Huxley's early work. One feels it did not derive from the courting of dairy-maids but from extensive browsing in the classics. His early avowed love of nature strikes the mind rather artificially. He came to Nature through Art because traditions urged him on. There is a story in *Limbo* about the return of Pan, which is very much like the kind of thing that Forster and Saki produced occasionally during the early years of the century. It was fashionable, up to 1930 and *New Signatures,* for the gods to reincarnate themselves among the English upper middle classes. There is a strong classical interest in the early poems. He dreams of the sudden appearance of Pan—or the spirit of Italy, it isn't quite clear. He translates " L'Apres-Midi d'un Faune " from the French of Mallarmé, and retells the story of Leda—and does it very well. He is already a fully fledged aesthete:

> Beyond all thought, past action and past words,
> I would live in beauty, free from self and pain.
> ("Stanzas")

And in a prose piece simply entitled " Beauty " he gives his credo: " It is not a far-fetched, dear-bought gem; no pomander to be smelt only when the crowd becomes too stinkingly insistent; it is not a birth of rare oboes or violins, not visible only from ten to six by state permission at a nominal charge, not a thing richly apart, but an ethic, a way of belief and of practice, of faith and works, mediaeval in its implication with the very threads of life. I desire no Paphian cloister of pink monks. Rather a rosy Brotherhood of Common Life, eating, drinking; marrying and giving in marriage; taking and taken in adultery; reading, thinking, and when thinking fails, feeling immeasureably more subtly, sometimes perhaps creating." Early in the same impression (it can hardly be called an essay) he refers to Faust and implies that one cannot rest with beauty. We can complete the picture of Huxley on Parnassus by quoting from a poem called " Life and Art ". Roses die, but from their death we distil

> The fullness of one rare phial,
>   Whose nimble life shall outrun
> The circling shadow on the dial,
>   Outlast the tyrannous sun.

Now I do not want to give an impression of mere easy superiority when discussing these poems. (Anyway, it is the attitude they embalm rather than the manner which is of interest at the moment.) They are the work of a young man who had not yet found himself. We can view these poems as exercises and must not load them with too much significance. But it is probably fair to say that Huxley genuinely did consider the pursuit of Beauty the major preoccupation of an artist, and that this pursuit lay through the suavity of Art rather than the crudity of Nature. The extract from " Beauty " states that the ideal may be found more easily in adultery than in oboes —but it ends with the wistful promise of creation. So far as sense can be made out of such writing, creation would seem to be the desired end. But the perplexity we feel in reading it is a measure of the essential indeterminateness of the ideas expressed. Huxley was not writing with passion; he was doing his best to make poetry out of a formula.

Did Huxley deceive himself ? Not all the time. The workings of his literary generator produced the Persona, and the Persona had an awkward habit of making some of his favourite notions seem dull and tawdry. I have already referred to Mr Topes, who managed to spoil everything by turning upon them the searchlight of artistic reference. Scogan, too, could be horribly frank and inconvenient. He knew everything there was to know about art before 1900. Did that make him any the more appreciative of art in general ? Not at all. He never felt a true aesthetic emotion—he only knew it existed from

what others had told him. It took him ten years before he
would honestly admit that pictures bored him. And then there
was another danger in the aesthetic game. It could conceivably
drive you to madness, as it did poor Eupompus. Starting with
the familiar ideas of organisation, balance, proportion, you
might continue along the path relentlessly until you discovered
yourself in a " glassily perfect universe of ideas, where all was
informed, consistent, symmetrical ". Many years later, in an
essay on El Greco, Huxley returned to this horror of perfection-
ism in art. As the Greeks said, a circle is a perfect figure; you
cannot improve on it. If you allow such considerations to
dictate to you, you will produce works as perfect as a red
circle inscribed within a black square—" yet even aesthetically
the perfect figure of a circle is less interesting than the perfect
figure of a young woman ". Quite early Huxley recognised
(though subconsciously, for the most part) the dangers of
extreme aestheticism.[1]

Misgivings about the value of art (or, at least, its value when
not the product of real feeling) became intrusive in *Those
Barren Leaves*. Francis Chelifer is worried by his too great
facility. He rarely has much of significance to say, but that
doesn't prevent him saying it. He clings pathetically (the word
is his) to art when he has thrown everything else overboard.
" Art for art's sake—halma for halma's sake. It is time to
smash the last and silliest of the idols." The doubt kept crop-
ping up in the writing of this period. The snobbery which
decrees that one must like Art (which means, pretend to like
Art) is as tyrannous as that which bids one visit the places
where one can see Life, he writes in *Along the Road*. Art has
acquired a bloated reputation because it has filled the vacuum
created by the decay of established religion. Hence the
enormous number of literary names in *Who's Who* and the
interviewers always lying in wait to ask the wandering novelist
his opinion about things of which he is not competent to speak.
And much later we find Mr Propter saying, " Art can be a lot

---

[1] In *Heaven and Hell*, Huxley expresses the fervent hope that non-
representational painting is finished. He was disappointed, but perhaps
because intellectuals are often accurate in ideas but inaccurate in tempo.

of things; but in actual practice most of it is merely the mental equivalent of alcohol and cantharides " (*After Many A Summer*)[1].

Eustace Barnack, in *Time Must Have a Stop*, expressed this new trend in one of his limericks:

> There was a young man of Peoria,
> Who to keep up his sense of euphoria
> Would don his Tuxedo
> And murmur the Credo,
> Along with the Sanctus and Gloria.

If this account of Art is true, what about Nature which was always seen through an artistic filter ? In *Those Barren Leaves* Huxley had a lot of fun at Mrs Aldwinkle's expense. Mrs Aldwinkle appreciated Nature as so many people appreciate Art. " The cypresses make such a wonderful contrast with the olives ", she said, prodding the landscape with the tip of her parasol, as though she were giving a lantern lecture with coloured slides. But perhaps the idea occurred to Huxley that he might not be beyond reproach himself in this respect. At any rate, later in the same novel we find Chelifer (who, like Philip Quarles and Anthony Beavis elsewhere, is one of the author's mouthpieces) giving vent to some heartfelt feelings on the subject of natural description. After describing the approach to Mrs Aldwinkle's palace he wrote, " The car drew up. And about time too, as I notice on re-reading what I have written. Few things are more profoundly boring and unprofitable than literary descriptions."

There is something forced about those early descriptions, as Huxley must have felt and caused Chelifer to admit. *Along the Road* is full of them. Hills, trees, foliage, mist and air are bullied into making pronouncements about North and South, England and Italy; Dutch farmhouses and English farmyards preach lessons in aesthetics; and in *The Olive Tree* (as late as

[1] The artist's place as priest-surrogate has now been taken by the crooner, comedian and TV artist. A sixteen-year-old Johnney Ray fan recently bathed her head and saved the water after Johnney had patted her hair. Other Ray fans wrote to her asking for some of the liquid, but she replied, " I'm not parting with it ". The new Holy Water baptises into the Communion of Crooners.

1936) English oak and Latin olive are raised to the rank of emblems. All the time, behind this hothouse treatment of Nature, lay his admiration for Chaucer, occasionally coming to the surface with a reproach that could not be ignored. And it was not only Chaucer. Edward Thomas, for instance, was " genuinely what so many others of our time quite unjustifiably claim to be, a nature poet. To be a nature poet it is not enough to affirm vaguely that God made the country and man made the town, it is not enough to talk sympathetically about familiar rural objects, it is not enough to be sonorously poetical about mountains and trees, it is not even enough to speak of these things with the precision of a real knowledge and love. To be a nature poet a man must have felt profoundly and intimately those peculiar emotions which nature can inspire, and must be able to express them in such a way that his reader feels them " (*On The Margin*). He returned to his theme in *Texts and Pretexts*, where he said that few poets had been content to set down baldly what they felt without at the same time expounding or implying some cosmic theory to explain why they felt it.

It was a crisis of a kind, and it was necessary to take some kind of action. But at this stage Huxley was in the position of knowing what he ought to do but being unable to do it. He would like to have emulated Thomas; he should have enjoyed Nature as Nature, been content with flower and landscape for their own sakes. In his tale of " Hubert and Minnie " (*Little Mexican*) we get a parallel from the everyday world of conduct. He describes a typical young modern couple who model their nature (i.e., their behaviour and personal relations, or what the world believes to be their nature) on literary patterns. They and their friends were convinced that Dostoievsky was a fair substitute for murder and D. H. Lawrence for sex. Huxley himself passed through this phase and makes no attempt to hide it. In his outlook on the world every external object and every internal feeling was a reflection of an ideal. Later he managed to reverse the relationship but he could not do it in one step, merely by

59

knowing it should be done. Instead he sent Calamy to the mountains (*Those Barren Leaves*—and still a vicarious experience!). For a time his characters acted for him, which was possibly an improvement on acting the wrong way. Calamy gazed at the mountains and drank in their beauty. But he couldn't stop there. "Beautiful, terrible and mysterious," he thought they were, "pregnant with what enormous secret, symbolic of what formidable reality." Thomas had beckoned but Wordsworth intervened.

It was a temporary throwback. Francis Chelifer had grown up in the shadow of Wordsworth. His father had walked him to the top of Snowdon and had pronounced the view " bloody fine ". But within him the Wordsworthian emotions had raged unchecked. And now it was Calamy, not Chelifer, who had returned. Chelifer was not capable of such a gesture, he was playing rather uneasily with the idea of living in the heart of human affairs and making the best of them. It is Calamy who takes up the challenge in this book—for in every Huxley novel there is someone who suggests a way out of the dilemma. But Huxley could have felt no great enthusiasm for Calamy's choice. He could never again treat Wordsworth seriously as a guide. When he visited the tropics he was only confirmed in his rejection of " old William's mild pantheism ". Nature gets drunk on tropical rain and sunlight. "If Wordsworth had been compelled to spend a few years in Borneo, would he have loved nature as much as he loved her on the banks of Rydal Water?" Huxley devoted a whole essay in *Do What You Will* to answering this question. His conclusion was that the Wordsworthian adoration of nature had two principal defects. Firstly, it is only possible in a country where Nature has been nearly or quite enslaved to man; and secondly, it requires a falsification of one's immediate intuitions of Nature. " Let Nature be your teacher ", says Wordsworth, and then proceeds to shut his ears and dictate his own lesson, distorting his intuitions rationalistically into the likeness of a parson's sermon.

The power of abstraction came late in man's development —probably somewhere in the course of the emergence of neo-

lithic man. The early " snapshot realism of his bisons " could
only be recovered when the art of abstraction, which made
civilisation possible, could be forgotten. By another route
Huxley was discovering the need to look at the world with
unprejudiced eyes, only he was doing it much earlier than he
is usually given credit for. " Nature does not change; but the
outlines that man sees in Nature, the tunes he hears, the
eternities he imaginatively apprehends—these, within certain
limits, are continuously changing " (*Texts and Pretexts*, 1932).

In this new state of disillusion with Art and alienation from
Nature, the most forceful expression comes from Mark Staithes
in *Eyeless in Gaza*. Mark was by no means a projection of
Huxley himself, being a once hearty, rugger-playing type who
had adopted an attitude of pessimistic asceticism, but he stood
for certain ideas that Huxley felt should be taken seriously.
Mark had nothing but contempt for aestheticism, and with
good reason when one considers the aesthetes he knew. " There
seems to be so little substance in it at all," he said, "Even in
the little that's intrinsically substantial. For of course most
thinking has never been anything but silly. And as for Art, as
for literature—well, look at the museums and the libraries.
*Look* at them ! Ninety-nine per cent of nonsense and mere
rubbish."

After *Eyeless in Gaza* there are not many good words to be
said for art. It is viewed as a pleasant and relatively harmless
drug. Most of the notable things that have been said or
written about it are delusive. Most of us find it much easier
to accept the truth of something that moves us aesthetically.
In fact, says Huxley in his address on " T. H. Huxley as a
Literary Man " (printed in *The Olive Tree*), literary art may
be associated with untruth. If only Plato had written as
badly as Kant, instead of bewitching us with beautiful nonsense ! And if Darwin had written as well as Samuel Butler,
Bernard Shaw's evolutionary doctrine would have been
sounder. In *The Doors of Perception* he goes so far as to say
that art is for beginners (in life, that is) or for dead-enders, who

are content with " the *ersatz* of Suchness ", the elegant recipe rather than the solid meal.

Another observation on art which later impressed Huxley as a rarely noticed truth was its irrelevance to life. Historians are too prone to use art as evidence in their accounts of life in the past, but with little justification. " From a collection of fifteenth-century Italian paintings who could possibly infer the society described by Machiavelli?" he asks in *Grey Eminence*. More often than not, the work of even the most " representative " artists shows what their contemporaries would have liked to be, not what they were. Most pictures and dramas merely illustrate bovaristic dreams. He returns to this theme (and how deflating it is to the ecstatic criticism of his youth!) in *Themes and Variations*. At every period, he says, there exists not a synthesis but " a mere brute collocation of opposites and incompatibles ". The aesthete becomes eloquent as he deduces from the art of the past the spirit " informing " the times. But he is deluding himself; there is no dominant spirit, only dominant dreams. Nevertheless, I feel that the dreams possess more importance than Huxley is willing to allow them.

The final stage is the condemnation of all art, which I referred to in the second chapter. Some God-centred saints have condemned art, root and branch. Aquinas, after achieving unitive knowledge of the Primordial Fact, ceased to write. In *Time Must Have A Stop* Sebastian Barnack reflected that " even the best play or narrative is merely glorified gossip and artistically disciplined day-dreaming. And lyric poetry? Just ' Ow! ' or Oo-ooh! ' or ' Nyum-nyum! ' or ' Damn! ' or ' Darling! ' or 'I'm a pig! '—suitably transliterated, of course, and developed." The way of an artist lies on a knife-edge. His gift is a gratuitous grace, in François de Sales's terminology, and not necessarily edifying. When I asked Huxley how he was managing to exist on such a precarious balance, he replied, " I do not feel impelled—nor am I financially able—to give up writing; nor do I think that writing is in any way incompatible with understanding. ' Knowledge ', says Lao-tsu, ' is adding to your stock day by day; the practice of the Tao is subtracting '. The secret of life is to do both—add and subtract—to the limit."

The net result of Huxley's misgivings on the score of culture is that he is no longer tempted to over-value it. Such over-valuation is today practised as policy in Soviet Russia, where Literature, Science and Art have become the three persons of a new humanistic trinity. Hard-boiled journalists in the capitalist democracies bow to Culture, if nothing else. " Advanced " educationists believe all will be well if only children and adolescents are allowed to " express " themselves. Classes are given in " appreciation ". These are Huxley's views, as set forth in *The Perennial Philosophy,* although my personal view is that, of his three persons, only Science has been deified to a dangerous extent. The deification of Art and Literature took place at an earlier date, and they have now sunk to a lower level in the Pantheon. They only retain their old influence as representatives of dead cultures which, lacking challenge, are readily acceptable as totems. Those Barren Leaves are now dead. Dr Obispo helped sweep them up.

Note: But Huxley was right. Since the war there has been a glut in deification: Art again, but this time at a popular level; Education; Sociology; and, of course, Statistics. 1966.

# Chapter 6

## THE HUMAN ORGY-PORGY

THE outstanding characteristic of Huxley's writing, for many people, lies in his horrified fascination with the human body and its physical functions. Here are three judgments from a symposium that appeared in the *London Magazine* for August 1955, all by reputable critics. Angus Wilson felt that the " pathological wallowing in physical disgust " that occurred in *Point Counter Point* and *Eyeless in Gaza* became tedious. Francis Wyndham felt that Huxley obliquely honoured the sensual life as a pornographer honours sex. And John Wain asked what on earth had the type of sex relationship described in *After Many A Summer* to do with the life of a normally poised human being ? In a 1946 broadcast Peter Quennell, speaking primarily of *Time Must Have A Stop,* said : " In the world that Huxley now evokes there would appear to be no intermediate stage between the ecstatic and the repulsive; no allowance is made for harmless human pleasures, for the mild afternoon sunshine of ordinary human life." These are the normal criticisms levelled at Huxley's work. Elizabeth Bowen, on the other hand, is more sympathetic. Those incidents which are usually dubbed " unnecessary " (e.g., the dog on the roof in *Eyeless in Gaza* and the moron's death in *Those Barren Leaves*) she calls the " moral pivots of the two books ". But she belongs to the minority.

Preoccupation with the flesh and corruption is found in Huxley's work from the beginning. It possibly accounts for his equal preoccupation with art, which usually managed to make the body appear beautiful and concealed the less pleasant aspects of life. We find him wishing that the body could be as quick (i.e., untrammelled) as the mind, and that will should find " release from bondage to brute things "

("The Reef", *Early Poems*).  But release was only a mirage, for the mind could never break loose from its partner, and

> Every earth to earth returns at last. ("The Elms")

He returned to this theme in the first of the well-known "Philosopher's Songs", published in *Leda* :

> But oh, the sound of simian mirth!
> Mind, issued from the monkey's womb,
> Is still umbilical to earth,
> Earth its home and earth its tomb.

Jove, lying in his high Olympian chamber, is appalled by the pattern of human flesh, wonders what strange deity ("so barbarously not a Greek") could have created such ugliness, Oriental and African :

> . . . a trellis of suppurating lips,
> of mottled tentacles barbed at the tips
> And bloated hands and wattles and red lobes
> Of pendulous gristle and enormous probes
> Of pink and slashed and tasselled flesh . . .
> > He turns
> Northward his sickened sight.
> > > ("Leda")

But not even Olympus is free of the body's stain.  As he stretches on his bed Jove is made aware of his own sweat.

Riding on a bus Huxley watches the smoke from his pipe streaming over his shoulder—" and my life with it ".

> I am a harp of twittering strings,
> An elegant instrument, but infinitely second-hand.

And what happened when this age-old plasm grew even older and prepared for the end of what it had not passed on? Beautiful women became repulsive.  Old men stank, their eyes were rheumy and rosiny.  Such were the thoughts that occurred to the young man as he caressed his mistress in " The Death of Lully " (*Limbo*).  It was this very decay, aided by disease, that had caused Lully to throw over his life of indulgence and become a hermit—the sight of his lover's breast, half eaten away by cancer, when she had stripped for his pleasure.

Huxley could not empty his mind of the incommensurables that seemed to govern sex, a reflection of the beauty that masked the cancer.  In a poem called " Morning Scene " he pictures a lady lying on a nuptial couch, with ribbed light beating on her naked bosom through a latticed blind, and above it " a red face, Fixed in the imbecile earnestness of lust " —a last line that makes a neat pair with that of " Frascati's " where lovers sit, " quietly sweating palm to palm ". The lust is at the same time abhorrent and insistent, overwhelming in its ardour and frightening in its animalism. Many years later, in *Time Must Have A Stop,* we find the young Sebastian churning out the images as he walks along the street, as much a victim as a victimiser.

> What bulls, what boys, what frenzy of swans and nipples,
> What radiant lusts like a red forge panting up
> From fire to brighter fire . . .

" Purple explosion of Bengal lights ", he feels, " rocketing up irrepressibly and uninvited into his throat." Huxley could not resist them, and he was ashamed. He was a man, and a man was supposed to live on a higher level than an animal.

He projected the same vision of pullulent rottenness into the mind of his dead friend John Ridley. He sits miserably in a café,

> Sunk to the eyes in the warm sodden morass
> Of his own guts . . .

He is

> Cesspool within, and without him he could see
> Nothing but mounds of flesh and harlotry.

But it is inescapable, the link between man and nature (not the charming felicities of nature as seen through art but its steaming, proliferating reality) is too strong to be broken. He, the promising young poet, watches the cows chewing, and knows that what they chew will one day form his body—

> My future body, which in Tuscan fields
> Yet grows, yet grunts among the acorns, yet
> Is salt and iron, water and touchless air . . .

And lightning flashes across the sky like "sudden sperm". He can find no relief from the obsession, almost an agony. He is cow and pig and fish and the very elements imitate functions he loathes yet cannot reject.

While giving full expression to this inner loathing (it was

really the familiar conflict between desire and reason raised to
an exceptional degree) in his poetry, Huxley managed to
restrain it in the earliest fiction. *Limbo* is practically free of
it and there is little in *Crome Yellow* beyond Henry Wimbush's
delight in the sanitation basis of Crome's architecture. Sir
Ferdinando, who built the house, placed the privies at the top
because " the necessities of nature are so base and brutish that
in obeying them we are apt to forget that we are the noblest
creatures of the universe ". Therefore the privies were to be
placed nearest heaven. There is no anguish in this, no com-
plaint to God that he should have constructed man in such a
way that excretion should be necessary. Nor is such a sentiment obtrusive in *Mortal Coils,* except perhaps in " Nuns at
Luncheon ". Challenged to make a story out of Melpomene
leaning over the castle bastions, the narrator causes her to
"look down and perceive, suddenly and apocalyptically that
everything in the world is sex, sex, sex. Men and women,
male and female—always the same, and all, in the light of the
horror of the afternoon, disgusting." But the narrator is
Huxley and the lady has just been seduced for the first time.
I would certainly not claim that lust and loathing and corruption are absent from this collection, but they are reasonably
under control.

In *Antic Hay* they thrust their way through. They become
incarnate in Coleman, with full licence to perform, to rave, to
trample on whatever beauty or decency may attempt to
insinuate themselves. Coleman howls with delight. " Does it
occur to you ", he says, " that at this moment we are walking
through the midst of seven million distinct and separate individuals, each with distinct and separate lives and all completely
indifferent to our existence ? Seven million people, each one
of whom thinks himself quite as important as each of us does.
Millions of them are now sleeping in an empested atmosphere.
Hundreds of thousands of couples are at this moment engaged
in mutually caressing one another in a manner too hideous to
be thought of, but in no way differing from the manner in

which each of us performs, delightfully, passionately and beautifully, his similar work of love. Thousands of women are now in the throes of parturition, and of both sexes thousands are dying of the most diverse and appalling diseases, or simply because they have lived too long. Thousands are drunk, thousands have over-eaten, thousands have not had enough to eat. And they are all alive, all unique and separate and sensitive, like you and me." Zoe, Coleman's trollop, when asked what she thinks of it all, merely jerks her head in his direction and says, " I think 'e's a bloody swine ".—" Hear, hear!" shouts Coleman, and waves his stick. Zoe continues to tag along.

It wasn't only the flesh, it was the volume of it. The aesthete felt he was in serious danger of being swamped by a never-ending flow of humanity, the inevitable consequence of the torrents of sperm. The horror of it pervades *Antic Hay*. Gumbril enters a train and finds himself sitting opposite an old gentleman who opens conversation with the words, " I see you agree with me, sir, that there are too many people in the world." (Gumbril had been gazing out of the window at the spreading rash of suburbia.) " What disgusts me is the people inside, the number of them, sir ", says the old gentleman. " And they way they breed. Like maggots, sir, like maggots. Millions of them, creeping about the face of the country, spreading blight and dirt wherever they go; ruining everything." It was clear that such proliferation was a menace not only to culture but to the life of the privileged as well, and the old man offered Gumbril a case of old brandy on the strength of it. And once again, when the older Huxley tries to revive the quality of his youth in *Time Must Have A Stop,* he causes Sebastian to be agonised by the awareness of millions and millions of bodies, dying, grieving, starving, sick and anxious, all as menacing as the images of lust were enticing. When Huxley discovered his social conscience the flesh may have grown numb but the statistics remained. Over-population was seen as the world's chief problem, the emotional horror became a sociological threat.

*Those Barren Leaves* substitutes the miserable certainty of death for the superfluity of life as a leading motif. The house party leaves Perugia and passes the family vault of the Volumni, who appeared to be proclaiming, through their fat, smiling faces, that they had enjoyed life and feared not death. But a little further on, at Assisi, lies the mummy of a she-saint, and it is her message that makes the deeper impression. " Think of death, ponder incessantly on the decay of all things, the transcience of this sublunary life. Think, think; and in the end life itself will lose all its savour; death will corrupt it; the flesh will seem a shame and a disgustfulness. Think of death hard enough and you will come to deny the beauty and the holiness of life."

Not long after this Cardan had occasion to participate in the exercise. His moron was dead, and it seemed to be a death-sentence for him. He had been going to marry her, or rather, her fortune. But she had eaten putrid fish and died vomiting. He thought of a favourite cat that had once eaten too many black-beetles and also died vomiting. There seemed to be nothing lovable about death, it carried with it neither consolation nor compensation. It was corruption, stark and simple, the one state you sought to avoid. Only the tragedy of the spirit can uplift or ennoble, he thought, but the greatest tragedy of the spirit is that sooner or later it succumbs to the flesh. The spirit has no real significance, there is only the body. " When it is young, the body is beautiful and strong. It grows old, its joints creak, it becomes dry and smelly; it breaks down, the life goes out of it and it rots away." Calamy told him it didn't matter, for salvation is in this world. One has no need of a spirit for any post-mortem adventures. But Cardan was not convinced. He wasn't even thinking of salvation.

The next phase in the debate is a continuation of Cardan's morbid reflections on the relationship of body and spirit. When Grace threw herself at Kingham's head (" Two or Three Graces ") she was committing " what is much more important than the intellect—the body." You can abandon a false intellectual position easily enough but to get the body out of a mess

is a difficult and often painful business. Again, the body
dictates, the mind must follow. The contrary is never essentially true. Elinor Quarles discovered the truth of this in the
cruellest way when her lover was murdered and her son lay
dying. Normal activities, such as eating and sleeping, seemed
almost cynical. But she possessed a body and it insisted on
rest and nourishment. It was useless to say nothing mattered
—the body was always there, with its demands. Throughout
*Point Counter Point* the flesh tyrannises over the spirit, makes
a mockery of its vaunted superiority. Quarles Senior felt himself to be at the heart of the battle when he dictated his notes
to a secretary whose skirt was tantalisingly above the knee.

" ' All my life ', he dictated, his eyes fixed on the lisle thread
(of the stocking), ' I have suffered from the irrelevant—no, say
importunate—interruptions of the wahld's trivialitah full stop.
Some thinkers comma I know comma are able to ignore these
interruptions comma to give them a fleeting but sufficient attention and return with a serene mind to higher things full stop.'

" There was silence. Above the lisle thread, Mr Quarles
was thinking, was the skin—soft, curving tightly over the firm
curved flesh. To caress and, caressing, to feel the finger-tips
silkily caressed; to squeeze a handful of elastic flesh. Even to
bite. Like a round goblet, like a heap of wheat."

It was the old men in particular who found the enticements
of the flesh so irresistible. John Bidlake, a wreck of his former
lusty self, depressed and bad-tempered, started painting again
and the result was orbism, by God, orbism! Enormous curves
and bulges, clouds like cherubic backsides, a hillside like a
belly, whole chunks of anatomy in leaves and vapour and
swelling earth. As their powers waned, so their imaginations
surrender to the goads and spurs of their animal instincts,
triumphantly asserting the primacy of the despised body. These
were the old men, the ones who had reached the traditional
time of wisdom, and their senses had obliterated the spirit.

In his next volume of essays, *Do What You Will,* Huxley
asserted categorically that we cannot escape our bodies. He
records a conversation between intellect, spirit and body. "You

don't really exist ", argues the intellect, poking the body in
the ribs. " You're not there at all; you're just a hole in the
infinite substance. There is no reality but the One."—" With
which ", adds the spirit, " I have made a personal and ecstatic
acquaintance." The body's reply is a faint rumbling in that
part of the corporeal illusion that we call the belly, signifying
it is time for lunch—or perhaps an image of bare thigh is
transmitted to the brain centre. The body tortures, whether
we call the experience pleasure or pain. Like the little Indian
girl in *Eyeless in Gaza,* dying of meningitis, we are " at the
mercy of skin and mucus, at the mercy of those thin threads of
nerves." And yet this carnal supremacy may be our protec-
tion against even worse pains. Suppose we did possess a
perfect and uninterrupted awareness of the self? Suppose
bodies did not act as barriers to understanding ? At least the
body guaranteed one's privacy.

It was inevitable that sooner or later Huxley would have
come to terms with Jonathan Swift, with whom he seemed to
have so much in common. The expected essay appeared in
*Do What You Will.* He starts by quoting the Dean's admitted
all Yahoos because of their sweat and excrement, genital
distaste for the word " bowels ", and referred to his loathing of
organs and dugs, groins and hairy armpits. He noted that
moral shortcomings were of secondary importance to the
Dean. He then considered the possible reasons for such combined fascination and horror. In some cases it derives from
a craving for excitement, a desire to be shocked out of life's
prevailing monotony. Then there are those who deliberately
seek pain and nausea for the sake of the pleasure they derive
from overcoming their repulsion. He cited Mme Guyon, who
once picked up a gob of phlegm and spittle and swallowed it,
discovering profound exaltation in the act. Nietzsche advised
men to be cruel to themselves because it was a good spiritual
exercise. Swift, said Huxley, belonged to a sub-species of this
second group. But why did he linger so long on what revolted
him ? Not to enhance his sense of power, nor for the love of
God. His real reward was the pain he suffered. " He felt a

compulsion to remind himself of his hatred of bowels, just as a man with a wound or an aching tooth feels a compulsion to touch the source of his pain—to make sure that it is still there and still agonising." Huxley attributed Swift's attitude to his refusal to accept reality. He was an inverted Shelley. He was a victim of man's abstractionising faculty, by which he invents symbols and labels them " soul " and " spirit " and then hates reality for not conforming to his inventions. It is a childishness equivalent to that of Ivan Karamazov, who returned God his entrance ticket to life because the real universe bore such little resemblance to the providential machine of Christian theology.

Huxley at least must have felt that his disgust with bodily functions was of a different quality from Swift's. There is undoubtedly a difference in expression; Swift never ceases to declare his nausea while there are times when Huxley appears to positively relish the smells and the faeces. Swift was absorbed in their contemplation, but masochistically. Possibly it was his pleasure, but it was a secondary pleasure, acquired through pain. One might say his pleasure was intellectual. Huxley often appears to gloat, treating the entrails as a particular affirmation of mankind's partly physical nature. You must accept it, he says—don't abuse it like Swift or ignore it like Shelley. In his later writings he came out with this explicitly. At the time of *Point Counter Point* he was still feeling his way, obeying unconsciously instructions that his conscious mind had not yet formulated. He is by no means a complete antithesis to Swift—as he himself says, that role belongs to Rabelais, who loved dung and the whole physical personality of an improbable world. My view is that Huxley is congenitally Swiftian but, perceiving the childishness of ranting against the given world, has made an effort of will to transform his response. The raw material of an attitude remains, of course, but he has done his best to alter its appearance.

Huxley's persistent honesty is always impressive. Having decided that facts will not disappear if you turn your back on them, he next considered how these facts could best be assimilated. What is literature to do about all the unmentionables which lie at the heart of our lives ? Miles Fanning discussed the matter with Pamela ("After the Fireworks", *Brief Candles*). You must write the truth, she said. (She was young and intellectual-flighty and knew that that was the thing to say, but had no intimate concern with the problem.) He agreed, but he didn't want to be lynched. Pamela was bewildered; you couldn't ignore them, they were so important, yet they were also humiliating and usually unpleasant. Huxley returned to this theme in *Vulgarity in Literature*. He had frequently been accused, by reviewers in public and by unprofessional readers in private correspondence, both of vulgarity and wickedness because he had reported his investigations into certain phenomena in plain English and in a novel —a scientific treatise would have been all right. "The fact that many people should be shocked by what he writes practically imposes it as a duty upon the writer to go on shocking them. For those who are shocked by truth are not only stupid, but morally reprehensible as well; the stupid should be educated, the wicked punished and reformed."[1]

In *Eyeless in Gaza* Mark Staithes read *Anna Karenina* and then listed its omissions. "Almost total neglect of those small physiological events that decide whether day-to-day living shall have a pleasant or unpleasant tone." Excretion, digestion, menstruation in particular. While preparing this study I came across a review of this novel by David Garnett, who poohpoohed Mark's strictures and said that Tolstoy was particularly aware of his duty in that direction. This simply cannot be maintained, although Tolstoy was less open to criticism of this kind than any other great novelist. But Huxley was not referring primarily to the lesser ailments, such as Napoleon's cold at Borodino, although Mark did mention them. One feels that Garnett missed the point, not because he could not grasp it, but because he preferred not to. This is significant, because he is an advanced and enlightened man, yet could not stomach

---

[1] This is certainly a true interpretation of the work of Huxley's contemporary, Llewelyn Powys.

Huxley's request for greater physiological truth, and so turned the problem aside with a half-truth.

Anyway, Huxley stuck to his guns. In *Themes and Variations* (1950) he reiterated the need for the " truthful and penetrating " expression in art of the unrationalisable facts of bodily existence—as Tolstoy had done for death in *Ivan Ilyitch*, Miller for sex in *Tropic of Cancer*, Goya for pain and cruelty in his *Disasters*, Mailer for fear, disgust and fatigue in *The Naked and the Dead*. And he returned yet again in *The Genius and the Goddess* (1955), when Rivers spoke of the harm done by simplified abstraction into " good " and " bad ". If you don't mention the physiological correlates of emotion, you're being false to the given facts. If you do mention them you're being gross and cynical. We need another set of words so that we can express the natural togetherness of things.

*Eyeless in Gaza* outdoes even *Point Counter Point* in its exploitation of the flesh and carnal unpleasantness. Huxley reaches his peak in the notorious incident of the dog which falls from an aeroplane on to a flat roof, spattering two naked lovers with its blood and torn flesh. But there is a lot more; Anthony heaves in church, because of the germs; the smell of poor children sickens him; Brian resents his "physical pre-destination to scatology and obscenity "; there is an account of nausea in a butcher's shop; and, as a sort of coda, Miller takes a shrewd look at Anthony, diagnoses intestinal poisoning and deduces from it a mood of scepticism.

In *After Many A Summer* physical appetite is dominant. Only Propter avoids its tyranny. Jeremy Pordage pays tribute to the mind but for him its real use lies in the refinement of the pleasure given by his senses. One of his simplest pleasures consists in picking the scabs off his scalp. Outside the castle frolicked the captive baboons in a special enclosure, watched by their human neighbours when they had nothing better to do. The millionaire Stoyte's pretty little mistress alternated her devotions to the Madonna with visits to the baboonery, where she could watch the creatures fighting and copulating, and clap her hands with delight, crying, " Aren't they cute!

Aren't they *human!*" She also screamed with delight when she picked up one of Jeremy's books and found some pornographic engravings. But she was positively disgusted by a garden nymph that spouted water from her polished breasts. The idea was primitive, indelicate, an affront to decency.

And finally *Time Must Have A Stop,* which begins with a piano-tutor laughing enormously because Sebastian vomits on the second-floor landing after trying to smoke a cigar, and ends with God (" the universal merriment ") guffawing from pole to pole, in Voltaireian yelps over stupidity and silliness and Rabelaisian rumbles over grossness and animality. At least Huxley is no longer agonised by the unmentionables; he has learnt to accept them and, if there must be emotion, to sublimate it into laughter. He has tried to get as close to Rabelais as he can because he fears the possible alternative, which would be a Swiftian pessimism. Natural inclinations pull one way, conscious will another. The result is a hybrid. For a consideration of the body as a part of Nature, something outside the self, I will wait till a later chapter.

## Chapter 7

### ROMANTIC PASSION AND PHYSICAL SEXUALITY

### A. The Conflict

THE opposition between body and spirit naturally finds its clearest expression in the field of sex. The two terms, sex and love, overlapping and to some extent involving the same set of relationships, imply the existence of tension.

There is a short poem called " Philosophy " among the *Early Poems* which says a great deal in a short compass.

> " God needs no christening ",
> Pantheist mutters,
> " Love opens shutters
> On heaven's glistening,
> Flesh, key-hole listening,
>> Hear what God utters " . . .
> Yes, but God stutters.

In the complex of love, religion and philosophy, all closely bound together through man's dual nature, his animal instincts and his search for the Unknowable, there is a great deal of stuttering. Even the most erudite speculation has a way of turning out to be sublime nonsense. Body continues to mock spirit. Huxley pictures St. Simeon on his pillar, looking down on the " harlots and human beasts "—he

> Cursed them and their unchasteness,
> And envied them in his heart.

At first Huxley could only see the perversity of love, the beautiful aspirations matched by the physical squalor. The couple " quietly sweating palm to palm " could also experience inexpressible beatitude. In Troy lived Cressid, " the feminine paradox . . . the crystal ideal—flawed." And then, in parenthesis: " But, bless you! our gorge doesn't rise. We are cynically well up in the damning Theory of Woman, which makes it all the more amusing to watch ourselves in the ecstatic practice of her. Unforeseen perversity." He continues, pinning woman down with a stark image: " Fabulous Helen! At her firm breasts they used to mould delicate drinking cups which made the sourest vinegar richly poisonous." ("Beauty ", *Leda*).

Where did this young man's cynicism come from? Huxley was constitutionally cynical, and his tastes led him to the works of cynics and pessimists of the past, poets like Quarles and Fulke Greville. A sensitive man's outlook is naturally emphasised by his reading, and his reading is a reflection of his outlook. From Greville in particular he picked up a pleasing sense of despair. No need to wait for the disillusion of experience when it already lay to hand so attractively in literary form. " Neere to the glories of the Sunne, clouds with most horrour burst," wrote Greville. The young Huxley could live his despair vicariously through the lines of the Elizabethan: " he most wretched is, that once most happy was "—it was worth knowing that love was a snare, would only bring pain, to stand aside and watch with a pitying smile or, if the animal insisted on action, at least not to be shocked and surprised by the outcome.

Lust was horrible, of course. It was the peculiar activity of the body, always dragging the nobler part down. It always won, always made the beautiful sentiment seem cheap and powerless. We find the attitude in the first volume of stories, *Limbo*, when Guy Lambourne kisses Marjorie and feels the urge to caress her. He shudders and pushes her away. " No, no, no. It's horrible; it's odious. Drunk with moonlight and sentimentalising about death . . . Why not just say with Biblical frankness, Lie with me—Lie with me?" It is the suffering of innocence, not necessarily of youth. Uncle Spencer experienced the same pangs as Guy when he adored Emmy Wendle but could not expel from his mind the horrible know-ledge of her seduction by that stage-door johnny at Wimble-don, those " endless embracements, kisses brutal ", which his suffering imagination insisted on conjuring up. A quarter of a century after Guy Lambourne, another of Huxley's young men feels the same unbearable incongruity destroying his pleasure. "In his fancy, love had been a kind of gay, ethereal intoxication; but last night's reality had been more like madness. Yes, sheer madness; a maniac struggling in the musky darkness with another maniac." And unlike Guy, Sebastian had experienced it (*Time Must Have A Stop*).

"Happy Families", a short play in *Limbo*, presents the conflict in stylised terms. The Freudian components of the two lovers are personalised, the Super-Ego and the Id working upon the Ego, beginning and ending by speaking through dummies. Another play, "Permutations Among the Nightingales" (*Mortal Coils*) is a cynical study of different types of sexual relations—sex in the service of avarice and worldly success, the vulgarity of lust, the childish display of sexual disappointment, the shifts and deceits of sexual manoeuvre.

But of course it is in *Antic Hay* that sex-hatred and sex-fascination first appear with full Huxleyan intensity. Once again the lusts and loves of Gumbril and Mercaptan, Coleman and Mrs Viveash, Rosie and Emily, are pointed in dramatic form. Gumbril and Mrs Viveash hear the Monster in the cabaret, after his encounter with the Prostitute, declaring: "Somewhere there must be love like music. Love harmonious and ordered: two spirits, two bodies moving contrapuntally together. Somewhere, the stupid brutish act must be made to make sense, must be enriched, must be made significant. Lust, like Diabelli's waltz, a stupid air, turned by a genius into three-and-thirty fabulous variations. Somewhere love like sheets of silky flame; like landscapes brilliant in the sunlight against a background of purple thunder; like the solution of a cosmic problem; like faith, somewhere, somewhere. But in my veins creep the maggots of the pox, crawling towards the brain, crawling into the mouth, burrowing into the bones. Insatiably." Mrs Viveash had given up any hope of harmony or sense, ever since her lover was killed in the war. His death was also the death of anything that mattered. And Gumbril had just forsaken the naïve but adoring Emily, forsaken her for the transient fascination of Mrs Viveash, and in so doing had destroyed his strongest connection with normal human decency. Sex corrupts, he might have thought, but undiluted lust corrupts undilutedly.

We are never told why Coleman hated sex so much, as we are told later in Spandrell's case. Sex is ugly enough for Coleman, but he feels impelled to make it even uglier. The sin against the Holy Ghost is so much the greater. Paradoxically, Coleman seeks the virtue of a thing and insists on intensifying it—only the virtue of sex is its viciousness. If you partake of sexual activity in the normal way it is merely dull. Tell yourself it's a sin, then you can enjoy its diabolic nature. The beauty of the grand passion, he told Rosie, is that it's revolting. He rejoiced in the pronouncements of the Fathers of the Church, especially Odo of Cluny, who called a woman a bag of muck. (After the Third World War woman would be universally recognised as a vessel of unholiness, we learn from *Ape and Essence*.) A little less elegant than Argonaut Huxley entering Troy, but amounting to much the same thing.

Sometimes Huxley felt that the fault was a racial one. Dwelling too much on the spiritual, transcendental aspect of love, the English fell an easy prey to the disgust inevitably aroused by the physiological aspect. Coleman's satanic attitude was really a mask, hiding his childish horror—or perhaps, like Spandrell, he was avenging himself—but on what? For the weakness inherent in this attitude, this indiscriminate lashing-out at the cosmos, or that part of the cosmos you felt to be in your power, was that the target you hit was so rarely the deserving one. Coleman hurt others, he hurt himself even more, but he never touched the true cause of his unhappiness, the vast, immutable fact of sexual intercourse, its thereness, its givenness, its reality. Perhaps the French were wiser. They saw the reality, shrugged their shoulders, and made no attempt to set up a smoke-screen of spirituality. The French writer " approaches his amorous experience with the detached manner of a psychologist interested in the mental reactions of certain corporeal pleasures whose mechanism he has previously studied in his capacity of physiological observer." His attitude is " dry, precise, matter-of-fact and almost scientific . . . (He) does not concern himself with trying to find some sort of metaphysical justification for the raptures of physical passion, nor is he in any way a propagandist of sensuality " (" Nationality in Love ", *On The Margin*). And it is in Crébillon that Huxley finds the perfect example of the scientific attitude to love. He manages to forget that love is a matter of the most intimate human concern, and treats it as though it were " as remote, as utterly divorced from good and evil, as spiral nebulae, liver flukes or the aurora borealis." His true message is that the basis of love is physiological and that the intense and beautiful emotions which it arouses cannot be philosophically justified or explained, but should be gratefully accepted for what they are : " feelings significant in themselves and of the highest practical importance for those who experience them "—but no more (*The Olive Tree*). The Englishman tends to reverse the values, and then to lose his temper when reality hits back.

But Huxley's young men were English and we must return to their divided loyalties, to flesh and spirit. It is the painful fate of almost every human being, writes Huxley in *Those Barren Leaves*. " Pull devil, pull baker; pull flesh, pull spirit; pull love, pull duty; pull reason and pull hallowed prejudice." And, running parallel with the conflict, was another obstacle : the devilish perversity of love. Francis Chelifer, as a young man, had desired all beauty, goodness and truth symbolised in one being. When he was ready to congratulate himself on getting them, he found he had simply got a young woman with a " temperament ". Later, of course, he knew better, but first of all he had to learn that it was possible to be profoundly and slavishly in love with someone for whom he had no esteem, whom he regarded as a bad character and who actually bored him. The lesson you learnt was that while love sometimes coexists with affection and admiration, worship and intellectual rapture, it more frequently exists apart from them.

But—there is a danger. The physiological interpretation of love may give peace of mind but it is not necessarily the truth. It may, in fact, be cynicism after all. The mere fact that lovers build such structures on the basis of their relationship suggests that there is something beyond physical pleasure. Perhaps the fault lies, not in our involvement of spiritual values, but in the manner of our involvement. The first sign that Huxley is having second thoughts about the purely physiological interpretation of love-making occurs in *Proper Studies,* where he refers to Anatole France's view of sex as a mere detached appetite.[1] France justified himself by an appeal to Reason. Huxley's comment is: "If this be reason, then let me be irrational." For this "Reason" condemned a man to forego the experiences resulting from the co-ordination of his sexual and intellectual and imaginative activities, and made for a reduction, not an increase of life. The difficult but rewarding task of incorporating sex organically into the whole personality is set aside. And if lovers suffer agonies unknown to rationalists, they may also enjoy experiences equally outside the rationalists' ken.

*Point Counter Point* examines the sexual conflict from every angle. Walter Bidlake at the age of twenty-two, "with the adolescent purity of sexual desires turned inside out", had believed that love was talk and spiritual communion and companionship. Sex was irrelevant. He took after his spiritual mother, shrank from his fleshly father, who could see little in women beyond what Rubens had shown him. Lord Edward Tantamount pretended bodies didn't exist when he made love; his love was "one long tacit apology for itself". This was due only partly to his Victorian shyness. He was really far more interested in grafting a newt's tail-bud on to the stump of its amputated foreleg. Marjorie liked the idea of love, but not of lovers. "A correspondence course of passion was, for

[1] Calamy, in *Those Barren Leaves,* had already given up the physiological interpretation, but his remedy seems to have been to forsake sex altogether. See last section in this chapter.

her, the perfect and ideal relationship with a man." Then there was the Shelley-type who, according to Rampion, pretended that going to bed with a woman wasn't really going to bed with her but just two angels holding hands. Beatrice wanted love, but the horror of being pawed about was stronger than her desire. And finally, Spandrell. His character is obviously based on that of Baudelaire. Neither of them ever got over the shock of their mother's second marriage. It was all mixed up in Spandrell's mind with what married people did to each other in bed, knowledge gained from his reading of *A Girl's School in Paris* at school, by electric torchlight under the bedclothes. He had grown up believing that the body was " a wild beast that devoured the soul, annihilated the consciousness, abolished the real you and me ". In his life he set out to be consistent, according to his lights. If that was how men and women were constituted, he would not try to stand in nature's way. The destruction of beauty, of the spirit or what pretended to be the spirit, of everything that tried to rise above the physical plane, this was his aim. He takes a prostitute for a walk in the country. Her starved sense of beauty is delighted, she smells the honeysuckle, goes into raptures over the foxgloves. This is the opportunity Spandrell has been waiting for. " Pleasingly phallic ", he says, and develops the conceit. She begs him to stop. His reply is to slash at them with his stick, until they all lie broken on the ground and his companion is in tears. " Damn their insolence ", he says. " It serves them right."

There is no sexual happiness in *Point Counter Point*. It is all madness, either the accepted, respectable madness of the idealists or the tolerated madness of the sensualists or the demonic madness of the psychologically unstable.[1] But where

---

[1] In one sense *Point Counter Point* can be regarded as Huxley's descent into Hell. It is a work of tremendous power, but the power is diabolical. There is not even a slender thread of positive good, as there is in *Eyeless in Gaza*, to which the reader can cling. In *Heaven and Hell* Huxley writes of the " negatively transfigured world " which is occasionally portrayed by the arts, and instances Van Gogh's later landscapes, Géricault's paintings, Browning's *Childe Roland*. *Point Counter Point* may be added to the canon.

lies sanity? In *Do What You Will* Huxley hinted that it might be found in the Rabelaisian approach. Rabelais transfigured muck by love. " He accepted reality in its entirety, accepted with gratitude and delight this amazingly improbable world, where flowers spring from manure . . . and where the violences of animal passion can give birth to sentiments of the most exquisite tenderness and refinement." But it is not an easy attitude to discover for oneself; the absurdities on either side are so inviting. As a reaction from Christian mythology, a sordid and ignoble realism tends to take its place, spending itself purposelessly and producing neither love nor even amusement in the long run. A new mythology of nature, an untranscendental mythology of Energy, Life and Human Personality, is required to create a new fashion in love. In modern times Blake, Burns and D. H. Lawrence have come closest to supplying it.

## B.  *The Retreat From Sex*

There was a moment in Huxley's development when he seemed to consider that perhaps, after all, sexual activity was not worth the pain it involved. This view is put fairly strongly in *Those Barren Leaves* and may have influenced his later approach to the subject. He was constitutionally incapable of urging sexual asceticism, but intellectually he could understand its social and even personal value.

In his " Autobiography " Francis Chelifer recalls his youthful determination to resist the " baser " desires. (In this respect he gives us a preview of Brian Foxe in *Eyeless in Gaza*—but Brian persisted in his asceticism until it was instrumental in causing his suicide.) The resistance was not very strong, he soon succumbed—and then, of course, wished he hadn't. But later he became rather weary of love. The excitement soon gave way to boredom. It wasn't difficult for a man to abandon love; he rarely possessed a woman's enthusiasm for it.

Now Calamy was an altogether different type of person. At the beginning of the book he makes his entry as a reasonably accomplished philanderer. He is still capable of falling in love. It is this capacity that worries him, for being in love is a form of enslavement. To be dependent on another human being in such a way is disgraceful. At Mrs Aldwinkle's he disgraced himself again. He fell in love with Miss Thriplow. As he kissed her he felt his anger rising. Why do I do this? he was thinking. There were other, more important things to do. At normal times he knew what he wanted to do. He wanted to devote himself to a study of—the " mystery of the universe ". There was no brief phrase that described his longings. But whatever name it might assume, it could not be reached so long as he remained inside the worldly tumult. He wanted to look into the depths of his mind but was hindered by preoccupation with his bodily appetites. And he deliberately tightened his bonds. His more intelligent part knew its work but refused to make the effort needed to break his enslavement. The disgrace was the greater because, like Chelifer, he knew that a man had less justification than a woman for failing to break the bonds. He needed freedom, to think and meditate. He could take it. But he allowed— yes, allowed—the image of Miss Thriplow to dominate his mind's eye.

So he ran away. He did not run away from sex as sex, but as an obstacle to other, in his view more valuable, activities. He took a room in a cottage among the mountains, where Cardan and Chelifer came to visit him. It was one of the eighty-four thousand paths of the Indian mystics. And what would happen at the end of three months' chaste meditation, Cardan wanted to know, when some lovely young temptation came toddling along the road, " balancing her haunches "? Calamy protested that his explorations of the inward universe would continue without interruption. Cardan suggested that he might manage to explore both temptation and interior universe simultaneously. Calamy agreed that if practicable it would be delightful, but all the best authorities denied its possibility. " In itself, no doubt, the natural and moderate satisfaction of the sexual instinct is a matter quite indifferent to morality. It is only in relation to something else that the satisfaction of a natural instinct can be said to be good or bad. It might be bad, for example, if it involved deceit or cruelty. It is certainly bad when it enslaves a mind that feels, within itself, that it ought to be free—free to contemplate and recollect itself."

So much for Calamy, whom we leave in the mountains. It is only an isolated incident in Huxley's work, and he does not repeat it in his fiction, as he repeats so many other situations and responses. But it does demolish the suggestion that has become current, that Huxley came to a consideration of the mystic's discipline suddenly. By 1925, at the latest, he was conversant (academically, at least) with the ways of mystics, and could even allow one of his characters to take the first steps towards the contemplative life. It is true, Calamy's approach was, at one and the same time, naïve and over-sophisticated. He still hoped to solve the mystery intellectually—at least, one infers that, for he says very little of his methods. But he had gone part of the way and so, one gathers, had his creator.

In no other novel do we come across such a determined effort to reject lust by someone who has given way to it and enjoyed its physical reward. In *Eyeless in Gaza* Anthony Beavis tries to conquer his desires because they deny human unity by insisting exclusively on particular individual experiences. In the same book Mark Staithes becomes an ascetic because he *wishes* to become *more* separate. In other words, the two men adopt the same means in pursuit of totally different ends. *After Many A Summer* advances us no further. Pete, under the influence of Propter, was puzzled by the same problem that drove Calamy to the mountains—but Pete was a schoolboy compared with Calamy, and his callowness brings no fresh light. He loved Virginia, but Virginia might actually be an obstacle between him and a higher cause. Whether your loyalty was of the worst kind (to your physiology) or of the best (to your higher feelings), it was still a loyalty to yourself and, as such, an obstacle to the greatest cause of all. (Pete wasn't sure what that was.) He also learnt from Propter that there was no one type of human sexuality that could be called " normal " in the way you can speak of normal vision or digestion. There was no absolute natural norm. Sexual behaviour could only be judged by referring it to the ultimate aims of the individual concerned.

In *Ends and Means* Huxley devotes a dozen pages to a discursive consideration of sex, which may be regarded as a summary of the position he had reached in 1937, and which he has probably adhered to since. Sex is evil when it takes the form of a physical addiction. It is evil because it compels the mind to identify itself with a physical sensation and prevents it from thinking of anything but its separate animal existence. It is also evil when it manifests itself as a way of satisfying the lust for power or the climber's craving for position and social distinction. In the latter case sex is the instrument of avarice and ambition. On the social plane, societies which provide the greatest opportunities for sexual indulgence show less intellectual energy than those where a degree of continence is imposed. History shows that no civilised society tolerates sexual continence for long, and in course of time such societies are replaced by others which grant greater opportunity. They, in turn, easily fall victims to more continent and therefore more energetic societies. (Huxley was here adopting the views expressed by Dr. J. D. Unwin in his *Sex and Culture*.)

His conclusion was similar to the one arrived at by Calamy, twelve years earlier—and he himself was now on Calamy's road, at least in matters pertaining to the spirit. He considered chastity a necessary pre-condition to a moral life superior to that of animals. In the past societies have either been continent and energetic, or they have preferred sexual indulgence to mental and social energy. But there was a third alternative that had never been tried, in which the energy produced by sexual restraint should be directed along channels more desirable than military aggression or economic expansion. The acceptance of pre-nuptial chastity and absolute monogamy must be combined with complete legal equality between men and women (only in this way could the periodic revolt against chastity be avoided) in the service of a social and political system that will be described in a later chapter.

## Chapter 8

### THE CYNICAL UNDERTONE

The leech's kiss, the squid's embrace,
The prurient ape's defiling touch:
And do you like the human race?
No, not much.

(Notice outside William Tallis's ranch,
*Ape and Essence*)

"I KNOW of no study which is so unutterably saddening as that of the evolution of humanity", wrote Professor Huxley. The grandson appeared to agree. He was no student of evolution as such, but he had a historical sense and life does not stand still. "The universe is vast, beautiful and appalling", he wrote in *Texts and Pretexts*. We must not expect our virtues to be rewarded and our vices punished. In such a universe there could be no disinterestedness, one of the distinguishing marks of humanity. Or conversely, there can be no humanity except in an inhuman world.

There is a great deal of despair and Worldpain in the early poems, most of it of a conventional, unfelt quality. After all, it was considered the young poet's duty to be pricked beyond bearing. But it would be stretching a point to say that Huxley found the pains "unutterably saddening". At times he seemed positively to gloat over man's unhappy destiny.

"World will always be hell. Cap. or Lab., Engl. or Germ. —all beasts. One in a mill. is GOOD", wrote Richard Greenow—but he was trapped in an asylum during the first World War, and could hardly be expected to be anything but pessimistic. He is only the first of a long series, however. In 1931 Hugo's reply to Enid's query, "How's life?" was a shrug of the shoulders and the reply, "Oh, as usual. Rather like death" (*The World of Light*). Enid tells him he takes pleasure in feeling like a worm, and he agrees.

Why is the world such hell ? For one thing, having glimpsed a destination you are never allowed to reach it. The notion comes to Huxley as he sits in a train, gazing out at furrows sweeping across the field like a drilled army on parade :

> Each line deliberately swings
> Towards me, till I see a straight
> Green avenue to the heart of things,
> The glimpse of a sudden opened gate
> Piercing the adverse walls of fate . . .
> A moment only, and then, fast, fast,
> The gate swings to, the avenue closes;
> Fate laughs, and once more interposes
> Its barriers.
> > The train has passed."
> > > (" Out of the Window ")

The Fifth Philosopher says it would have been better had we never been born; each of us takes the place of a better man. The Ninth can only sip his misery dram by dram because he cannot take shelter behind the delusions enjoyed by others. Troilus quotes some lines of poetry to himself but cannot remember the correct epithets. " Not that they mattered— any more than anything else."

The idea that only one person in a Million is really worth anything was certainly a strong one in those early days. We have seen Greenow entertaining it, and the Fifth Philosopher (or the Philosopher's Fifth Song, I never know which) reprimands the "froward Homunculus " for elbowing out a possible saviour of the race. Chance rules that one out of a million shall be selected—and it turns out to be You, a two-legged worm! Mr. Jacobsen even refused to talk seriously to the nine hundred thousand odd who were incapable of profitable thought! (" Happily Ever After ", *Limbo*).

The fools are always attempting to solve the problem of life. " Living is hard enough without complicating the process by thinking about it " (" The Bookshop ", *Limbo*). Much better to take for granted the " wearisome condition of humanity, born under one law, to another bound." (Later, this quotation from Fulke Greville appeared on the fly-leaf of *Point Counter Point*.) Jacobsen got a perverse pleasure from the support of organised religion—not because it even approached a solution but because it provided a solidity and an unchangeableness that were among the few hopes for a humanity that thirsted after evil. (There was no doubt about the thirst; this was no youthful desire to shock. See *Ape and Essence*.) He loved to contrast the power and pretension of the Church with the childish imbecility of its representatives. How sincere were the outpourings of intellects only slightly less limited than that of an Australian aborigine! In *Texts and Pretexts* Huxley argues that, after all, a sermon may be better than the drivel people leave behind to hear it.

I have already remarked that *Crome Yellow* is a gayer, more light-hearted novel than the others; its action does not take place on the edge of the bottomless pit, as does *Antic Hay*'s. Everyone is slightly foolish, only two are irredeemably foolish. Mr Wimbush complains that human contacts involve a terrible expense of time and he is looking forward to the day when he will be able to live in dignified seclusion, "surrounded by the delicate attentions of silent and graceful machines, and entirely secure from any human intrusion." It is a gentle thought, put without the fierce animosity that developed later in Huxley's writing.

Huxley showed himself capable of pity. Spode is genuinely sorry for Tillotson, the pupil of the great Haydon, who had lived on into another world, forgotten and half-starved, barely existing in a basement overrun by beetles. Spode persuades Lord Badgery to give a banquet for the old man. But it is not a kindness, it is merely a stunt. It would be splashed in *World's Review,* it would bring in the snobs. Tillotson is dragged out of his basement, fitted into a dinner jacket, and carried off in a Rolls Royce. The artistic élite of London come to gaze at him. But he turns out to be a bore; he gets drunk, he rambles on for too long, and finally collapses (*Mortal Coils*).

This is an important story for our understanding of the

younger Huxley. Not a single character does anything he can be proud of. The most we can say is that Spode feels qualms of conscience, but only for Tillotson's poverty, not for the spectacle he helped make of the old man. The story is amusing, but its humour stems from cruelty. Exactly the same can be said of " Nuns at Luncheon " in the same volume. In each story the characters are either vicious or foolish. The link with the more kindly Jacobsen and Wimbush lies in an identity of outlook: people are imbeciles or bores, and they deserve what they get. The Bad Joke as Literature recurs in " Uncle Spencer " (*Little Mexican*) where the wretched Dravidian is hoaxed into believing that he has been freed from the prison camp. Disillusion kills him.

There is a great deal of punishment in Huxley's fiction, and it possesses a peculiar irony of its own. The case of the moron in *Those Barren Leaves* is one of the most significant examples of Huxley's delight in the paradox of fate. Miss Elver, whose mind has never developed out of childhood, has been left £25,000. Her brother, a disappointed man, covets it and takes her to live in some malaria-infested marshland. The intent is obvious. But Cardan meets them accidentally, hears of Miss Elver's fortune, proposes to her and is accepted. So far, so good. Cardan takes Miss Elver away with him, in preparation for the marriage—and she dies of food poisoning. This is not just a simple case of wickedness failing in its object. Cardan is frustrated, of course, but the brother gets what he wants—and without even the burden of conscience to hound him. Cardan did his dirty work for him.

Take the case of Moira in " The Rest Cure" (*Brief Candles*). She fell in love with an Italian, whom her husband called " a black-haired pimp from the slums of Naples ". The insult only intensified her desire. Then comes a quarrel with Tormio, the lover, after which Moira finds her purse has disappeared. Her husband's taunt comes back to her and, in despair, she kills herself. When her body is removed from the bed the purse falls with a thump to the floor. It had got stuck between the bed and the wall.

E

Chance again had played havoc with people's lives. Huxley has always been impressed by the importance of accident in human affairs. He prefers to believe, for instance, that artistic progress can usually be attributed to the chance appearance of a genius rather than to the action of impersonal forces. It is the Theory of the Creative Millionth. Chance intervenes at every point of a person's being, in his gene-structure as well as in the pattern of his activities. Its influence spreads out fanwise and involves thousands whom the world calls innocent. But there is no innocence. Chance moves on its own track, divorced from any human conception of right or wrong, responsibility or irrelevance. There is another example of this amoral chain-reaction in *Time Must Have A Stop*. Sebastian's desire for a dress suit led to personal deceit, the punishment of a little girl, the death of a dog and Bruno's arrest.

The only possible consequence of such a random scheme of cause and effect was perpetual disillusionment, such as experienced by Mrs Viveash and Mary Amberley. You could never be sure where any particular action would lead you. (Huxley's criticism of the utopian planners was that they pretended to know all the effects of the causes they set in motion.) Experience was no guide, or only a very imperfect one. What delighted once could certainly not be counted on to delight the next time. Orvieto used to be so heavenly, said Mrs Viveash. But now it tasted like a " bad muddy sort of Vouvray ". It was not only wine; the same applied to truth and love. " It was one of those evenings ", thought Gumbril, " when men feel that truth, goodness and beauty are one. In the morning, when they commit their discovery to paper, when others read it written there, it looks wholly ridiculous. It was one of those evenings when love is once more invented for the first time. That, too, seems a little ridiculous, sometimes, in the morning " (*Antic Hay*). Flatness is all, Gumbril might have said. When he wrote his autobiography he would name the eminent people he had met and then say of them what he had said after his first love affair: Is that all? As Mark

Staithes said, in a later novel, of the wonderful things of life,
" They give you just a taste of the next world, then let you
fall back, flop, into the mud ". Even when he's in heaven he
finds himself echoing Gumbril: " Is that all? Like time, the
river of life flowed stanchlessly from the world's side."

Huxley's typewriter once found the correct term for man's
condition: the Human Vomedy: " Was there ever a
criticism of life more succinct and expressive?" (" On
Deviating Into Sense ", *On The Margin*). In this volume he
was much concerned with the part played by ennui and
accidie in literature. He pointed out that whereas they had
once been regarded as sins they had now become inspirations
for literature. He attributed the change to the failure of the
ideas of the French Revolution, the progress of industry with
its filth and misery, and the futility of political enfranchise-
ment, despite the dreams it had given birth to. Life outside
the big towns became increasingly insipid, inside them increasingly restless. And then, to complete the chain of disasters,
the first World War. " We can claim with a certain pride a
right to our accidie. With us it is not a sin or a disease of
the hypochondries; it is a state of mind which fate has forced
upon us." We might add Miller's theory that increase in
meat-eating has poisoned people into scepticism and despair.
It used to be a privilege of the rich. It was extremely difficult for a sensitive man brought up in the nineteenth and early
twentieth centuries to avoid first disillusion and then
despair. His teachers insisted that men were naturally good,
spiritual and lovely. His first contact with human reality
at its worst or even its average caused him to fall down in
the mud and rub his nose in it. Uncle Spencer in the story
of that name (*Little Mexican*) was a typical example of such
horrified disillusion, except that he preserved his romantic
optimism much longer than most.

An essayist gives us himself, not imagined fictions. In *On
The Margin* Huxley admitted that recently he had been incapable of enjoying any poetry whose inspiration was not
despair or melancholy. He thought it might be due to the

chronic horror of the political situation! He meditated on the possibility of compiling an Oxford Book of Depressing Verse, in which Fulke Greville would naturally be well represented. Greville's view that the best a statesman could do was to patch and prop the decaying fabric of society in the hope of staving off for a little longer the inevitable crash, was very much to Huxley's taste. He did not mention Quarles in this essay but I think there is sufficient evidence elsewhere to conclude that Quarles would have appeared alongside Greville. " The world's a bubble "; " When not himself, he's (i.e., man) mad; when most himself, he's worse "; " 'Tis glorious misery to be born a man "; these would all have met with Huxley's warm approval. He admits there are consolations, though he only mentions minor ones. It is comforting and refreshing, for instance, to consider that our civilisation is not yet as idiotic as Tibet's. When he feels that life is not worth living he reads Edward Lear. Nonsense is an assertion of man's spiritual freedom.

But you can't think of Tibet or read Lear all the time. Chelifer, in *Those Barren Leaves*, decides that, like it or not, one must immerse oneself in " reality " and make the best of it. Only, with typical consistency, he decides that making the best of it is the colloquial, deceptive phrase for making the worst of it. We live in a mean city, and it is useless trying to escape it. If it is our destiny to live meanly we must live intensely meanly. Some people find evidence of kindliness, charity and pity in the midst of the squalor. But of course they do; men have not yet fallen below the brutes and parents are still devoted to their offspring. Every obituary notice mentions the subject's " heart of gold ". And they are right. One never meets a man with a really bad heart. He would be a freak, as rare as a Mozart. But the ordinary human virtues are nothing to be inordinately proud of, because we share them with the animals. It is the truly human, non-animal virtues we lack: open-mindedness, absence of irrational prejudice, complete tolerance and a steady, reasonable pursuit of social goods. The jolly, optimistic fellows are quite content

for us to be good in the way that whales and bees are good.
If we ask for evidence of more human sapience, they rebuke
us for intellectual coldness and general "inhumanity".

The trouble is, being imaginative, men often act far less
sensibly than animals. Huxley noticed this in India. At
Benares he saw a million people who had come vast distances,
suffering fatigue, hunger and discomfort in order to perform,
in a certain stretch of very dirty water, certain antics for the
benefit of a fixed star ninety million miles away. At the same
time he saw a bull scoop with its tongue the food from a sleeping beggar's bowl. He felt that the bull, because of its brain-
lessness, was acting much more rationally than its masters.
" Man is so intelligent that he feels impelled to invent theories
to account for what happens in the world. Unfortunately, he
is not quite intelligent enough, in most cases, to find correct
explanations. So that when he acts on his theories he behaves
very often like a lunatic. Thus, no animal is clever enough,
when there is a drought, to imagine that the rain is being with-
held by evil spirits, or as a punishment for its transgressions.
Therefore you never see animals going through the absurd
and often horrible fooleries of magic and religion " (*Texts
and Pretexts*).

The deepest of all realities, wrote Chelifer, was stupidity,
the being unaware. At that time there was a great deal of
optimism about the beneficial effects that would result from
increased leisure for the ordinary man and woman. Improved
social and industrial organisation, more equitable distribution
of goods and greater equality of wealth, would allow the individual's personality to flower, and the problems that beset our
civilisation would melt away like snow. But how could greater
leisure reduce the effects of basic stupidity and unawareness,
Huxley wanted to know. The principal occupations of a
working-man's leisure were watching other people play games,
going to the cinema, reading newspapers and indifferent fiction,
listening to the radio and going from place to place in trams
and buses. These occupations only differed from those of the
rich in being cheaper. " Prolong the leisure and what will

happen? There will have to be more cinemas, more news-papers, more bad fiction, more radios and more cheap auto-mobiles. If wealth and education increase with the leisure, then there will have to be more Russian Ballets as well as more movies, more *Timeses* as well as more *Daily Mails,* more casinos as well as more bookies and football matches, more expensive operas as well as more gramophone records, more Hugh Walpoles as well as Nat Goulds " (" Work and Leisure ", *Along the Road*). There would be a corresponding increase of the spiritual maladies — ennui, restlessness, spleen and general world-weariness—that to date have only afflicted the rich.[1] Mark Staithes had joined the Communist Party to get rid of the people at the top—but what would happen after that was something he didn't care to think about too closely. " More wireless sets, more chocolates, more beauty parlours, more girls with better contraceptives. The moment you give people the chance to be piggish, they take it—thankfully." Russia had so far avoided this state because circumstances had forced the people to be ascetic. But suppose the experiment succeeded ? Would the result be a civilisation of soft, piggish Babbitts? (*Eyeless in Gaza.*)

But it is not always easy to detect stupidity or mediocrity. Some people have a special talent for concealing them, a quick, superficial manner which dazzles their audience. This is particularly true of the fashionable world, of artistic and literary circles where a desire for constant stimulation and amusement allows a particular type of flashy second-rateness to rise to the top. Rodney Clegg, the " brilliant " and " witty " artist, was one of these (" Two or Three Graces "). He kept a little repertory of jokes which he polished and refined, to bring them out " spontaneously " at the next party. He would practice a particular kind of art in his notebooks, and then " dash off " an example before an admiring circle of friends, who would gasp and say: Isn't he wonderful? and, Is there

[1] The Inventions Office is stuffed with plans for labour-saving processes, the World Controller told the Savage in *Brave New World*. Why weren't they put into execution ? For the sake of the labourers; it would have been sheer cruelty to afflict them with excessive leisure.

any other living artist (always barring Picasso) who could improvise so brilliantly? In *Point Counter Point* Molly d'Exergillod was another. She prided herself on her conversation. She practised paradoxes in bed, recorded anecdotes and witticisms in her diary, and laboriously mugged up Cocteau's epigrams about art, Mr. Birrell's after-dinner stories, Yeats's anecdotes about George Moore and what Charlie Chaplin said to her the last time she was in Hollywood.

And with *Point Counter Point* we come to the peak of Huxley's misanthropy. Starting with a conviction of man's helplessness in the condition in which he found himself, Huxley now discovered that man himself was loathsome Man was not to blame, but such an extenuating circumstance could not cause you to love him more. Huxley merely differed from the conventional misanthrope in believing that man could not avoid his own evil. He prefaced this novel with some verse by Fulke Greville. Continuing the poem, we come across these lines:

> If nature did not take delight in blood,
> She would have made more easie waies to good.

This novel makes a greater impact than *Antic Hay* because it is more massive. The theme and tone are much the same, but they have been expanded in their reference. In the earlier novel we see the Bright Young Things of the day falling into the abyss. Their elders are at times lovable and even capable of self-sacrifice. In the later novel the whole society seems to be tumbling. The only people who have the vision to forestall the event are the Rampions (D. H. Lawrence and his wife), and they are powerless. The others are divided into two categories: those who are consciously and cheerfully hell-bent, and those who cannot help themselves. In the first group are Spandrell and Lucy Tantamount. The second and much larger group all suffer from some defect of character (Nature taking delight in blood) which causes them to aid their own self-destruction. Philip Quarles can only come to terms with the world on the intellectual level; Illidge is mentally warped by his social background and his scientific monomania; Walter Bidlake is negative and lacks courage; Burlap is an unconscious but thoroughgoing hypocrite; Webley allows some valid ideas to fall victim to his undirected dynamism; and so on with the other characters, who erect walls of gadgetry or mysticism between themselves and the world, and the minor ones, who bewail their fate or are simply gulled by externals.

The general view of Huxley as a confirmed pessimist has a good basis in fact, but it needs diluting on closer acquaintance. No other contemporary writer is more critical of the society in which he lives, and yet he frequently expresses a conviction that this society, however rotten, has the power to improve itself. It would be truer to say that, man being what he is, improvement is improbable. He is a victim of his own perversity, which so often makes him insist on doing what he does not want to do, such as making love to a woman he does not like and whose intimacy will bring him nothing but vexation, or stubbornly declining to do what he has been passionately desiring, merely because the opportunity of doing what he wants is not presented in exactly the way he had anticipated. (Huxley had already referred to this fatal flaw in the human make-up in *Little Mexican*.) One might summarise his attitude as follows: modern society is in a state of transition, and it is at such times that the less attractive aspects of existence show through the gaping seams. The Victorians had all our faults in potential but their defences and masks were sounder. But no society is doomed until it stagnates. There are few signs of stagnation in ours.

This view of Huxley is partly a quantitative matter. He is best known for his novels, which depict a world that is vicious and stupid. This is what he sees; he cannot also give us what he might see in a few hundred years' time—at least, not in the same novels. But he has done this in two other books, *Brave New World* and *Ape and Essence*—and the pessimism seems to be proved. But these novels are meant to tell us what the world will be like *if* certain contemporary trends continue.

It is true, if you read the novels only, you are not likely to arrive at this conclusion. But if you read the essays you will frequently come across the raw material of the future-books, or the tentative observations which are later filled out and developed. And very often you will find that alternative futures are set forth, divided by large *ifs*. Then why does he appear to favour the less pleasant, the less hopeful alternatives, when he tries to detail mankind's near future? Well, for one thing the unpleasant and the unhopeful have a greater dramatic appeal. For another, he may have allowed the visionary within him (as opposed to the very skilful entertainer) to perform a social service. And, of course, he may after all be a *considered* pessimist—he may, after much thought and observation, believe that this *is* the path that mankind will take, because mankind cannot help itself. But, if so, the decision was not arrived at quite so facilely as the critics sometimes appear to believe.

But my argument may be based on externals only. What Huxley tells us in his essays is the fruit of ratiocination. The real Huxleyan desires are those that find expression in the novels, which increasingly emphasise all that is rotten, diseased, demoralised. Whether it is fair to call states rotten that are natural to normal men and women is another matter. But in *Eyeless in Gaza,* for instance, there is little encouragement for the liberal-minded optimist and humanitarian. Even when Huxley emerges for a while from the subterranean torrents of desire and selfishness, hypocrisy and cowardice, into the lighter world of young love, we are faced with the equal rottenness of spirituality. There are no personalities in this world, whether Huxley's or our own, but only states. Either Huxley gives us an accurate picture of what exists in us and around us, and in the process explodes our own more attractive (and self-gratulatory) view, or he is more hopelessly at the mercy of dark forces than Lawrence ever was. Again and again we come across the point of view here expressed by Mary Amberley: " I did what I didn't want to do. One's always doing things one doesn't want—stupidly, out of sheer perversity. One chooses the worst just because it is the worse. Hyperion to a satyr—and *therefore* the satyr."

Huxley is a cynic about the universe rather than about man in isolation. He is cynical about men as playthings of the universe. Hence there is a greater concentration of cynicism in the novels than in the essays, because there he is dealing with men as embodiments of nature. The novels appear to be written by someone of immense experience, someone who is a little jaded by what the world can offer. On the other hand, his essays, though brilliantly perceptive in places, do not seem to come from the same olympian mind. He finds a great deal to attack and even to despise, but it is usually done with sympathy. There is not much sympathy in the novels.

Huxley's sheer intellectual capacity was probably overrated in the early days. Up to the time of *Proper Studies* (1927) one feels he knew a great deal about the life of the artistic world, the arts themselves and the world of abstract thought, and he had correspondingly strong views on them. In other fields, religion and politics, for example, he knew less, his attitudes were less formed, and he walked more gingerly. He could allow himself to be cynical in the novels, but elsewhere he was aware of his limitations and was not prepared to expose himself by making immature gaffes. A lot of preparation went into the writing of *Proper Studies* but it did not show anything like the grasp of its subject that *Point Counter Point* did of the contemporary world of sophistication.

Of course, Huxley has found a way out—that is why it is wrong to refer his cynicism to man directly. Let us consider the incidence of disinterested action in the novels. There are, in fact, very few examples, especially in the earlier fiction. Gumbril Senior's friend Mr Porteous performs one—but it is for his son, and the disinterest is open to question. Nevertheless, his action is regarded with awe. But nearly every other character, when confronted with a choice between good and evil, knows the good and chooses the evil. Anthony Beavis and Sebastian Barnack are outstanding examples. Anthony tells himself he will do what decency demands, but he procrastinates endlessly, until Brian commits suicide. Sebastian is in an even better position to act morally, because he has been made aware of the " genealogy of an offence " (the spreading-out of chance) but self-interest, even if delusory, is too strong. In the later fiction there are characters who are capable of behaving well because they have become aware of eternity (the God in them). These are men like Miller (*Eyeless in Gaza*), Propter (*After Many A Summer*) and Bruno Rontini (*Time Must Have A Stop*). The inference is that man is redeemable, but first of all he must find God. As no one in the early novels even believed in God (or if he did, he did so shamefacedly) it is obvious that they were beyond redemption.

But I am leaving Huxley's solution to a later chapter. Meanwhile he went on searching. In *Do What You Will* he diagnosed the ills that threatened the world and suggested how they could be guarded against. They included monotheism and the superhumanist ideal, the worship of success and efficiency, and the machine. He urged us to emulate the Greeks, to live in a state of balanced hostility between our component elements, and to regard all manifestations of life as divine. Although it was too late to reject the machinery we should make a concerted effort to de-mechanise leisure. He recommended Greek pessimism, which perceived, behind the beauty of the world, that it was finally deplorable. It is our duty to make the best of the world and its loveliness while we can— at any rate, during the years of youth and strength. "Hedonism is the natural companion of pessimism."

Before reaching the decision that the required change can come only through individual surrender to God, Huxley considered the possibility of working through social and political reform. In 1934, when *Beyond the Mexique Bay* appeared, such ideas were particularly strong. In this book he declared that most people prefer boasting, hating and despising others to living at peace. A high proportion of every human being is an automaton; a sense of inferiority always calls for over-compensation. Man, who is generalised by nature, is maiming himself by specialisation. He congregates in large cities, which cannot avoid being ugly and in consequence produce a narrow suburban mentality. Meanwhile, the proportion of talented men to the reading and listening public is much lower than it used to be, thanks to universal education. The result is that we must pay the price, vulgarity, for the benefits of prosperity, education and self-consciousness. It is a question of taste, what we see in life—either irremediable senselessness or potentialities for good. A reconstruction of social and political institutions might assist the good in its human realisation—but Huxley never seemed either very enthusiastic or very hopeful about such a possibility.

One dangerous consequence of revolutionary sentiment was that it tended to lead to cynical acceptance of the very evils it attacked. If we emphasise the existence of corruption we are liable to accept it as inevitable, like the weather. He pointed to the centuries preceding the Reformation, when cynical acceptance of the evils of ecclesiastical corruption was widespread among all classes. Boccaccio, Chaucer and Poggio denounced the evils—but they also laughed. Bruno Rontini (*Time Must Have A Stop*) said it was waste of time denouncing others and instanced Dante, who spent his great gifts threatening his enemies with hell-fire and, once he reached heaven, caused Benedict and Peter Damian to do the same.

All the same, cynicism has an important part to play, providing you know when to stop. You've got to be cynical, Propter told Pete. " You've been taught to worship ideals like patriotism, social justice, science, romantic love. You've been told that such virtues as loyalty, temperance, courage and prudence are good in themselves, in any circumstances. You've been assured that self-sacrifice is always splendid and fine feelings invariably good. And it's all nonsense, all a pack of lies that people have made up in order to justify themselves in continuing to deny God and wallow in their own egotism. Unless you're steadily and unflaggingly cynical about the solemn twaddle that's talked by bishops and bankers and professors and politicians and all the rest of them, you're lost " (*After Many A Summer*). It is folly to be optimistic about social reforms, to imagine that good can be fabricated by mass-production methods. People cannot remain as they are and inhabit a world which is conspicuously better than the world they live in at the moment. The wise man will be pessimistic about the things most people are optimistic about, and optimistic about the thing they're so pessimistic about they don't even know it exists—the possibility of transforming and transcending human nature. " It's the kind of pessimism and the kind of optimism you find in all the great religions. Pessimism about the world at large and human nature as it displays itself in the majority of men and women. Optimism about the things that can be achieved by anyone who wants to and knows how."

This novel is full of examples of the pessimism we should cultivate. We are in the company of highly respected men— men such as Dr Obispo, who says he's in the racket for the fun he can get out of it and detests the " high-moral culture " stuff; or his employer, millionaire Jo Stoyte, who periodically murmurs " God is Love " to keep on the right side of the Almighty, runs a Children's Hospital while putting through a legally valid but morally squalid estate deal, and takes a sick child into the Hospital as a kindness to its father whom he has grossly underpaid for information worth a million dollars.

There is a final warning. Cynicism about the universally respected and admired captains of industry and leaders of society can easily lead to unjustified feelings of moral superiority. But " practically all of us are capable of practically anything ", says Huxley in *The Devils of Loudun*. " There are no limits. Everybody's capable of anything— but *anything* ", says the Arch-Vicar of Belial in *Ape and Essence*. In a *New Statesman* review of *Woman* by Ploss and Bartels, as long ago as 1936, he had noted the " unbelievable sum of ingenuity spent by men and women in making themselves suffer and in devising means for inflicting pain, discomfort and misery upon their fellows." And in *The Olive Tree*: " there is no dogma so queer, no behaviour so eccentric or even outrageous, but a group of people can be found to think it divinely inspired." The behaviour may be devilish or insane, but the people who commit it are, to outward seeming, ordinary decent human beings. But evil is contagious. No man can concentrate his attention on it and remain unaffected. But equally true, and less widely understood, is the fact that no man can consistently oppose evil and remain unaffected. An obsession imparts the poison, whether it expresses itself as absorption in evil or rejection of it. Devils derive their strength from the very violence of the campaign waged against them. And so, in another way, revolutionary sentiment and reforming zeal are liable to produce results quite different from those originally intended, and to corrupt their possessors into the bargain.

# Chapter 9

### NEXUS, OR COMMON GROUND

O N E difficulty that literature has to contend with is its inability to give a simultaneously whole picture of the object, whether it be person or event.    Literature's method must be consecutive.  Wholeness of impression cannot be given although it can be re-established by the reader. In this respect the writer is at a disadvantage compared with, say, the composer of music.  Huxley has always felt this shortcoming of the literary form acutely and has frequently cast about for methods to compensate for it.  As a result his work is fairly full of passages where perception dances in a kind of synthetic melée and all the senses are taxed in an effort to give wholeness to the representation.  This is rare in English literature, which is predominantly bare and skeletal, rationalised and consecutive.

The same difficulty occurs, of course, in writing about Huxley, and rather more so than in the case of a writer who deliberately takes one thing at a time.  I have referred to the young man's reverence for art, his fascination with bodily functions, his attempt to find a meaningful frame for sex, his pessimistic attitude towards man's chances in an appalling environment.  All these characteristics belonged to the same man at the same time, but to attempt to deal with them simultaneously would lead to incoherence.  One has to hold in reserve the various facets of his personality and allow them to shed what light they can on the part under review. Writing about a man is rather like shelling peas.  Meanwhile, we can see how Huxley himself attempted to portray wholeness of perception—and to remember, while we are doing it, that at best it can only be done fitfully.

Men have always sought for the sole reality, a vantage point from which they will be able to view life as a whole; to be, for a moment, one with God. Various technical methods have been tried out as an aid to this search, from the continued chanting of OM to the rhythmical whirling of the dervishes, from the use of drugs to exclusive concentration on an image. In itself it does not require a theology, though a theology is inherent in it. In Huxley's early attempts to find a nexus for all thought and feeling lies the seed of his later theological speculation. But an artist can feel the need for this spiritual oneness with reality as keenly as a metaphysician. It is, in a more rarefied form, the search for the philosopher's stone, the alchemist's elixir. And in Huxley's first book of stories, *Limbo,* Eupompus believed that the secret lay in number. Number seemed to him to be the sole reality. Art, to have any value at all, must ally itself with reality, i.e., have a numerical foundation. He painted pictures which were merely variations on a selected number, and went mad.

Love and sexual union have also been regarded as avenues to the moment of revelation. The mating of Leda and the swan, of humanity and divinity,

> Whose different grace in union was a birth
> Of unimagined beauty on the earth

was a spark from which all things could emanate. It was a mathematical perfection. Normally we live in the middle regions, suspended between godhead and annihilation. During rare moments of beauty (" that moment of descent when apotheosis tilts its wings downwards into the gulf ") we experience a sensation barely communicable, and then only by metaphors. But it is the hint of greater knowledge, greater power, and it has always tantalised man.

The writer who searches for this truth and tries desperately to convey its quality in the guise of love or beauty or number, is naturally envious of the musician. Without being able to say why, we know that music approaches closer than any other art to the moment of truth. It is an instinctive revelation, and we feel compelled to trust our instincts. John Ridley, listening to a lute, considers

> Music's endless inconsequence that would reveal
> To souls that listened for it, the all
> Unseizable confidence, the mystic Rose —

and here we go round the mulberry bush, relating music to beauty so that we may grasp the meaning of truth. When Gumbril takes Emily to a concert at the Albert Hall he muses more cynically than Ridley, but the same sensation of merging grips him: music renders body and soul indivisible and brings them nearer to God. Somehow the personality slips its groove and discovers unimaginable acquiescence. And any sequence of sounds can be music, even the dripping overflow from a cistern. It establishes its pattern, drugs the mind, and trembles on the edge of meaning. It is the symbol and type of the whole universe. There is just the one missing link: if he could only grasp it he would understand " the whole incomprehensible machine, from the gaps between the stars to the policy of the Allies " (" Water Music ", *On The Margin*).

Just as the One contains everything, so all things can coalesce into the One. Lypiatt, the artist in *Antic Hay,* is convinced of this. He will storm God with painting, verse and music. Alas ! poor Lypiatt was agonised by an idea and hadn't the talent to give it life. His assault on Reality was like a bear's attack on a Maginot Line.

And, in fact, no one save the mystic or the very greatest artist can know the coherence in himself, and then only in rare moments of vision. Most of us can only surmise it from the outside, and know intuitively that it exists—but always there is that missing link. Like a scientist in a divine laboratory, Calamy meditated on his hand. It existed in a dozen different ways—as electrical charges, as chemical molecules, as living cells, as part of a moral being, the instrument of good and evil, in the physical world and in mind. Then what relationship existed between these different modes of being? That's where the gulf opened (*Those Barren Leaves*).

There must be a principle of harmony, and until man discovered it his condition would remain appalling. John Donne had known it. He could " skip from the heights of scholastic philosophy to the heights of carnal passion, from the contemplation of divinity to the contemplation of a flea, from the rapt examination of self to an enumeration of the most remote external facts of science, and make all, by his strongly passionate apprehension, into an intensely lyrical poetry" ("Subject-Matter of Poetry", *On The Margin*). He could have knitted Calamy's hand together. To sense the union of opposites requires no great intellectual capacity; it rises from a state of mind, harmonious in itself, dependent on emotional grace. Emily knew it when she was with Gumbril, when she discovered that being happy was also melancholy—but a delicious, dream-like melancholy. Edward Thomas could create it in his poetry: "quiet happiness, which is at the same time a kind of melancholy". At such moments past and future can be abolished. It is this that causes men to doubt the independent existence of time. It can be annihilated, and with it die all the accidents which require time as a platform. There were moments when nothing existed, when everything was swallowed up in a vast "omnipresent Nil, world-soul, spiritual informer of all matter". Everything became nothing. It could even happen in a night-club, as Gumbril discovered. It couldn't be dismissed as a mere "feeling", for on what grounds could any "feeling" be dismissed as mere?

When these emotions strike us with such intensity we feel insufficient in ourselves, we regard them as evidence of the Reality underlying the accidents of existence. This is particularly true of the emotions aroused in us by the contemplation of beauty. To explain the phenomenon poets have involved the universe, asserting that they are moved by the contemplation of physical beauty because it is the symbol of the divine. Emotions are therefore described in terms of theology. Huxley's attitude to this process is rather ambivalent. At times he accepts it as inevitable, at others he praises poets like Thomas for avoiding it. But he is aware that all thoughts and feelings are interdependent, and it is this interdependence that suggests an integrating principle that exists beyond our normal range of perception. The integrating principle is glimpsed through transcendental experience, and the ways to it are various. Writing much later, in *Heaven and Hell,*

Huxley re-affirmed this intuition in more definite terms when he advised the aspiring mystic to turn for technical help to the specialists in pharmacology, in biochemistry, in physiology and neurology, in psychology and psychiatry and para-psychology—and they in turn should make contact with the artist, the visionary and the mystic. In God's house are many mansions, but it should not be forgotten that the mansions make the house.

Once again, *Point Counter Point* is the work where these considerations are given their fullest expression. It is, in every way, the centre of Huxley's achievement, the mode by which his earlier works were related to each other, and the creative store from which his later work developed. In this novel he tackled the great problem of artistic simultaneity,[1] mentioned earlier, and set up a network of symbols which acted and reacted on each other like the parts of an organism. The idea is put in scientific terms by Lord Edward Tanta-mount. Everything was perpetually changing its mode of existence. Bits of animals and plants became human beings. " Perhaps when I was at Vienna last year I actually consumed a piece of Mozart's substance. It might have been in a Wiener Schnitzel, or a sausage, or even a glass of beer. Communion, physical communion. And that wonderful per-formance of *The Magic Flute*—another sort of communion, or perhaps the same really. Transubstantiation, cannibalism, chemistry. It comes down to chemistry in the end, of course. Legs of mutton and spinach . . . all chemistry ". The " of course " and the " all chemistry " mark the specialist, who convinces himself that his little nook is the universe and, if the monomania develops, finally discovers he's God Almighty.[2] Lord Edward felt he had had an apocalyptic vision. Philip Quarles believed that the whole story of the universe was implicit in any part of it. " The meditative eye can look

[1] In his next novel, *Eyeless in Gaza*, he took time to pieces and re-assembled them. But this method, although affirming a superficial independence of consecutiveness, could not solve the problem of simultaneity.

[2] A process described by C. S. Lewis in *Voyage to Venus* (*Perelandra*).

through any single object and see, as through a window, the entire cosmos." Quarles was a novelist and tried to apply his discovery to his art. The problem was " to produce diaphonousness in spots, selecting the spots so as to reveal only the most humanly significant of distant vistas behind the near familiar object." Fiction might be musicalised, viz., the novelist could modulate from one aspect of his story to another, as from the aesthetic to the physio-chemical aspect, from the religious to the physiological or financial. This would be the opposite pole from simultaneity. Reality, the unitive principle, would be passed through a prism.

The life-worshipper must live intensely. The harmony of life is built up of many elements. " The unity is mutilated by the suppression of any part of the diversity ", wrote Huxley in *Do What You Will.* Each separate melody in the counterpoint of life is indispensable. We live in a world of *non-sequiturs,* in which different aspects of the same event appear to be juxtaposed and are only seen in union by the artist and the mystic. The only reason for supposing that there is any connection between the logically and scientifically unrelated fragments of our experience is the fact that the experience is *ours.* But as yet we can do no more than hop from one to the other.

Such a view seems impossibly remote from the common man, yet in *Ends and Means* Huxley attempts to bring it down to earth. Of course, he cannot. It belongs to the whole cosmos and cannot be grounded. Nevertheless, an approach to integration can be made, even if in a manner that appears hopelessly crude. Our civilisation is a technical one. Man blunts his perceptions in the technical schools. Their products come into the world unprepared to deal intelligently even with the facts of experience. There is virtually no network of cognitive relationships. Bits of information exist like stars in a gulf of black incomprehension. A principle of integration is needed and Huxley suggests it should be one that could be approached through normal human interest. Mechanicians must be taught how machinery affects men and women; the link between down-draught carburettors and education in Mexico, between aluminium alloys and the slaughter of Abyssinians. And later, perhaps, the interdependence of ethics and metaphysics might be approached, and from that the close relationship of each to politics and economics, education and religion.

Every good idea can be murdered by misapplication. The idea of the principle of integration was murdered by Paul De Vries in *Time Must Have A Stop*. He had been touring the leading universities of Europe and Asia. " Getting in touch with the really significant people in each. Trying to enlist their cooperation in his great project—the setting up of an international clearing house of ideas, the creation of a general staff of scientific-religious-philosophic synthesis for the entire planet." (Perhaps he had read H. G. Wells. And Lord Curryfin had had the same idea : " he had been caught by the science of pantopragmatics, and firmly believed for a time that a scientific organisation for teaching everybody everything would cure all the evils of society ", Peacock tells us.[1]) De Vries was the crank who seized on a good idea and murdered it because he was so busy thinking about values he had no time to experience them.

[1] *Gryll Grange*

## Chapter 10

### EN ROUTE TO MYSTICISM

UNLIKE most of his contemporaries, when Huxley discovered meaning in life it was formulated in religious terms. During the nineteen-thirties those writers who did not take refuge in a mild aestheticism turned to politics. Huxley was the most eminent of the few who looked for a spiritual salvation. Yet at the start of his career neither he nor his readers would have regarded such a development as at all likely. As we follow his progress from spiritual indifference to a spiritual interpretation of the universe, we have a strong intuition of a mind grappling reluctantly with matters it would prefer to ignore, but which impress themselves the more persistently as the years go by, until at last they appear to overcome his defences with an air of inevitability. The society Huxley described was hopelessly corrupt. It was the intensity of the corruption, sensed more keenly by him than by any other writer of the time, that drove him to the other extreme.

Dick Greenow confessed to a " feeling about his soul ". It troubled him because he didn't know what to do about it. He had all the feelings of Bunyan without his religion. Guy Lambourne, in the same volume (*Limbo*), felt the same. " Intellectually he was a Voltairean, emotionally a Bunyanite." It seems to have been a familiar condition for Huxley's young men. Wise after the event, we can now see why the author and his characters later explored and fostered an urge that was so easily missed by the early readers. But it was a noumenous feeling that left God out. On the analyst's couch Dick was asked to respond immediately to a list of words read out to him. The word " God " left a blank in his mind. Then he said " Wilkinson ", for he remembered a boy he had known at school named Godfrey Wilkinson, called God for short. He was told he had an almost religious passion for someone named Wilkinson.

Although one's subconscious mind leaves God out, the conscious mind is not allowed to. One cannot ignore a being that crops up perpetually in literature and the press. But if this God existed, who or what was he ? Huxley gave the answer in a short piece called " The Merry-Go-Round ", published in *Leda*. The riders clamber on to their symbolic beasts, Ram, Scorpion and Goat, and tear round in a ceaseless Bank Holiday of drunken life and speed. " But I happened to look inwards among the machinery of our roundabout, and there I saw a slobbering cretin grinding at a wheel and sweating as he ground, and grinding eternally. And when I perceived that he was the author of all our speed and that the music was of his making, that everything depended on his grinding wheel, I thought I would like to get off. But we were going too fast." Dick Greenow, unwilling to worship a cretinous god, told the tribunal before which he appeared as a conscientious objector that he had no religion. When the court expressed disbelief in such a position, he told them to put him down as an Albigensian or Bogomil or Manichean. The court, he said, gave him a profound sense of the reality and active existence of a power of evil equal to, if not greater than, the power of good. The court found this irrelevant.

Huxley belonged to the kind of family that still admired Wordsworthian pantheism. Long after Wordsworth himself had declined into Anglican lethargy his youthful ideas still appealed to men who could find no comfort in institutional religion. Matthew Arnold is a case in point. In *Those Barren Leaves* there is an account of a Wordsworthian father tramping his son over God's symbolic mountains, and this passage has a reality that suggests a basis of experience. In a poem called " Scenes of the Mind " Huxley was still sufficiently under the influence to write:

> I have seen God in the cataract.
> In falling water and in flame,
> Never at rest, yet still the same,
> God shows himself.

This was probably little more than filial acknowledgment, a gesture towards the fathers of the tribe. In *On The Margin*

Huxley tells us how, as a child, he had been taught to believe " that a Sunday walk among the hills was somehow equivalent to church-going: the First Lesson was to be read among the clouds, the Second in the primroses; the birds and the running waters sang hymns, and the whole blue landscape preached a sermon of ' moral evil and of good '."

At the same time as the old orthodoxies disintegrated the religious impulse was finding a new outlet through spiritism. Huxley, however, set his face against this alternative very firmly. He did not deny the existence of the phenomena but he could not accept them as evidence of survival or of any other kind of religious truth. In *Crome Yellow* he mocked the spiritualist journalist, Barbecue-Smith, with his pipes connecting his Subconscious to the Infinite. Guy Lambourne was convinced there was no after-life. Speaking of " Last Things " (*Leda*), Huxley asks the old monk Hildebert whether he did not envy the new generation who knew only one ultimate: death annihilates us " with all our shame and all our folly, leaving no trace behind ".

Although Huxley's views on survival (and even on messages from " beyond ") have changed, his attitude towards " spiritualist " and trance phenomena has remained the same. In *The World of Light* Hugo admits that clairvoyance and telepathy are facts. But to connect them with dead people is a matter of taste. " The facts of psychical research simply do not warrant the adoption of anything remotely resembling a harp-and-scream conception of survival; the only rational interpretation to which they lend themselves is an interpretation in terms of some kind of squeak-and-gibber theory ", i.e., the ravings of the subconscious (" Squeak and Gibber ", *Music at Night*). And in *Grey Eminence* he commented on the phenomenon that worship of the odd is to be found among very simple and credulous people and among the highly intelligent. Scientists in particular fall a prey to occultism. They are trained to concentrate upon events in the world of space and time, and are more concerned with " signs " than with the " kingdom of heaven within ". Events which cannot be explained according to their rational and physical criteria tend to be regarded as miracles.

This subject was more closely investigated by Huxley after his own conversion to the Perennial Philosophy. In *Time Must Have A Stop* part of the " action " actually takes place in some other, post-mortem world. Eustace Barnack does in fact send messages to his relations through a medium, but they are distorted and garbled by the latter's worldly and trivial consciousness. And although these messages come through it does not follow that all the pronouncements of mediums come from the same source. The subject is inextricably entangled with wish-fulfilment. In a conversation with Bruno, Eustace accuses the other of believing in survival because it comforts him. Bruno points out that others, such as Eustace himself, get equal comfort from the idea of annihilation. When we come to the séances, Eustace finds that his messages (the messages whose existence he had, while living, denied) had to pass through the filter of another's intermediate knowledge. The result was usually unadulterated nonsense.

Bruno explains to Sebastian his theory of these phenomena. Eustace had been a body plus some unknown quality, $x$. His body was abolished. At the séance $x$ plus the medium's body equal a pseudo-Eustace. But we know nothing about $x$ when it isn't connected with the medium's body. " Most of the consolations of spiritualism ", he said, " seem to depend on bad logic—on drawing faulty inferences, from the facts observed at séances." And many years later Sebastian tried to establish a working hypothesis for religion that would take all the facts into consideration. Among his data he places the mingling of unreliable and often valueless intuitions of psychics into lower levels of non-sensuous existence with the infallible intuitions of great saints into the highest spiritual reality, leading to confusion and public derision of the whole subject. His conclusions will be mentioned in a later chapter.

To complete Huxley's treatment of " spiritual " phenomena, we can refer to *The Devils of Loudun*, where he is concerned with manifestations that have much in common with the medium's. Access is rarely gained to the Divine Ground of all being but to that " queer ' psychic ' world which lies, so to say, between the Ground and the upper, the more personal levels on the subconscious and conscious mind ". The psychic states resulting from such access are often confused with spiritual enlightenment. But the self-transcendence in question is horizontal, not upward. In certain states it is probable that trance mediums go beyond the personal subconscious, beyond the " verminous realm of Original Sin, into an area of sub-liminal mind in which, like a radiation from some distant source, the influence of Original Virtue makes itself faintly but distinctly felt." This would account for the high moral tone, yet unbearably dismal style, of most mediumistic utterances. More often, however, they only make contact with inferior entities, some indigenous to their own personal subconscious, others existing " out there " in the psychic medium, some harmless or positively helpful, others highly undesirable. In *Heaven and Hell* he sums up his position: " My own guess is that modern spiritualism and ancient tradition are both correct. There *is* a posthumous state of the kind described in Sir Oliver Lodge's book, *Raymond;* but there is also a heaven of blissful visionary experience; there is also a hell of the same kind of appalling visionary experience as is suffered here by schizophrenics and some of those who take mescalin; and there is also an experience, beyond time, of union with the Divine Ground." Again, for a fuller discussion of these matters we must wait until Chapter 14.

To return to the Huxley of the twenties, we find him fully aware of mystical literature but equally puzzled about its value. Scogan read the mystics and found nothing but the most deplorable claptrap. They could be nothing else to someone who had not felt the same emotion. " The mystic objectifies a rich feeling in the pit of the stomach into a cosmology ", he says. When Calamy went to the mountains he discovered the same difficulty. " How is a man to give an account of something entirely unlike the phenomena of known existence in a language invented to describe these phenomena? You might give a deaf man a most detailed verbal description of the Fifth Symphony; but he wouldn't be much the wiser for it, and he'd think you were talking pure balderdash." Huxley's original difficulty in accepting the conclusions of the mystics lay in their different interpretations, according to whether the author was a Buddhist, a Brahman, a Mohammedan, a Taoist, a Shamanist, or a Neo-Platonist. At this stage he had not realised that the essential truth was always the same and its outer garb of little importance. In so far as each of them claimed to reach the unattainable Truth, and all of them postulated a knowledge of the unknowable Absolute, they were all equally ill-founded, he said in *Do What You Will*.

This inability to transmit the mystic's experience has always been a matter of significance to Huxley. You are placed in the position of having to accept the conclusions before you can appreciate the statement. Once again, in " Music At Night ", he draws a comparison with music. The introduction to the *Benedictus* in the *Missa Solemnis* is a statement about the blessedness at the heart of things. But you cannot *say* any more about it. When the mystics attempt to describe their experiences the result is often lyrical nonsense in the style of the analytical programme-makers. It was not until he took mescalin that he really understood what the Buddha had meant when he said that the hedge at the bottom of the garden was the Dharma-Body. In India he was reminded of the difficulty again. In this case he felt that Hindu artists tried to express in terms of form what could only be expresed —and imperfectly at that—in words. Ultimate Reality cannot be expressed in art.

Even after Huxley accepted the mystics at their own valuation he continued to doubt the possibility of transmitting their truths to others. The essence of the Perennial Philosophy is that it must arise out of one's own experience. Propter, in *After Many A Summer,* is insistent on this. " The only vocabulary at our disposal is a vocabulary primarily intended for thinking strictly human thoughts about strictly human concerns. But the things *we* want to talk about are non-human realities and non-human ways of thinking." He gives us some examples of the words that baulk us. *Ecstasy*: a technical term that refers to the soul's ability to stand outside the body—but it carries the implication that we know what the soul is and how it is related to the body. *Infused contemplation*: there is somebody outside us who pours a certain kind of psychological experience into our minds—but it implies that we know who that somebody is. The terms are derived from the language of metaphysics, and the people who use them are committing themselves to an explanation of entities whose existence is purely hypothetical. We must remember that words are " signs of things " and avoid the fatal mistake of making things the " signs of words ".

Before Huxley managed to convince himself of the truth of mystical philosophy by personal contemplation, he was unable to accept it at its intellectual face value. He admitted that mystical emotions might have a conduct value, in so far as they " enable the man who feels them to live his life with a serenity and confidence unknown to other men " (" A Wordsworth Anthology ", *On The Margin*). But intellectually they might be worthless, even harmful. At this stage, therefore, he considered the emotion as being more important than the theology.

Probably, like Cardan, Huxley distrusted the automatic quality of much modern mysticism. Scientific modernism had destroyed the certainties of nineteenth-century materialism, and even quite intelligent people sought a way out through a new faith in the unknown. Huxley wanted proof, and there was none — except of panic. Chelifer considered the various escape-routes adopted by his contemporaries — into space or the future or Platonic eternity, the ideal. But, he concluded, " an escape into mere fancy dress does not prevent facts from going on; it is a disregarding of the facts."

During the twenties Huxley constantly weighed the good and evil consequences of religious interpretations, and usually found them balanced. He wanted something more than a philosophical equilibrium. In *Jesting Pilate,* for instance, he referred to the anthropomorphic view that religion is a device employed by the Life Force for the promotion of its evolutionary designs; but against that one might claim it was also a device employed by the Devil for the dissemination of

118

idiocy, intolerance and servile abjectness. In fact, India set up strong resistances in his mind to all forms of spirituality. It was, he felt, the primal curse of India and the cause of all her misfortunes. A little less spirituality would have brought with it less dirt and more food. He felt it was wrong to attack materialism. The failure of Western civilisation was, surprisingly, that it was not materialist enough. The remedy was more materialism and not, as false prophets from the East asserted, more spirituality : " more interest in this world, not in the other." The fault of the average Westerner was that he was too little interested in the world about him. Despite the opportunities offered by modern technology, the lives of the vast majority of men and women among the Western peoples are narrow, monotonous and dull.

The argument swayed to and fro in Huxley's mind but, despite his negative reaction to Indian spirituality, he found it impossible to say either yea or nay to religion. With Spandrell he could wonder : " Why should one class of psychological intuitions be credited with scientific value and all others denied it ? A direct intuition of providential action is just as likely to be a bit of information about objective facts as a direct intuition of blueness and hardness." In *Do What You Will* Huxley wrote : " Science is no ' truer ' than common-sense or lunacy, than art or religion . . . . . it tells us nothing about the real nature of the world to which our experiences are supposed to refer."

Religious intuitions *may* be true—that was all that Huxley was willing to accept at the time. But others go further. All feelings are temporary. After a while they are succeeded by other feelings. Nevertheless, men are prepared to base metaphysical systems on them. It is not only the religious who do this, organising what Melville called " all-feelings " into symbols of eternal truth. Scientists also feel justified in making universal application of the " temporary feeling " they have during their occasional observations and in basing upon it a whole theory of molecular behaviour—despite the fact that they live their daily lives with the ultimate conviction that molecules not only don't move but don't exist.

When people experience the " all-feeling " they begin to talk about infinity. But infinity, in their mouths, tends to become mere sound and fury, signifying nothing but a personal emotion. Writers like Hugo and Verhaeren have practically talked it out of existence—the word is the sign of a thing that is completely unknown. Chelifer remembered his boyhood and his father grandiloquently quoting those awesome words, " A sense of something far more deeply interfused." It took him a long time to discover that they were as meaningless as so many hiccoughs.

The religious feeling, then, was very suspect. It had no provable contact with reality and it had been made ridiculous by attempted explanation in too many idle words. When Huxley looked at the practice of religion by its organised neophytes, he felt he was getting further still from any acceptable truth. The contrast between spiritual aspiration and mundane conduct was too great to ignore. At the funeral service of Grace Elver there was no hint of sanctity. " The priest reeled off his Latin formulas as though for a wager; the bearers, in ragged and tuneless unison, bawled back at him the incomprehensible responses. During the longer prayers they talked to one another about the vintage. The boy scratched first his head, then his posterior, finally picked his nose. The priest prayed so fast that all the words fused together and became one word. Mr Cardan wondered why the Catholic Church did not authorise prayer wheels. A simple little electric motor doing six or eight hundred revolutions a minute would get through a quite astonishing amount of pious work in a day and cost much less than a priest.

" ' Baa baba, baa baba, Boo-oo-baa ', bleated the priest.

" ' Boooo-baa ', came back from the bawling flock."

It was defilement of religion. (It is only fair to add, however, that in *Jesting Pilate* Huxley stated that, whereas we Northerners are revolted by such exhibitions, the Southerner overlooks the trivial details and enjoys the fine general effect of ecclesiastical ballet. But it brings us no nearer religion to enjoy such performances as art.) Hugo, in *The World of Light,* was as much appalled by the Northern, Protestant variant. " That smell of a congregation on a wet Sunday morning—I wish *I* could feel it was the odour of sanctity. But no. I really prefer the smell of cows. And then the service—so far as I'm concerned, the divinity it's addressed to is dead, stone-dead."

There are times, of course, when ritual can uplift. A ritual gravely performed is overwhelmingly convincing, for the moment at any rate. And then there is the fact, frequently mentioned by Huxley, that the letter can sometimes produce the spirit, the rite can bring God. He first commented on this in *Jesting Pilate.* In the following year, in *Proper Studies,* he stated that natural Quakers could not understand this and condemn those who adopt such a method as idolaters and formalists. But you might as well blame people for the colour of their eyes or the shape of their noses. " Substance conditions form; but form no less fatally conditions substance ", he wrote in his Introduction to *Printing of Today.* He modified his opinion in *Ends and Means.* A ceremony cannot create a *lasting* sentiment. To create a ritual, as Comte did, in the hope that it would create in its turn a religious emotion, was to put the cart before the horse. We are told that Biran de Maine refused to make ceremonial gestures because he felt it would be cheating. He wanted to explore the unknown. To induce in oneself, by physical means, an unfounded conviction that one already knew the unknown was not a reasonable or honest way to conduct the search.

He also noticed that religions which despise ritual, images, music and the various pomps calculated to produce *bhakti* (the Indian term for heavily charged devotional feeling) are peculiarly liable to outbreaks of revivalism. Revivalism is much commoner in Protestant than in Catholic countries, for irregular emotional stimuli seem to be required to take the place of those slight but regular recurrent stimuli provided by ritual. " As a believer in order and the decencies ", he wrote, " a lover of the arts, I prefer the Catholic method to that of the corybantic Protestants " (*Proper Studies*). On the whole, he felt that Catholicism was the most realistic of all Western religions, as its practice was based on a profound knowledge of human nature in all its varieties and gradations. It provided something for everyone—except the minority who desire liberty.

He had rejected the writings of the mystics because they were unable to transmit their intensely personal experiences. He could not accept the validity of a system based on anything so transient as the " all-feeling ". Organised religion at its worst debased spiritual sentiment, at its best stood between the spirit and reality. Perhaps a way might be found through abandonment to contemplation ? Calamy felt increasingly the irrationality of attempting to run with the hare and hunt with the hounds. He must either stay in society, and accept its laws, or retire from it altogether. He felt that, given time and freedom, he might arrive at the truth. By dint of several months' hard thinking he might burrow right through the mystery. One had no right to make definite statements about life until one had thought a long time, in freedom, unattached. One might discover nothing. But merely to satisfy one's curiosity about the unknown universe within would be worth doing. And it might lead to something more important. The idea of Calamy's retreat probably came to Huxley as he stood near the monastery of Montesenario, looking out over the mountains. " Here at the heart of it (solitude), I thought, a man might begin to understand something about that part of his being which does not reveal itself in the quotidian commerce of life; which the social contacts do not draw forth, spark-like, from the sleeping flint that is an untried spirit; that part of him, of whose very existence he is only made aware in solitude and silence " (*Along the Road*).

Calamy was a sign of things to come, but in 1925 no more than a false alarm. Huxley so often seemed on the brink of the contemplative life but was not to go over the edge for many years. Perhaps he was too deep in the affairs of this world. Yet again and again he approached the mystery. In India he asked himself, Why are we on this planet ? Surely not to go about collecting dung, as so many Indian peasants were doing ? It seemed an inadequate reason for the first cousin of the angels, the brothers of Buddha and Mozart and Newton. The Hindu philosophy was too " high " for him, by which he certainly did not mean beyond his mental reach (one could not imagine the Huxley of 1926 admitting such a thing) but hung too long, like a pheasant. When he met an Indian holy man he was appalled by his unpleasant dirtiness. Huxley certainly saw no reason why godliness should be divorced from cleanliness. His conclusion was that one is all for religion until one visits a really religious country. All philosophies, he decided, are imperfect. He found his inclinations turning towards drains and machinery, and on leaving India he felt that Ford was a greater man than Buddha. About the only good word he had to say for mysticism after his Eastern travels was that it constituted a rule of moral health. He felt fairly safe in assuming that religious mystics do not in fact unite themselves with " that impossible being, a God at once almighty and personal, limited and limitless", but that by their discipline they attained serenity and integration.

It should be borne in mind that during this period Huxley was coming more and more under the influence of D. H. Lawrence. Rampion (*Point Counter Point's* portrait of Lawrence) despised mysticism and asceticism as enemies of life. " The fornicator's hatred of life in a new form ", he called them. The beatific experiences were often the imagination's reply to the body's denial of life. When the Fairy in " Chawdron " (*Brief Candles*) had a headache she pretended it was worse than it was. Then her imagination took control and she began to regard herself as a martyr. Finally the pain, now greatly magnified, became the raw material of a mystic, spiritual martyrdom on a higher plane. An intelligent person would know her for a pathological case, but there were others who took her at her own valuation. These " spiritual " people, whether they are regarded as " genuine " (whatever that may mean) or not, revert to a state of crass non-existence. Mrs Bidlake in *Point Counter Point* ended up by doubting her own existence and, of course, everybody else's. She used to wander round the garden, repeating her own name over and over again. The syllables had lost all significance. And this was where the retreat from life led to.

Huxley was fully aware that the practice of mystical religion was unlikely to gain many followers in modern times. It entailed asceticism, and it is the first duty of every good citizen to consume as much as he possibly can. But it remained an intellectual challenge to him. He knew, as Calamy said, that the most important mystics have been men of the highest intelligence. He instanced Buddha, Jesus, Lao-Tze, Boehme and Swedenborg, and also reminded Chelifer that Newton abandoned mathematics for mysticism. On the other hand, a lot of intelligent people didn't believe in God at all, but regarded him as " a sensation in the pit of the stomach, hypostasised . . . the gratuitous intellectualist interpretation of immediate psycho-physiological experiences." If you've never had a religious experience, said Philip Quarles, it's folly to believe in God. You might as well believe in the excellence of oysters when you can't eat them without being sick. Far better to be certain about the pit of your stomach.

Huxley was whirling like a weathercock, intelligent and imaginative enough to see all the viewpoints and to condemn all the dogma. What he lacked was the only thing he knew to be necessary: a personal experience which he could diagnose and analyse with the full weight of his intellectual honesty. Failing this, he had to fall back on his rational powers. *Do What You Will* tackled the religious problem in a dozen essays, some direct assaults, others marginal skirmishes. In them he cleared the ground for the next stop.

First of all he examined the Judaic-Christian-Islamic predilection in favour of monotheism. He felt it was not essential to religion, even " true " religion, but that it was a fashion that sprang from the bare, undiversified desert. Today Europeans believe in One God, not because they have thought about it, but because they have taken it from an old tradition and because their neighbours have done the same. Later, in *The Perennial Philosophy,* he wrote that there could only be monotheism where there is singleness of heart. In fact, monotheism barely exists in the modern world. It is theoretically enthroned but in practice Western man worships a multitude of gods. But Huxley appears not to have grasped this in 1929. Returning to his essay " One and Many " we read : " We are aware of existing; therefore we are not merely one. We are conscious of remaining ourselves through inward and outward change; therefore we are not merely diverse. Given these peculiarities of human nature, it is easy to infer the peculiarities of divine nature. Men are both simple and diverse; therefore there are many Gods and therefore there is only one God." The modern trend of our civilisation has been towards a unitarian mythology, i.e., to a position where the God of man's simple nature is regarded as a truer description of reality than the Gods of his diversity. But the only reason Huxley can adduce for this choice lies in taste, not in logic. This tendency is regarded as a spiritual progress because its consummation has been *Us*. Man's arrogance, and a historical accident, have together combined to displace polytheism.

But in the process God dies. He has degenerated into an algebraical formula, a pure abstraction. " The modernists have all but spiritualised him out of existence. From polytheism to monotheism, from monotheism to the worship of an abstraction, from the worship of an abstraction to the worship of nothing at all—such are the several stages in the progressive 'spiritualisation of man's conception of the divine ' ". The old polytheism did at least answer the needs of man's peculiar condition. The new monotheism does nothing of the kind. Our present tendency is to overvalue the instrument and to undervalue the food which alone give us the vital power and health to use the instrument properly. Contemporary monotheism is an expression of the abstract knowledge which enables us to predict and organise, but it gives no sustenance. Huxley concludes that man's needs can only be met on the spiritual plane by a recognition of man's diversity and a return to polytheism. We need a new religion of life, with many Gods but also One. " It will have to be Dionysian and Panic as well as Apollonian; Orphic as well as rational; not only Christian, but Martial and Venerean too; Phallic as well as Minervan or Jehovahistic." It will have to symbolise the whole of life, not merely one of its aspects.

Life-worship, an idea which resulted from his intimacy with Lawrence, required the deification of Human Personality. At least we know something of it, which is more than we know of God, he says in another essay in the same volume ("Fashions in Love"). It is necessary to classify our experiences, as Pascal classified them into body, mind and charity, but the life-worshipper must never forget that reality is an organic whole. Abstractions have no existence outside the classifying intellect; they merely distinguish between different states of the total reality as experienced by different individuals, and by the same individual at different times. The many Gods of the new pantheon will only have their being in communion with the One God of Human Personality. Huxley then gives us the creed of the life-worshipper. " His fundamental assumption is that life on this planet is valuable in itself, without any reference to hypothetical higher worlds, eternities, future existences." Next, that the end of life is more life, that the purpose of living is to live. He quotes Lotze: " our virtue and happiness can only flourish amid an active conflict with wrong." Life is inconceivable without contrast and diversity. The perfection of the Hindus is Nirvana, the extinction of life.

This is where Huxley stood in 1929. From then until the publication of *Eyeless in Gaza* in 1936 he added little to this conception. In the latter year we find him moving once again towards a more mystical interpretation of man and nature, taking over from where we left Calamy in 1925. But this time the change was to be permanent. *Ends and Means* showed that he had completely rejected the attitude expressed in *Do What You Will* and adopted the Perennial Philosophy. Henceforth every book he published demonstrated its mystical base, some more than others. He could not deny the many Gods but he knew that man could not reach salvation through their worship. I will take up the thread of his religious progress again in Chapter 14.

# Chapter 11

## A. *Early Laurentian Trends*

NO ONE can permanently assume an alien personality. Before they find their true selves young men are apt to flirt with bovarisms, pseudo-Lenins or pseudo-Hemingways. But it takes time to discover the natural self. In many ways Huxley was the antithesis of Lawrence—rational, tolerant and scientific in outlook where the other was instinctive, condemnatory and apocalyptic. Yet there was something in Huxley's make-up which responded to the Laurentian view of things. Under the influence of Lawrence's personality this was fostered to a degree out of harmony with Huxley's essential nature; after the other's death the influence faded yet left a valuable colouring to his opinions.

All of us, even the most inhibited, have a Laurentian strain. If this were not so, Lawrence would have been of little importance, a literary freak. Huxley, dubious at first, later realised that Lawrence had something valuable to say. His tolerance (except for stupidity, which he has always derided) allowed him to listen to views that frequently contradicted his own. Frieda Lawrence wrote that most people couldn't grasp her husband's ideas easily, and became hostile. " There were a few like Aldous and Maria Huxley who patiently listened " (" D. H. Lawrence As I Knew Him ", *New Statesman and Nation*, 13 August 1955).

Laurentian behaviour is to be found in almost any novel. Lawrence attracted attention because he made it the basis of a way of life. We find a Laurentian in one of Huxley's earliest stories, " Happily Ever After " (*Limbo*). George White had no prejudices, no theoretical views about conduct; "he just lived, admirably, naturally, as the spirit or the flesh moved him." Guy, the involved intellectual, envied him. When Guy was killed George had no silly qualms about loyalty to the dead or to memories—he made love to Marjorie, George's fiancée. The devil-may-care Ivor in *Crome Yellow* was a Laurentian who had been through a course of upper middle class conditioning, without being essentially altered.

Barbara (in " Green Tunnels ", *Mortal Coils*) felt her flesh crying out for more air, more sunlight. She had not learnt the lesson that such desires are wicked. She wanted to run about with no clothes on but Mrs Topes made her wear shoes and stockings and a frock even at the hottest hour of the Italian day. Mrs Topes had been in India. " In India ", she said, " we always made a point of being properly and adequately dressed. An Englishwoman must keep up her position with natives, and to all intents and purposes Italians *are* natives."

In *Antic Hay* there was the artist Lypiatt. Now Lypiatt could never be mistaken for a portrait of Lawrence but he might well be a caricature of the Laurentian attitude. " Passionately I paint passion ", boomed Lypiatt. " I draw life out of life ". And yet there was no life in his work. No one could be intentionally unkind to Lypiatt, but he was obviously a man with excellent ideas only he hadn't the talent to express them. So he became a laughing-stock, and a pathetic one because he was so easily hurt. At this stage Huxley had not fallen under the Laurentian spell. Lypiatt's feminine counterpart was Rosie Shearwater: " life, life—it was there to be lived—life—to be enjoyed." But in the hands of such people the Laurentian idea was vulgarised because they didn't know how to live. They called their existences " life ', but the life was subordinated to the ego. Underneath the boasting they were frightened. Lawrence would never have said he regarded enjoyment as a duty. That immediately introduced the moral element. Life was to be enjoyed, not because it was right, but because a properly constituted body could behave in no other way. In one of his later poems, " The Cicadas ", Huxley expressed the Laurentian wisdom which refused to refer bodily action to moral precepts :

> Clueless we go; but I have heard thy voice,
> Divine Unreason ! harping in the leaves,
> And grieve no more; for wisdom never grieves,
> And thou hast taught me wisdom; I rejoice.

It was Huxley's conviction that Lawrence was a true artist that swayed him more than anything else. The artist was a priest-surrogate, the modern man with a message. In this he disagreed with Middleton Murry, who attributed the conflict in Lawrence's work to the Oedipus Complex. Huxley denied this. If Lawrence's views were the product of a psychological accident they lost a great deal of their interest. In *Those Barren Leaves* he poured scorn on the psycho-analytical interpretations of art, according to which Filippo Lippi was no longer what used to be understood by the word "artist", but had become an incestuous homosexual with a bent towards anal-erotism ! If Murry were right, Lawrence was no artist because he subordinated the whole to a part. Huxley became convinced that Lawrence's art was the work of the whole man, and therefore could not be dismissed without the most serious consideration.

## B. The First Portrait: Kingham

Richard Aldington, who knew Lawrence, said in his study of him, *Portrait of a Genius, But . . . .,* that Kingham (" Two or Three Graces ") is a perfect picture of Lawrence in certain " awkward " moods. Rampion (*Point Counter Point*) is less accurate because more idealised.

Kingham was morbidly sensitive to anything that might be interpreted as a reference to his social origin. He was always on the look-out for insults from " gentlemen ". As is the way of such people, he was intensely proud of his working-class background. (Incidentally, in " The Claxtons ", *Brief Candles,* there is a portrait of another, much more familiar type of bright boy who has worked his way up from humble beginnings. Herbert Claxton serves as a significant contrast to Kingham. He was a very serious young man who was burdened by the weight of his own intelligence. He read William Morris and Tolstoy as others used to read the Bible. " He's one of the very few people I've met who feel *responsible* about things. Everyone else is so terribly frivolous and self-centred and indifferent ", his wife wrote in her diary. " He's conscious, he's aware, he accepts the burden." He

was also dull, exhausted and half-dead.    Kingham knew
instinctively that the " burden " became heavier the more you
were aware of it.    In fact, there should have been no
" burden "; it was the figment of a mind too conscious and,
despite Mrs Claxton's view, too egoistic.)   Kingham liked to
feel abased so that he could react with the greater violence.
" I know that my father was a plumber, and that I was
educated at the expense of the State and by scholarships for
the encouragement of clever paupers, etc., etc."

The result was frequent scenes—and he liked scenes.   He
liked to flounder in emotion—his own and other people's.
He never considered the consequences, he simply enjoyed the
intoxication.   But his emotions were genuine, only they were
aroused too easily.   He needed occasional orgies of passion,
to humiliate and be humiliated.   The other people concerned
became instruments which he could play upon.   It was always
easy for him to give free rein to his emotions by brooding on
his loves or grievances.   He could do this by intense concentration on the object of his desire or hatred.   He needed no
dervish tricks.

Then, having provoked a storm, he was astonished when
others were hurt.   He could not understand the inability of
the world at large to tolerate what he called his frankness.
As a result, it was impossible to feel indifferent towards
Kingham.   People either loved or hated him.   But his power
lay in his brilliance.   He could charm you even when he was
saying things with which you disagreed or doing things of
which you disapproved.   And you could never pin him down
in argument.   You could never prove him wrong because he
never stayed long enough in one intellectual position.   When
you raised your logical cudgel to smash him he escaped
" through some little trap-door of his own discovery, clean out
of the argument."   Aldington said this was a perfect exposition
of Lawrence's methods of evading an argument.

Kingham's denunciation of the modern vices of triviality
was eloquently Laurentian.    " Everything that's easy and
momentarily diverting and anaesthetic tempts—people, chatter,
drink, fornication.   Everything that's difficult and big, every-

thing that needs thought and effort, repels. It's the war that did it. Not to mention the peace. But it would have come gradually in any case. Modern life was making it inevitable. Look at the young people who had nothing to do with the war—were only children when it happened—they're the worst of all ". But he hated these vices because they were his own, and he could not eradicate them. This was a misunderstanding of Lawrence—or, conversely, Kingham at this point ceases to be Lawrence.

Finally, we are given some passages from one of Kingham's books. There was a tirade against " those silly prophets and Utopia-mongers who offer us prospects of uninterrupted happiness." In order to know happiness and virtue man must also know misery and sin—a view put forward by Huxley in *Do What You Will,* as we have seen. The Utopia he offered would be one of unbridled pleasures, the cruelties and dangers of the ancient world, the ecstasies and fears of Christianity. Not " a sterilised nursing home, with Swedish drill before breakfast, vegetarian cookery, classical music on the radio, chaste mixed sun-baths, and rational free love between aseptic sheets", the heaven on earth of a Herbert Claxton. He concludes with the creed of the Life-Worshipper in abbreviated form: " Nothing that intensifies and quickens life is futile." It was this assertion that sunk deep into Huxley's mind and produced, some years later, Laurentian ideas in a Huxleyan mode.

### C. The Second Portrait: Rampion

Lawrence praised *Point Counter Point* (where he appeared in the guise of Rampion), but added, " No, I don't like his books: even if I admire a sort of desperate courage of repulsion and repudiation in them. But again, I feel only half a man writes the books—a sort of precocious adolescent." Undoubtedly Huxley's novels came from the intellect, which could hardly have been expected to please Lawrence. Huxley was trying to write the right books in the wrong way. Rampion is a very favourable portrait of Lawrence (the only balanced man in the novel), but it has been passed through a rationalising filter. There is this difference between Kingham and Rampion: Kingham is a rounded character while Rampion is no more than a mouthpiece.

Rampion's first words are, " What I complain of is the horrible unwholesome tameness of our world." In his view we all ought to be " atavismuses with all modern conveniences. Intelligent primitives. Big game with a soul." (Frieda Lawrence's father had called her an " atavismus " when she ran off with D.H.). In other words, we should live in a harmony of body, mind and spirit. Blake was his model because he managed to live without being lopsided. Any kind of lopsidedness, of intellect or body, of soul or feelings, was barbarian. From being barbarians of the soul we are becoming barbarians of the intellect.

As the preoccupation with intellect pushes the body into the background, so our disease expresses itself in a hatred of sex. Sex hatred characterised the fornicator as much as the puritan. Rampion called it Jesus's and Newton's and Henry Ford's disease, because between the three of them they had made of sex something shameful. Huxley reiterated this view in " Spinoza's Worm " (*Do What You Will*). The superhumanist ideal has made man feel ashamed of all but a small part of his multifarious being. Normal activities are regarded as degrading or sinful. Men do what their instincts command, but apologetically. " The result, naturally enough, is that the quality of their instinctive, passional and physical life degenerates ". Even Rampion was, at bottom, half a puritan. It had been in his upbringing and he could never completely throw it off. (The same had been true of Lawrence.)

Rampion preached phallism but insisted that it was something utterly remote from unimpassioned civilised promiscuity. The former was Greek, balanced, sane; the latter was just Christianity turned inside out. " The ascetic contempt for the body expressed in a different way." The moderns hate life and their only alternatives are promiscuity or asceticism, which are two forms of death.

132

Rampion had drawn a cartoon of a grotesque procession of monsters, starting with dinosaurs and pterodactyls and leading to human monsters, without limbs or bodies, creeping slug-like on vaguely slimy extensions of chin and neck. The faces were mostly those of eminent contemporaries, and included J. J. Thomson, Bernard Shaw, Sir Oliver Lodge, Sir Alfred Mond, John D. Rockefeller, Dr Frank Crane and Mrs Eddy. The lizards died because they had too much body, said Rampion. But what about mental size ? " These fools seem to forget that they're just as top-heavy and clumsy and disproportioned as any diplodocus. Sacrificing physical life and affective life to mental life." Again the idea is returned to in *Do What You Will*. Modern man is trying to reduce the soul to singleness by violent means. The object of the true humanist, on the other hand, should be to keep all his parts, if not at peace, at least in a condition of balanced hostility.

Another idea expressed by Rampion and subsequently developed at length by Huxley was that words shut one off from the universe. Most of the time we are not in contact with things but with the words that symbolise them. We can go further, preferring " some poet's damned metaphorical rigmarole about a thing " to the simple words which, even if they are only symbols, at least don't disguise reality unnecessarily.

Rampion could see no genuine cleavage in the programmes of the modern political parties. They existed simply to decide whether we should go to hell by communist express train or by capitalist racing motor car, by individualist bus or collectivist tram running on the rails of state control. The important thing, which no-one of influence seemed to challenge, was that they were all agreed on the excellence of the industrial stink. Industrial progress must lead to over-production, and the results would inevitably be a search for new markets, international rivalry and war. The problem would be solved, but by annihilation — and that seemed a poor kind of solution. Rampion thought there might be another, a temporary one, while the system was being modified in the direction of a permanent solution. People must learn to live dualistically, in two compartments: in one as industrialised workers, in the other as human beings. At the moment, they live as idiots and machines all the time, at work and in leisure, and they persuade themselves they're living like gods.

Rampion gave the existing situation ten years. " After that the most appalling and sanguinary bust up that's ever been." It is a fact that Lawrence accurately forecast the outbreak of the second World War at a time when politicians were rejoicing over Locarno. Huxley has drawn attention to the naïvety of worldly men, particularly in those spheres where they might be expected to have exceptional insight. Politicians and journalists acclaim some trivial piece of diplomacy as though it inaugurated a new era, business men foresee Prosperity and Plenty at the moment the slide to Ruin and Inflation begin. There was bound to be trouble, said Rampion. Love of death was in the air. His own children had a passion for machinery. " It's as though the young were absolutely determined to bring the world to an end—mechanise it first into madness, then into sheer murder." Huxley felt the same thing. In *Music At Night* he said the new romanticism, including the passion for machines (regression to second boyhood), the " collective mechanism " of the Bolsheviks, the dehumanisation of art, was leading straight for death. In fact, what he called death the new romantics called life. Their popular songs in particular had a horrible tang of putrefaction about them. In them human emotions intrinsically decent were ignobly parodied. They made him feel like a man who, having asked for wine, is offered hog-wash.

Rampion was right; Philip Quarles, who comes as close to Huxley himself as anyone in the novels, was convinced of that. Moreover, Rampion lived his ideas. He didn't think one thing and practice another, like Burlap, who was a malicious portrait of Middleton Murry[1]. And later he gave two reasons why he

[1] The later Huxley, preaching love and charity, is probably now appalled by the viciousness of this earlier attack on Murry. Whether Murry could forgive and forget I don't know, but there is a hint in one of Huxley's later books that Huxley at least would like to wipe out the past. Murry is quoted with approval in *Science, Liberty and Peace*. The quotation is apt but not at all striking, and a similar one might have been borrowed from any of a score of other writers. This certainly could not have happened twenty-five years ago.

believed Rampion to be right : first of all, Rampion lived in a more satisfactory way than anyone else Quarles knew, and secondly, because so many of Rampion's opinions agreed with his own. This wasn't mere vanity. Quarles felt it significant that someone so different, and starting from such a different point, should yet come to the same conclusions as himself.

There is of course no reason why we should expect either of these portraits to be accurate. They are characters in fiction who were recognised as being tolerably close to Lawrence, but to criticise them for their lack of fidelity to the model would be inexcusable. Huxley knew Lawrence better, more sympathetically anyway, than any other man. The fact that Rampion is not the Lawrence of the biographies may mean that the biographies were wrong but probably means that Huxley didn't attempt an absolutely perfect reproduction. As Rampion is also not the Lawrence revealed in his letters, this is probably nearer the truth. The vast rages are lacking, his expression is too academically articulate, he is too patient with opposition, he is not sufficiently irritable to be D.H.L. Rampion is less accurate (as a copy) than Kingham, but he is more appealing. By the time *Point Counter Point* was being written Huxley was listening eagerly to Lawrence, wanting to understand him, to give him the benefit of every doubt. Aldington says the two men " became as near friends as was possible without the risk of explosions." Huxley's mind was an excellent foil to Lawrence's. There were others, but they were too egotistical to make a partnership possible. Lawrence supplied all the egotism that was permissible. I imagine Huxley had sufficient confidence in his own outlook to be able to listen to abuse without replying in kind. He felt Lawrence had something to offer, however wrongheaded some of his views might be, and he did not press his own views unduly. He had enough sense to enjoy Lawrence's gaiety and wit, and to pass over his faults.

Apparently Maria Huxley typed *Lady Chatterley's Lover* for Lawrence, making many " little mistakes " on the way. The Huxleys stood by him during the fuss over its distribution. It was unfortunate that *Point Counter Point* was getting such good notices at the time, and Lawrence was envious. It was necessary to conceal this reaction somehow, and he did it subtly by the prediction that before the year was out Huxley would be in the lunatic asylum. At least, that is Aldington's story. Personally I think it fair comment; Huxley could not have concentrated on stupidity and evil much longer without risking a mental breakdown. And Lawrence probably did believe, quite sincerely, that Huxley carried too great a load of cerebration for any one man to bear. Whatever his motives Lawrence was being, as usual, much more perceptive than the world of commonsense gave him credit for. After all, Edgar Allan Poe was driven mad not by drink but by an over-active analytical capacity. But no pettiness could come between them; the Huxleys were with Lawrence to the end and it was Aldous who called in the doctor on the last day.

## D. The Influence of Lawrence

Huxley found Lawrence extremely persuasive. On their first meeting, although embarrassed by sincerities of a kind to which his upbringing had not accustomed him, he agreed to go to Florida to help start a new " colony of escape ", as he called it. Heseltine (later to be the model for Coleman in *Antic Hay*) was also chosen. Fortunately for Huxley the scheme fell through. From 1925 to the year of Lawrence's death they were frequently together, usually in Italy or France. In his diary for 27th December 1927 Huxley made this entry: " He is one of the few people I feel real respect and admiration for." When Lawrence wanted to start a little magazine called *The Squib* (" just squibs to have little darts of revenge and send little shots of ridicule on a few solemn asses "), he told Aldous he would be " Al at it ". They argued, of course, especially about science. Lawrence wouldn't accept any evidence he didn't feel in his solar plexus. Despite his sympathy, this was an attitude Huxley was incapable of adopting. His psychophysical constitution wouldn't allow it. Each age of man, he felt, has its suitable philosophy of life; Lawrence's was not a very good one for old age or failing powers. In his Introduction to Lawrence's *Letters* Huxley speculated whether Lawrence might not have been happier if he had disobeyed his *daimon* and forced himself into mechanical and external connection with the body of mankind. This is the path followed by most of us, including Huxley, but then our personal *daimons* are not so insistent as Lawrence's. Huxley criticised Lawrence's " bird's-eye view " because it tended to ignore all tiresome details, all the difficulties of social life, to judge too sweepingly and to condemn too lightly. In method the two men were poles apart but in outlook (like Rampion and Quarles) they were very close. In a letter to Huxley, written in 1928, Lawrence praised the other's idea of the " grand perverts ". He mentioned St. Francis, Leonardo, Kant, Louis Quatorze, Baudelaire and Proust and added: " they all did the same thing, or tried to: to kick off, or to intellectualise and so utterly falsify the phallic consciousness, which is the basic consciousness." This was the very idea attributed by Huxley to Rampion.

The ripest fruit of Lawrence's influence is to be found in *Do What You Will* and *Brief Candles*. In the former Huxley made a Laurentian hero of Pericles—Rampion had praised the Greeks where Lawrence would have chosen the Etruscans. But Huxley had to take his examples from among the known; his particular type of integrity would not allow him to attribute qualities to a race of whom so little is known as the Etruscans. Lawrence could do this and, being what he was, could also do it without loss of integrity. Huxley wrote: " What Pericles took for granted was briefly this: that men should accept their natures as they found them. Man has a mind: very well, let him think. Senses that enjoy: let him be sensual. Instincts: they are there to be satisfied. Passions: it does a man good to succumb to them from time to time. Imagination, a feeling for beauty, a sense of awe: let him create, let him surround himself with lovely forms, let him worship. Man is multifarious, inconsistent, self-contradictory; the Greeks accepted the fact and lived multifariously, inconsistently and contradictorily." There must, on occasion, be the exercise of restraint, but it should not come from religious spirituality. There should be no pretence of a conflict between a diabolical Lower Self and certain transcendental Absolutes, but between a part of the personality and the personality as an organised whole. Such restraint would be fundamental and emotional, not artificial and intellectual.

If we try to repress certain elements of the personality, spiritual blood-poisoning will result. It explains why so many important and influential people are nevertheless fools in certain areas of thought and feeling. Chawdron, in *Brief Candles,* had spent so much of his energies making money out of New Guinea Oil, he was taken in by any little girl-child that crossed his tracks. Tilney also admitted that, because he himself had spent his life reading the Best that has been Thought or Said, he was an easy prey for any bitch. Neither of them had lived, completely and intensely, on every plane of existence as a human being ought to. Part of their being had atrophied in each case.

The same thing is said of Sir Watney Croker, the eminent physician in "The Rest Cure". He was a bit of a baby because too much preoccupation with the duodenum had prevented his instinctive part from fully growing up. (Dr Obispo, in *After Many A Summer,* realised that he could do practically as he liked with his employer Stoyte because, outside of business, he was frightened, ignorant and stupid.) Martha Claxton was the product of long years of wilful self-denial, of stubborn aspirations towards the highest, of conscious and determined love for humanity and her enemies. She irritated by her aloof air of superiority, ill-disguised by fake humility. No instinct was ever willingly allowed expression. But they cannot be dammed up indefinitely. They " rose and rose behind the wall of voluntary mortification, deep and heavy with the potentialities of force." Martha's love of power was usually strong enough to maintain control but sometimes her greed would gain outlet in an unexpected way. She would buy and secretly polish off in a single day a whole pound of chocolate creams. These orgies became more frequent with the passage of time. She was trying to bring up her daughter Sylvia on the same admirable model. But by training her as an angel, or as her idea of an angel (i.e., by repressing her " lower self ") she was transforming her into a devil.

In " Holy Face " Huxley declared that Pascal was mad in his excess of conscious wisdom. The men and women he despised so much, though incomparably grosser and stupider than he, were " wise with the unconscious wisdom of the species." They responded to the commands of life, of their own natures, instead of an intellectualised part-view of it. Pascal had to be consistent, but a sincere person cannot be consistent. He has to obey the dictates and satisfy the claims of all the many people who live inside him—his fluctuating states or conditions, in psychological terms. The life-worshipper is therefore a man of many principles. " He does not select one single being from his colony of souls, call it his ' true self ', and try to murder all the other selves. Each self, he perceives, has as good a right to exist as all the others ". Once again Huxley uses the phrase " equilibrium of balanced excesses " to describe the good life. We should not attempt to adopt the Aristotelian doctrine of the golden mean, which results in doing everything by halves, living in a state of perpetual compromise. "The life-worshipper knows that nothing of any significance has ever been achieved by a man of moderation and compromise " (" Pascal ").

Huxley insisted, more and more vehemently as time passed, that he didn't advocate a return to Primitive Man. " Primitives are horrible ", said Tilney. But Primitive Man and Natural Man are not the same being at all. Primitive Man is raw material, Natural Man is the finished product. He is a work of art, and our trouble today is that there is so much bad art about. Too many Ary Scheffers, not enough Manets. Fanning told Pamela she could hardly hope to be natural at her age. " Naturalness is something you learn, painfully, by trial and error."

There are one or two other observations on this view of human nature to be found in *Brief Candles*. For instance, while it is true that self-stultification will result in humiliation you probably won't recognise it, as by that time you will have already been reduced to a sub-human condition. That is why Nemesis sometimes seems to reward. And then there is Fanning's theory of the point of culture, which only becomes obvious when you meet practical business men or workmen from the big towns. They make you see the point of culture as the Sahara makes you see the point of water: they're arid. Fanning's definition of culture was " knowing and thinking about things that have absolutely nothing to do with us ". He concluded with a Laurentian eulogy on the Etruscans.

There is a great deal of Laurentian reflection in *Brief Candles,* if not application—for however impressed Huxley was by the Laurentian thesis he could never have become an active apostle himself. In " After the Fireworks " he was already considering the pitfalls that beset the path of the would-be Laurentian. Miles Fanning is an apparently Laurentian author—his women work from impulse. He is attracted by a woman thirty years his junior, and she is more than willing to respond to his advances, having been moulded by Fanning's fiction. But there are doubts and misgivings. We learn that Pamela's mother had been " unnatural by nature "—she urged herself to act from a simulated instinct, derived from certain fictional heroes. (Huxley refers several times to the power fiction—and also history—have of creating outside themselves, in life or " nature ". To take one instance only, there is Bob Briggs in *Ape and Essence,* who fancied himself as all the Romantic Poets rolled into one—"Beddoes committing suicide, Byron committing fornication, Keats dying of Fanny Brawne, Harriet dying of Shelley.") Then the life-passion must organise its own restraints, as we have seen — and this may bring us perilously close to the Podsnapian outlook. After all, there was that thirty years' difference, and no personality remained its " self " for long. Both Fanning and Pamela would change or, in Huxleyan terms, there would be a progression of discontinuities. This, in fact, is realised when, against his wiser promptings, Fanning allows himself to take Pamela as his mistress. Three months later we find him planning to leave her. Once again, Huxley has been unable to find the satisfactory answer. A balanced response to the claims of the different elements that make up the human personality may have seemed satisfactory to Rampion or Lawrence, but for Huxley there was always another element left unassuaged. And the conclusion seems obvious: happiness is unattainable.

In Lawrence's footsteps Huxley visited the Caribbean and Mexico, recounting his experiences and reactions in *Beyond the Mexique Bay*. Again he confessed that he was not attracted by primitive people. (Incidentally, Lawrence came to the same conclusion, though this has generally been obscured.) But apart from the people, a return to primitivism as a way of life was impracticable. In Mexico Lawrence had to refresh himself continually by contacts with western books, civilised men and women. He hated the misapplication of science so much he thought science itself should be abolished. But the correct strategy was a science of better quality. " If Miahuatlan were the only possible alternative to Middlesborough ", Huxley wrote, " then really one might as well commit suicide at once. But luckily it was not the only alternative." He concluded the book with a reference to the artistic failure of *The Plumed Serpent*. Lawrence found that it was psychologically impossible to give up the life of the intellect and spirit, which a contented primitivism demanded.

There are a few more reflections, all antipathetic to the primitivist idea though not to Lawrence personally, in *Eyeless in Gaza*. Anthony Beavis wondered if Lawrence's views would have remained the same if he had looked through a microscope and seen biological energy in its basic undifferentiated state. Lawrence had insisted that the raw material should be worked up to a certain pitch, but no further. Yet ulterior purposes and organisations existed and could not be ignored. Lawrence's arrest of the evolutionary process took place at an entirely arbitrary point. It is not quite clear what Beavis meant. He was deeply moved by the swarming life revealed by the microscope, and he felt he had experienced a revelation. Like all revelations, it was overwhelming yet not very lucid in detail. It turned his thoughts to spiritual possibilities, which made him shudder from habit. But one thing seemed certain: there were Life Forces stronger than any Lawrence had imagined.

Although Lawrence's influence appeared to grow thin after his death, the part that remained helped to keep Huxley's later thought more firmly based in physical reality than it might have been. The danger of conversion lies in the extremism it gives rise to. From his early indifference and positivism Huxley might easily have leapt to a position from which he condemned nature and all her works. Thanks to the lesson he derived from Lawrence he has never forgotten that man is partly an animal. Lawrence's most valuable gift was not his worship of instinct and " dark forces ", which could easily degenerate into diabolism, but his sensitiveness towards nature and his insistence that man must never attempt to cut the links between him and it. Surin, in *The Devils of Loudun,* did this and his reward was madness. We are helped by three kinds of grace, Huxley says in *The Perennial Philosophy*—animal, human and spiritual. " Animal grace comes when we are living in full accord with our own nature on the biological level—not abusing our bodies by excess, not interfering with the workings of our indwelling animal intelligence by conscious cravings and aversions, but living wholesomely and laying ourselves open to the ' virtue of the sun and the spirit of the air ' . . . But of course, the fullness of animal grace is reserved for animals. Man's nature is such that he must live a self-conscious life in time, not in a blissful subrational eternity on the hither side of good and evil. Consequently animal grace is something that he knows only spasmodically in an occasional holiday from self-consciousness, or as an accompaniment to other states, in which life is not its own reward but has to be lived for a reason outside itself."

## Chapter 12

### NON-ATTACHMENT

THE solitary ideal of life-worship did not outlast Lawrence for long. It received its fullest expression in 1929, by 1936 it was obviously considerably diluted, and in 1937 its place had been taken by the ideal of non-attachment. It was not a mere replacement, for I have shown how Huxley retained his respect for " animal grace ", but it gave a new direction to his thought. Non-attachment was the attitude that symbolised the latest spiritual turn.

Huxley started *Ends and Means,* subtitled " An Enquiry Into the Nature of Ideals and into the Methods employed for their Realisation ", with a description of the ideal non-attached man. He is non-attached to his bodily sensations and lusts, to his craving for power and possessions, to the objects of these various desires, to his anger and hatred, to his exclusive loves, to wealth, fame, social position, to science, art, speculation, philanthropy. The practice of non-attachment entails the practice of all the virtues: charity, courage, intelligence, generosity and disinterestedness. This ideal has been preached consistently over the last three thousand years by Hindus, Buddhists, Taoists, Stoics, Christians and moralists outside the Christian tradition, such as Spinoza. The non-attached man puts an end to pain, not only in himself but also, by refraining from malicious and stupid activity, to such pain as he may inflict on others.

What caused this change of direction ? Huxley quotes Nurse Cavell's statement on patriotism: it was " not enough ". He had tried so many moral positions that were not enough— indifference, aestheticism, rationalism and life-worship, and each of them left a void. He had always shied away from " spiritual " solutions but there could be no doubt that the inadequacy he experienced had nothing to do with physical or intellectual deficiencies. In fact, so far from being deficient in any way, his bodily, mental and emotional life may have suffered from a surfeit of activity. When trying to " balance his excesses" he realised that one part of him had never experienced excess, had scarcely been exercised at all—and it was that very part that Lawrence had loathed for its traditional over-excitation. But most " spiritual " activity, he found, was pseudo-spiritual. Even when he believed in God, the average modern man knew next to nothing about the connection with God.

Modern society praised intelligence, for intelligence kept the turbines working and the aeroplanes flying. But mere intelligence knew no more about spiritual life than did stupidity. Very few people today are capable of living on their own spiritual resources but have become abjectly dependent on incessant stimulation from without. But more important than the fact is the failure of most people to see any danger in this.

No author has given us a more vivid picture of modern restlessness, surrender to distraction and refusal to think than Aldous Huxley. Towards the end of *Antic Hay* Gumbril and Mrs Viveash tour the West End in a taxi, driving round and round aimlessly like lost souls, constantly retracing the same ground. There is nothing else to do and if they kept still they might have to think about something. It is the perfect setting for Mrs. Viveash, with the sky signs dancing over Piccadilly, always repeating themselves in their imbecile patterns. " Too lovely ", she sighed. Gumbril knew better. Gumbril was the type of man, a perfect Huxleyan, who could not help following the worse when he knew the better. " These things are the epileptic symbol of all that's most beastly and idiotic in contemporary life ", he said. He liked to talk like that and Mrs Viveash liked to listen.

In his early essays Huxley frequently deplored the modern " life of pleasure ". Like Gumbril, like so many characters in the stories, like Philip Quarles even, he was partly a slave to it himself. Yet " I would rather put in eight hours a day at a Government office than be condemned to lead a life of ' pleasure ' ", he wrote in *On The Margin;* " I would even, I believe, prefer to write a million words of journalism a year ". He had to earn his living, which served as a deterrent, but no-one could write so well of the Gumbrils and Viveashes without personally knowing something of the life they led. Without any philosophical consolations to buoy them up they believed, with Bill Hamblin in *The World of Light,* that it is " our business to make the best of this world while we're in it ". No-one can dispute that, but what they meant by " the best " was the most agreeable to the bodily senses and the emotions. Super-attachment was their key to fulfilment.

In Los Angeles Huxley found a society which had sur-rendered itself completely to this creed. It was the great Joy City of the West. There was every conceivable delight to taste and swallow and digest or, more likely, to bring up again; rushing about, always being busy, never having time to think, being too rich to care, shouting and dancing, singing *Yes, sir, she's my Baby,* talking about nothing at the top of your voice, being always in a crowd, getting a kick out of uplift—in short, having a Good Time.

But Los Angeles is still exceptional and most men still have to work. The intense enthusiasm for outer activity, the emasculation of the inner life, therefore occur within a frame-work of business rivalry and careers that possess auras of something akin to holiness. Socially recognised success, Hux-ley says in *Proper Studies,* is professional success; a man im-poses himself on society by doing well at his work. This requires qualities of reason, will and intuition, and it is natur-ally these that are developed. But success in this field of activity is impossible without well-organised acquisitive tendencies. Covetousness, which used to be a deadly sin, is now a cardinal virtue. Four qualities are therefore required in a personality coordinated for social success : reason, will, intuition and covetousness. The other elements of the per-sonality are outlawed from normal professional and occupational life. No attempt is made to link up sex and the other feelings with the organised personality; they remain un-coordinated discontinuous states. Their irrelevance constitutes their charm; they are not associated with any notion of responsibility.

Huxley was probably first brought to a close examination of the idea of non-attachment when he prepared his essay on Pascal for *Do What You Will.* This may have been contemporary with or immediately after the writing of *Point Counter Point,* and Pascal's personality must have contrasted strangely with, say, Lucy Tantamount's. Pascal's hatred of attachment was so great that he would not even allow anyone to love him, "for I am no man's goal and have nothing wherewith to satisfy them." At the time Huxley was repelled by Pascal's lack of humanity, but he was never able to put aside the fascination which the theologian's personality exerted on him.

Non-attachment, however, is valueless unless it belongs to a fully responsible person. Loyola was wrong to adopt a militarist-type organisation, for unquestioning obedience and non-attachment cannot be practised simultaneously. The attitude of non-attachment is a choice. No man can be compelled into it, nor is a corpse a sound model. Non-attachment is also incompatible with a high income. "The possession of considerable wealth causes men to identify themselves with what is less than self." But extreme poverty is equally a barrier. The requirement which attracted Huxley more than any other was that of intelligence, the kind that sees the general implications of particular acts. He thought Buddhism decidedly superior to Christianity in this respect because in the Buddhist ethic stupidity, or unawareness, ranks as one of the principal sins. Intelligent appraisal of long-range consequences of one's actions is not insisted upon by Christian moralists. One result of this is that there are scarcely any examples in imaginative Western literature of intelligently virtuous, adultly non-attached characters. Most of our literary examples are idealisations of the average sensual man. The virtuous have usually been feeble-minded or infantile, eccentric or dull.

Huxley himself has not been very successful in his obvious attempts to create a non-attached character. Propter in *After Many A Summer* is the best, but, as with Bruno Rontini in *Time Must Have A Stop,* we rarely see him in action and never at a point of tension. They are mouthpieces, and do not make good fiction.

In addition to these qualities and conditions, we can add bodily fitness. Pain causes the owner of the body to identify himself with his faulty physical processes. Even where maladjustment does not cause pain it sets up psychological strains which modify the mind's relations with external reality. The internal reality, the overself which mystics have identified with God or the integrating principle, is also affected[1]. There can also be no non-attachment without inhibition. The truly non-attached person will know no need of inhibition, but such are very rare. As a life-worshipper Huxley had said that the inhibitory mechanism was set in motion by the whole personality, acting on a part that has become refractory or overstimulated. Now he declared that the person practising non-attachment must be prepared to inhibit on various levels emotionally, by checking malice and vanity, lust and sloth, avarice, anger and fear; intellectually, by rejecting irrelevant thoughts; and physically, by refusing to be satisfied with our normal, maladjusted actions.

Non-attachment demands great reliance on personal resources, which is less easy today than at any previous period in history. Young people are exposed to a much more intense barrage of suggestion and temptation than ever before. They should be taught, as much as possible, to dispense with newspapers, wireless and films, and to subject the devices of propagandists to critical analysis. But this will not be easy in a society where ambition is regarded as a virtue. The lust for power creates a state of attachment, which is intrinsically separative from the integrative principle. The spiritual vices are always the most harmful and the hardest to resist, and

[1] Its nature cannot be altered, of course, but its light can be dimmed.

many of them are fostered by the most respectable propagandists of our society.

Mr Propter, in *After Many A Summer,* said that time and craving are two aspects of the same thing, the raw material of evil. Potential evil is *in* time, the longer you live the more evil you automatically come into contact with. It is different with good, which isn't found merely by living longer. Time is potential evil, and craving (attachment) converts the potentiality into actual evil. That is why, in *Ends and Means,* Huxley said that an association which tried to create a working model of a society unobsessed by lust for power and success would be creating a working model of a society having no reasons for war. The Good Society of the social philosophers is a chimera, because we cannot actualise good. But at least we can prevent the actualisation of evil. Propter was interpreting Eckhart's " Time is what keeps the light from reaching us ". Sorrow is the unregenerate individual's life in time, the life of craving and aversion, attachment and separation. The highest ideal is that of liberation from personality, from time and craving. Men are frequently confused in their minds about what they call selflessness. They speak of the selflessness and devotion of the artist or scientist, and imagine they are attaching themselves to the highest. But this is not so. The ideals they pursue are merely projections of their own personality, and therefore not liberation at all but a concealed bondage.

In this chapter I am largely concerned with one aspect of Huxley's spiritual progress, his new-found conviction that absorption in self, projections of the self, and the outer world stand as barriers between man and what he has always called his salvation, and what we might call a state of blessedness. In the next chapter I shall deal with another aspect, his treatment of the greatest social evil of our time. I regard these as paths which helped him to the full acceptance of the Perennial Philosophy: disillusion and fear working on a sensitive mind which had always been subject to intuitions from " out there ". He had at first been reluctant to admit the true source of these intuitions because his upbringing and environment made it difficult for him to appreciate what " science " had discredited. Now, almost by elimination, he had come to the conclusion that God was much more than a sensation in the pit of the stomach. Union with God was not a romantic fiction, but it laid down certain definite conditions. One of these was that the soul cannot approach God unless it is in a state of perfect detachment. Anxiety, even when it was concerned with God's work, separated. And there was another way in which direct experience or reality could be clouded. This was by the action of " distractions ", the horde of purposeless and irrelevant thoughts, notions, memories and images which assail the mind whenever an attempt is made at concentration. They are imbecilities, waste products of psycho-physiological activity, and they are what Christ meant by " idle words ". They can be annihilated, along with the passions and intellectual vanities, but only when the action followed is intrinsically good or ethically neutral.

In *The Perennial Philosophy* Huxley admitted that the majority of people sought attachment because they found the world dull and often disagreeable. For those who have transformed the world by making themselves fit to see God within it as well as within their own souls, it wears a very different aspect. Traherne's "the corn was orient and immortal wheat" gives only a dull glimmer of the blessedness he experienced. Normal, unregenerate man believes he is being asked to pursue " self-naughting " as an end in itself, and understandably declines. It possesses merely an instrumental value, as the indispensable means to something else. It is the " something else " that must remain a mystery until it is personally experienced. Too many turn in disgust from the Puritan who practises all the cardinal virtues and remains a thoroughly bad man. The mistake lies in identifying stoic austerity with holiness. Holiness is the total denial of the separative self, in its creditable as well as discreditable aspects, and the abandonment of the will to God. Holy indifference is not stoicism but active resignation. We are to renounce particular attachments so that the divine will may use the mortified mind and body as its instrument for good. There can be no real love where the mind is imprisoned in private preferences and aversions.

## Chapter 13

### PACIFISM

THE social expression of Huxley's new outlook lay in pacifism. As he had been semi-blind during the first World War his attitude to war was of importance only to himself. But in fact he was not at that time much attracted by the pacifist viewpoint. To hold it one must put a high valuation on human life and activity and there is little reason to suppose Huxley cared much about either in general terms. It is true, Richard Greenow was a conscientious objector in 1914 but he had little love for his fellow pacifists, who seemed not to take the faintest interest in the welfare of humanity at large and were wholly absorbed in the salvation of their own souls and in keeping their consciences clear from the faintest trace of blood-guilt. Even when Dick refuses military service and is sent to work on the land he finds himself wishing that Tolstoy, one of the High Priests of Pacifism, had never been born. In fact, Tolstoy as a thinker comes in for constant reproof throughout Huxley's work—and as an artist for constant praise, with the possible exception of his physiological shortcomings. We find that the Claxtons disapproved of the war on partly Buddhistic, partly Socialist-International and partly Tolstoyan grounds (*Brief Candles*). There was nothing admirable about their attitude, it was really nothing more than a declaration of superiority to bolster self-esteem and nourish their mock humility.

It is doubtful if Huxley had any strong opinions, one way or the other, about war at this early stage. But there was one thing he could always be relied upon to do, and that was to uncover and attack hypocrisy wherever he found it. He could not work up a passion about the mass-suicide of humanity but he could be made angry by someone else's pretence that it was all for the best. There is a good example of this in Chapter Nine of *Crome Yellow*. It consists of a sermon written by the Rev. Bodiham, and it was based on an actual address that had been given to a meeting of clergy in 1916. The author was not really appalled by the slaughter. Instead, he regarded it as the necessary preliminary to the forthcoming Armageddon, and rejoiced in it as a condition of God's merciful will. Fifteen years later Huxley wrote that there were plenty of pious churchmen who believed that God approved of killing, provided it was in war, but would be horrified at the suggestion that fornication and adultery could be anything but detestable in His eyes. But such falsity did not make Huxley love the pacifists any more. In fact, in *Vulgarity and Literature* he singled out Romain Rolland for the "emotional soup" of his wartime pacifist pamphlet. It is clear that Huxley cared more about Rolland's style than his opinions. He disliked both, though he argued that the latter were " politically valuable ".

The important change was first noticeable in *Eyeless in Gaza*, where Anthony Beavis came under the influence of a minor prophet named Miller and turned pacifist. He made the discovery that national policies are large-scale projections of individual desires. In consequence, political changes can only be worked through individual channels. He formulated four empirical facts: we are all capable of love for other human beings, we impose limitations on that love, we can transcend the limitations, and love breeds love just as hate breeds hate. It was part of the general search for sounder moral foundations that marks the Huxley of the early thirties; it also took place in the shadow of Hitler's, Mussolini's and Stalin's aggressive and disciplinarian tyrannies. Huxley said that the philosophy of Constructive Pacifism was based on these axioms.

Because of the individual, human basis of politics, no important political progress could be made until people were treated as human beings, Miller said. If you treated people as savages, he had found in his work as a missionary, they would behave like savages.   Similarly, if you regarded people as hands, mouths, statistics, sheep or wolves, they would behave in the manner expected.   Like produces like.   If you want peace and justice, you must use means that are just and pacific. People have to be trained to act in this way.   The real obstacles to peace are human will and feeling, human convictions, prejudices, opinions.   The causes of war are primarily psychological and we must tackle them first.

Beavis concluded that we are all ninety-nine per cent pacifists.   The other one per cent, which allows us to exterminate our own particular enemies, is the great barrier to peace. We are all convinced of our own rightness and, by implication, of the other man's wrongness.   " Peace, perfect peace, so long as we can have the war that suits us.   Result : everyone is the predestined victim of somebody else's exceptionally permissible war.   Ninety-nine per cent pacifism is merely another name for militarism."   In addition to incomplete pacifism there was negative pacifism.   This was normally associated with bad economic conditions, and was not to be relied upon.   Suffering from poverty and unemployment, people willingly swear they will not fight again.   Feed them, employ them, and they resume their worship of the conventional idols, Empire, National Honour and the rest.

The greater part of Huxley's pacifist ideas are expressed in *Ends and Means, An Encyclopædia of Pacifism* and his six-penny pamphlet, *What Are You Going To Do About It* ? *Eyeless in Gaza* shows Anthony Beavis finding his way towards pacifism, in the manner that Huxley himself must have approached it.   Just as Propter is the non-attached man, so Miller is the pacifist.   Miller has one advantage over Propter; he acts.   We see him at a meeting, being challenged by a heckler, knocked off a wall several times but always climbing back, until at last the young man turns away, frustrated and jeered at by the crowd.   Pacifist propaganda, which was so strong before the war, is practically non-existent today.   The organisations and the literature still exist, but their impact is practically nil.   Yet the arguments are as powerful and cogent as ever they were, and I therefore propose to summarise the views set forth by Huxley in the three publications mentioned above. They must form part of any study of Huxley, but at the same time it should be recognised that they were also the views of a movement, not of an individual only. In Huxley's case, pacifism involved more than the prevention of war. Pacifism could not succeed without a revolution in man's way of life. A part-time pacifist was inconceivable. (Unfortunately a part-time militarist wasn't.) Something much more radical than a political instrument or a social technique was required. Hence a study of Huxley's pacifist thought leads naturally to, and is engulfed by, something much larger; a study in metaphysics and the kind of society it entails.

First of all, man is probably unique in making war on his own species. Other creatures fight among themselves but do not make war. When it is said that man is a " fighting animal ", what is meant is that he is a " scrapping animal ". There is little relation between individual scrapping and the mass murder we call war. In fact, war is no more natural than the sanguinary manifestations of sexual jealousy that are found among primitive tribesmen but which have been set aside by civilised peoples. Nor can it be claimed that war leads to the survival of the fittest. War selects dysgenically, i.e., eliminates the young and strong. Furthermore, the triumphant culture is just as often that of the vanquished as of the victorious. The Hebrew and Greek are excellent examples of influential cultures that had suffered complete military defeat.

Not every civilisation has been warlike, as is often claimed. That of the Indus Valley, as rich and elaborate as those of Sumer and Egypt, knew nothing of war. Neither weapons nor fortifications have been found by the archaeologists. The rise of war is probably correlated with an abrupt change in human consciousness. The correlation may have been with increased sexual continence on the part of the ruling classes.

It is often claimed that peace and justice can only be

imposed by force. But force cannot impose permanent order on a people which is hostile to the wielders of force. In the last resort the real sanctions for order and justice are public opinion and the desire felt by every individual to be thought well of by his fellows. But even if we accept the necessity of police forces, we acknowledge that the end of police action is restraint. The end of war is destruction and it employs unrestricted violence as its means. The vital interests of the community cannot be defended by war. For this reason the condemnation of war is no longer a heresy among Catholics. Although they may not condemn war as war, they know that under modern conditions a population is certain to suffer more from war than from non-violent resistance. Huxley therefore refused to support the idea of military sanctions, according to which the non-committed nations would combine against the aggressor, or of an international police force, which he called an international massacre force. In the language of the stud book, it would be by Machiavelli out of News From Nowhere.

Huxley took his standpoint on the view that means determine ends. However excellent intentions may be, bad means must inevitably produce results quite unlike the good ends orginally proposed. War leads to injustice, injustice to resentment and hatred, and a desire for revenge. We have reached a crisis now because a new possibility has presented itself: the chance of annihilation. History supports the pacifist. The " iron dictatorship " of the Jacobins produced war, military tyranny, the rise of nationalistic idolatry; Tsarist oppression and World War I produced the " iron dictatorship " of the Bolsheviks. The threat of revolution begot Fascism, Fascism begot re-armament, re-armament led to the de-liberalisation of the democracies. Another way in which war produces war comes from the desire for an im-proved strategical position. A " natural " frontier is one lure; also, " we must use our forces now in order that we may be in a position to use them to better effect next time."

These are certain virtues which apologists claim belong

155

G

naturally to war: courage, self-control, endurance, a spirit of comradeship, readiness for sacrifice. It is true that these virtues may be stimulated by war, but at such a gigantic price that it is madness to excuse war on their behalf. In war, such virtues can only be cultivated by means of coexistent vices. Also, the " military " virtues can and do exist in individuals who are devoted to peace. Huxley favoured a system of peace-time national service which would give young men the opportunities for rough and tough behaviour that they require: fire-brigade service, lifeboat service, light-house service, sea fishery, etc. Those who demand a cause they can live for and even die for might find it in such activities. They would, of course, require as much propagandist effort on their behalf as war receives at present.

The foundation of the pacifist faith was the conviction that if you treat other people well, they will usually treat you well. One might go further and say that, if you continue to treat others well they will always reciprocate, because it is only initial suspicion that has to be broken down. There have been numerous historical examples of this truth: the early Christians and the Imperial authorities, Penn and the Indians, the Hungarians and Emperor Francis Joseph, Gandhi in South Africa and India, all serve as illustrations of successful preventive pacifism. It is humanly impossible to go on attacking people who offer no resistance—this was the point of the Miller episode I have referred to. But non-violent resistance is useless once war has broken out. Modern war is waged almost exclusively with long-range weapons, which do not allow any human contacts between opponents. The pacifist must prevent war from breaking out.

Despite the immense ingenuity expended in an attempt to prove the opposite, an unprejudiced reading of the Gospels leaves one in no doubt that Christ condemned war. If the Gospels were not sufficient, there would be the conviction of the early Fathers during the first three centuries of our era to support the view. Owing to the close association of Christian doctrine with the Old Testament, " righteous indignation " has come to be regarded as a virtue and has justified Christians in the commission of many atrocities. Buddhists, on the other hand, regard anger as always and unconditionally wrong. Modern Christians justify their support of war by a distinction between the " spirit " and " letter " of Christ's teachings, i.e., they argue that Christ meant them to ignore his words completely.

Among the causes of war Huxley includes the fact that many people find their peace-time occupations either humiliating and frustrating, or just boring. War provides an escape. During wartime the suicide rate among non-combatants falls to about two-thirds of its normal figure. Life becomes simpler, one lives in a state of chronic enthusiasm, war brings " prosperity ", there is greater sexual freedom. Nationalist idolatry, which thrives in war and periods of inter-national tension, acts as an antidote against the inferiority complex. Even the most unfortunate member of the Chosen People or Master Race is entitled to think himself superior to any outsider, however gifted. Huxley believed that the applica-tion of the principle of self-government to industry and business would do something to deliver men from their frus-trations and humiliations and their pathetic recourse to a vicarious sense of self-importance through the medium of national arrogance.

Huxley certainly did not believe that the causes of war were either exclusively or predominantly economic. In this he was true to the official pacifist interpretation but opposed to the dominant revolutionary temper of the time, which was Marxist. He did not even believe that there was any valid economic reason for the class struggle. It persisted because some men desired power over others, and they could best realise their ambitions in the framework of class rivalry and hatred. The belief that wars are made solely by capital-ists and armament makers for their own private interests is too naïve to be entertained, for the capitalists never have any difficulty in finding non-capitalist troops to fight their wars for them.

In *Ends and Means* Huxley listed the various causes of war. In addition to those already noted (boredom, nationalism, strategy) we find the desire to further a religious or political creed (ideological war). The personal vanity or thirst for glory of a leader is another (Alexander, Napoleon). Unfortunately it is often felt that the rest of the people share this glory, and therefore they make no attempt to resist the search for it. And although the economic causes are not so predominant as the Marxists claim, it is true that they exist: desire for fertile territory, the need for foreign markets and also areas where capitalists can invest their savings. Arms manufacturers can foment war scares by false reports, bribery and patriotic propaganda. The nationalisation of the arms industry, often recommended in those days, would not reduce the danger of war, although it would destroy the influence of socially irresponsible capitalists. On the contrary, it would to some extent legalise and justify an intrinsically abominable traffic. The only solution lay in the complete abolition of arms manufacture and that would only come when the majority wished it. Huxley suggested that a start should be made by the total destruction of our bombing fleet. Returning to the causes of war, he mentioned the speculative investors who, though less mischievous than the armament makers, preached imperialism because of the profits it brought the financiers. The nation as a whole probably does not profit from the possession of colonies.

Violent attempts to change the existing structure have not been very encouraging. The most important modern example was the Russian Revolution. The result of the violent means employed is that contemporary Russian society is not communist (the desired end of the revolution) and the principle of coercion has survived. Individuals can no longer coerce as owners but they can coerce as representatives of the State.

" The pacifist's alternative to militarism is a policy that has the double merit of being not only morally right, but also strictly practical and business-like ", Huxley wrote. The star example of non-violent settlement on the international level is the history of relations between Norway and Sweden since 1814. But on the whole the method has been proved most successful in less formal fields of activity. Administration in the Belgian, Dutch, English and French colonies had become more humane and at the same time more efficient by the application of non-violence in place of the old-fashioned combination of prejudice and fear of the " savage ". The same method has been used in the treatment of domestic problems. The modern and more enlightened approach to criminals and the insane is essentially non-violent, i.e., a mixture of trust and goodwill.

But the movement of reform must come from individuals, as it always has done. They must persuade their fellows that pacifism is preferable to militarism. The official mind is not capable of such a revolutionary sentiment. Unfortunately, few " peace-lovers " also love the indispensable conditions of peace. These are disarmament, renunciation of empire, abandonment of economic nationalism, and systematic training in non-violent methods. These things must be shown to have value in themselves, beyond being means to an end. We are reminded of the " negative " pacifists in *Eyeless in Gaza* who only hated militarism because it did not bring them prosperity.

On the diplomatic and international level Huxley hoped that the monopolistic powers could be persuaded to call a conference at which the unsatisfied powers could state their claims. But no progress could be made without sacrifice—of economic advantage and of prestige (viz., pride and vanity). In *Ends and Means,* however, Huxley admitted that little could be hoped for from international conferences. The National Persons were too jealous of their sovereign rights. Yet one generous gesture on the part of a great nation might be enough to set the world free. There seemed to be no other way out of the impasse. And Britain, he felt, was in a better position than anyone else to make the gesture. If the gesture were not made, however, pacifists should cease to cooperate with the State. " The State is not God and its demands are not categorical imperatives. The State was made for man, not man for the State. The State is a convenience, like drains or the telephone; its demand that it should be treated as an all-wise divinity is inadmissible and leads, as the history of tyrannies and dictatorships shows, to every kind of crime and disaster " (*An Encyclopædia of Pacifism*).

In his pamphlet Huxley urged the need for the organisation of a Constructive Peace Movement. He suggested the formation of local units of between five and ten people, who would meet regularly for discussion, mutual help and criticism. Each group should be an unlimited liability company, in which each member would assume responsibility for all the rest. Ideally the members of these groups should live in common, possessing nothing as individuals, everything as joint owners of communally held property and communally produced income. In 1934 Canon Sheppard's letter to the press had produced immediate response, and later led to the formation of a Movement which partly satisfied Huxley's requirements. He became one of the sponsors of the Peace Pledge Movement, along with Vera Brittain, Storm Jameson, George Lansbury, Rose Macaulay, Lord Ponsonby, Bertrand Russell, Siegfried Sassoon, Sheppard, Donald Soper, Arthur Wragg, Wilfred Wellock and others. All members took the simple pledge: " We renounce war and never again, directly or indirectly, will we support or sanction another."

Huxley knew that a pledge and membership in an organisation were not enough by themselves. Pacifism could not live unless it became a way of life, a personal ethic. It was impossible, for instance, for a man to be a true pacifist if he were mild and generous in politics yet a tyrant at home or a bully to his employees. Pacifism must enter into a man's being and not be merely an attitude, like most political opinions. For this reason Huxley wanted the members of the Movement to practise spiritual exercises in common, that their beliefs might gain a religious intensity and be united with something stronger than prejudice. When an association of individuals sets out to initiate desirable changes the first condition of success is that they shall accept the same philosophy of life. In addition to spiritual discipline and communalisation of property and income, there would have to be various arrangements governing democratic organisation, practical work and study. (Incidentally, we hear no more of aristocracy at this stage. It simply leaked away from Huxley's thought and, without any public pronouncement, seems to have been replaced by the democratic ethic.)

Members should also guard against the kind of high-flying idealism which leads to a disregard of mundane matters. For instance, no organisation can exist without capital; if the organisation is going to participate in industrial or agricultural production, as Huxley envisaged, capital needs would be great. " Good intentions and personal devotion ", he wrote in *Ends and Means,* " are not enough to save the world; if they were, the world would have been saved long before this—for the supply of saints has never failed. But the good are sometimes stupid and very often ill-informed ". Propter, in *After Many A Summer,* was trying to put Huxley's ideas into practice. He had a few machines, a small workshop, a few acres with greenhouses, and two or three men working with him. But the main difficulty was financial. Rich men would give lavishly to art schools but were not interested in helping small communities to be self-supporting. There were a lot of other problems awaiting solution but they would depend on practical experiment. They included the best method of combining workers' self-government with technical efficiency, the elimination of boredom, disposal of wealth created by machine production, the investment of superfluous wealth, and so on. The Peace Pledge Movement never developed along these lines, however. It remained a rather amorphous aggregation of people, the majority of whom never felt more than an emotional distaste for war at a time when peace still prevailed.

At the time of his conversion to pacifism Huxley wrote an essay entitled " Words and Behaviour " (published in *The Olive Tree*), which demonstrated how the reality of war is masked by the words we use to describe it. This is an early example of semantic method. It shows how the language of politics and strategy is designed to conceal the fact that war consists in the murder and suffering of individuals in quarrels which are not their own. Military writers use the terms " sabres " and " rifles " instead of " cavalrymen " and " foot-soldiers ". As Huxley says, the accounts of some battles read like a clash of ironmongery. Or sometimes we get battles fought between ideas: " forces interact; weights are flung into scales; masses are set in motion." Or it may be geometry. Or the combatants become personifications. " The enemy " is singular, " he " makes " his " plans, strikes " his " blows. Conflict becomes mythological, and no blood flows. Later in the same essay Huxley translates a passage from politico-military jargon into direct, unveiled language. I have only space to quote the first sentence, but it will suffice. Napoleon-Joffre-Churchill says: " You cannot have international justice unless you are prepared to impose it by force."[1] The translation is longer but it conceals nothing: " You cannot have international justice unless you are prepared, with a view to imposing a just settlement, to drop thermite, high explosives and vesicants upon the inhabitants of foreign cities and to have thermite, high explosives and vesicants dropped in return upon the inhabitants of your cities."[2]

The belief that the way to peace lies through war (a success-ful war, of course, though every successful war is also, by definition, an unsuccessful war for someone else) is one of the most pathetic yet persistent illusions the human race is sub-ject to. History is full of examples of its failures, but what-ever the use of history may be, it is certainly not the provision of unacceptable truths. In *Grey Eminence* we find Father

[1] It is interesting to note that Bertrand Russell, one of Huxley's co-sponsors of the Peace Pledge Union, also supports this view now.

[2] Article XXXVII of the Anglican Church says: " It is lawful for Christian men at the commandment of the magistrate, to wear weapons and to serve in wars." Coleridge's comment was, " This is a very good instance of an unseemly matter neatly wrapped up. The good men recoiled from the plain words: 'It is lawful for Christian men at the command of a king to slaughter as many Christians as they can '."

Joseph writing to a friend: " The King's intention is to bring about as soon as he can a general peace with guarantees for the future—a peace which will be a golden age and, as it were, a new era of Augustus. His means for achieving this are as follows: to back up by the action of several armies every promising negotiation and opening for peace." The King's " golden age " was to be, of course, the submission of Europe to the Bourbons. As for its nature, the illustrations of Jacques Callot are the best testimony.

When war came pacifists would be helpless, Huxley had written. War did come, most pacifists supported the war effort in one capacity or another, and Huxley himself ceased any active propaganda. His view today is that the pacifist position will never be accepted on ethical or religious grounds, but it may be forced upon the world by the logic of techno- logical advance. Meanwhile the best way in which a writer can further peace is by calling attention to the psychological and demographic factors making for war. Huxley has adopted this method himself, particularly in *Science, Liberty and Peace,* an essay in *Themes and Variations,* and *Ape and Essence.* In the first of these books he expressed the belief that *satyagraha* (non-violent resistance as practised by Gandhi) might be resorted to in the West. This would not be the consequence of a change of heart but of the realisation by the masses that it has become the only practicable form of political action in a society where the rulers control massive resources. He pointed out that the Germans adopted this method in the Ruhr in 1923. It broke down, just as Gandhi's earliest efforts broke down, because it had not been adequately prepared for. But it lasted long enough to prove that a Western people, even one traditionally associated with mili- tarism, is capable of non-violent direct action.

## Chapter 14

### THE DIVINE GROUND

> "Some day, it may be, the successful novelist will write about man's relation to God, to nature, to his own thoughts and the obscure reality on which they work, not about man's relation with woman."
> ("Uncle Spencer", *Little Mexican*)

B Y 1936 Aldous Huxley was a pacifist and a convert to the Perennial Philosophy. These two allegiances were part of the same process, the mind working from different starting points to the same end—or, *sub specie eternitatis,* diverging along different paths from the same centre. *Eyeless in Gaza* marks the beginning of the process. The subjects are treated polemically in *Ends and Means*. Then follow two novels, *After Many A Summer* and *Time Must Have A Stop,* where the contemplative approach is presented in the most favourable light. The movement reaches its peak with the publication in 1946 of *The Perennial Philosophy,* an anthology of mystical writings with a commentary by Huxley. All his other writings of the period, and continuing up to the present, bear the same marks of something "more deeply interfused".

Anthony Beavis was first attracted by the fundamental theory of mysticism while an undergraduate. The orthodox explanations were "obviously idiotic", but direct union with the truth was a possibility. He wanted to *be,* completely, and to *know,* but he wasn't interested in the experience of the mystical discipline. (This was the kind of half-baked dilettantism that both Cardan and Calamy had seen through and rejected in their different ways.) Anthony was content merely to *know* about the way of perfection without working for it. The price of experience was loss of liberty, which was too high. Twenty-two years later, when he had come under the influence of Miller, Anthony realised how impossible it was to get something for nothing. To become aware you must know good and bad use. The proper use of self is the basis of right action and right thinking. Quietism, " the contemplative life ", can be a kind of highbrow substitute for Marlene Dietrich. If there is to be contemplation it must be the fruit of a discipline. Meditation should not be merely a pleasurable end but a means for effecting changes in the personality and mode of existence.

Huxley had come to a dead end. He was no longer convinced that the world was meaningless. Looking around him, he was struck by the number of philosophers and mystics, belonging to so many different cultures, who had come to the conclusion, by inference or direct intuition, that the world possessed meaning. An obviously untrue materialist philosophy of life was leading to disaster. People brought up on " abstract reasoning " demanded fact and evidence, and rejected convictions that required an act of faith. Yet every time we frame a scientific hypothesis we are resorting to a faith that a few observed phenomena are representative of all phenomena, past, present and future. Repugnant as it may be, we are no less justified in accepting a faith in theism or pantheism without logical proof. Some such mental process was no doubt responsible for the increased interest in oriental psychology and philosophy. The danger, emphasised by the rationalists, that they might easily lead to a recrudescence of superstition was not an essential argument against their truth.

In an introduction to Swami Prabhavananda's and Christopher Isherwood's translation of " The Song of God " from the *Bhagavad-Gita*, Huxley stated that there are four fundamental doctrines at the core of the Perennial Philosophy: (1) the phenomenal world of matter and of individualised consciousness is the manifestation of a Divine Ground; (2) human beings are capable of realising the existence of the Divine Ground by direct intuition; (3) apart from his phenomenal ego man has an Eternal Self, which is the spark of divinity within the soul; and (4) the purpose of man's life on earth is identification with his Eternal Self and hence a unitive knowledge of the Divine Ground. In *The Devils of Loudun* he also summarises the theory of man's relation with God. There is a primordial Fact ("That art thou", expressing identification with the Divine Ground) and a primordial Duty, which consists in allowing the Ground to come to the surface of the finite consciousness. The soul seeks transcendence, which may only satisfactorily be found through union with (employing Christian theology) God as a Trinity, simultaneous union with the Father ("the source and Ground of all being"), the Son ("the manifestation of that Ground in a human consciousness") and the Holy Ghost ("the spirit which links the Unknowable to the unknown"). Union with any single person of the Trinity, to the exclusion of the other two, is not realisation. Obscurely, he concludes, we know what we really are—hence the passionate desire to break the bonds of the imprisoning ego. But other forms of self-transcendence, "downward" and "outward", exert their lure and usually warp the desire.

Brought up in a Christian environment as he was, Huxley's mind was naturally exercised by speculation on whether God is a person or not. Anthony Beavis sidestepped the issue by denying its practical importance. Only revelation could tell. But much more significant was the question: Which gives a man more power to realise goodness—belief in a personal or an impersonal God? He decided that it was a matter of taste. Different minds required different techniques. *His* mind could not think in terms of personality, but there was no doubt about the effectiveness of the Imitation of Christ. Speaking for himself, at the conclusion of "Justifications" in *The Olive Tree*, Huxley pointed out the dangers consequent on belief in a personal God. While it tends to heighten the believer's energy and to strengthen his will, these faculties are merely instruments which can be misused and misdirected. And there is also the danger that a personal God will be thought of as similar to a human person, with all the moral weaknesses inherent in human personality. Such a God will be regarded as completely transcendent and distant, and will be capable of Kierkegaard's " teleological suspensions of morality ". Devotees of the personal God tend to believe in the supreme importance of grace and the corresponding use-lessness of works and the inner life. Therefore although the Perennial Philosophy does not demand the depersonalisation of God, as Patanjali admitted, the alternative tends to a Calvinistic lack of charity and identification of virtue with material wellbeing.

Mr Propter knew that through the medum of a personal God, unquestioning faith in a set of opinions, and the one true church, it was easy enough to convince anyone of his sinful-ness, and to explain what he ought to do about it. Without these aids, unsleeping goodwill and unsleeping intelligence are necessary. And even intelligence is not sufficient; there must also be " the recollection which seeks to transform and transcend intelligence." Each person must try to actualise his more-than-personal consciousness. Psychologically, adherence to a person, an Incarnate Word or the Virgin, can-not bear the same fruit as adherence to ultimate reality. It is a path to virtue and to intense, affective devotion, but not to union. It leads to a concentration on moralism, though the acts of virtue may be accomplished " more through relation and homage to Jesus Christ than out of desire for the same virtue in itself ", as Pierre de Bérulle put it. The substitution of a person for the undifferentiated Godhead of the early mystics makes the highest state of union impossible. The notion that God is a personal and all-powerful ruler leads to ritualistic legalism. The best that can be said for it is that it improves conduct. It does little, however, to alter character and nothing of itself to modify consciousness.

One of Huxley's chief critics in this field used to be C. E. M. Joad who said, in his *The Recovery of Belief,* that " the most persuasive form of the belief that individuality is not a perman-ent but a transitory category, in its application both to the human soul or spirit that pervades the universe ", was to be found in Huxley's writing. He objected chiefly to Huxley's belief that God is not a person and that, being expressions of the universal spirit, our individualities are temporary and will be ultimately merged. In both *Jesting Pilate* and *Proper Studies* Huxley had expressed his concern for the free expression of individual freedom, but his new attitude certainly implied, as Joad said, that conduct should be directed to the overcoming of individuality. Joad gave three reasons for his inability to accept Huxley's views: what point could there be in the universal consciousness splitting itself into many individual consciousnesses? what could be the point of a process whose end was the same as its beginning? and why should the individual strive to deserve immortality if it was not to be his? He felt that this view had immense attraction for the modern mind because it denied all limitations. Its major deficiency was that it could not possibly affect one's life. " What is a universal impersonal consciousness that it should help *me,* even if it is aware of my existence, or why, after all, should I desire to lose my individuality by merging into it, or even believe that the resistance of temptation would assist my merging?"

Joad, who was a facile assimilator and frequently inaccurate in his appreciation, was in fact putting forward the unregenerate man's egotistical objections, never stopping to consider either their rightness or their relevance. He accused Huxley, by implication, of finding the Perennial Philosophy " attractive ", and then complained because he, Joad, found it " unattractive ". He made of his religion not a cosmic truth but a personal support. Why should he care for something that didn't care for him? Joad was really looking for an ally in his private struggle with sin. There are many Joads in the world and in the churches, and Huxley was thinking of them when he wrote in *Ends and Means*: " Those who persist in having emotional relationships with a God whom they believe to be personal are people who have never troubled to undertake the arduous training which alone makes possible the mystical union of the soul with the integrating principle of all being." For the viscerotonic the way is truly hard. And as hardly anyone " ever troubles, etc. ", there is not a great deal of force in the criticism. Huxley on his peak and Joad in his slough could do little but hurl insults at each other.

It is impossible to transcend personality unless we first learn control of the self. Huxley advised the modern Western man to practise the technique of physical training developed by F. M. Alexander. By conscious control of the body we can develop physical self-awareness which will lead in turn to mental and moral self-awareness and control. The purely psychological methods are easy to know, difficult to apply. They include self-analysis, periodical analysis by others, habitual self-recollectedness and unremitting efforts to resist the temptation to become completely identified with the thoughts, feelings, sensations or actions of the moment. Carlo Malpighi, in *Time Must Have A Stop*, said that the wise man's transformation of himself must be the base for any improvement of the human race. Given the divine spark, man can do nothing until he works in harmony with it.

The moralist's and reformer's obsession with sin, frequently the sin of others, is bound to lead to preoccupation with the self. Sin is the fruit of self-will, and the scourging of it a feeding of the will. The aim of union with ultimate reality is incompatible with a mental emphasis on sin. It is well to know that one is a sinner but the remedy lies in avoiding sin by the raising of consciousness first to self-awareness and then to awareness of God, not by a morbid self-flagellation which will stand as a barrier between souls and their God. The author of *The Cloud of Unknowing* said that the idea of sin must not be analysed by the contemplative: " Hold them all whole these words; and mean by sin a lump, thou knowest not what, none other thing but thyself."

One must cling to unity. Many men have regarded the self as the indivisible unity that must be upheld, forgetting that such egocentrism cuts them off from God. Even in *The Art of Seeing* Huxley noted that the truth discovered by the mystics that " the more there is of the *I*, the less there is of God " has been rediscovered and confirmed time and again on the physiological level. The more there is of the *I*, the less there is of Nature—of the right and normal functioning of the organism. The action of the conscious *I*, with its fears and worries, cravings, griefs and ambitions, is responsible for a great deal of physical and neural mal-functioning. The major enemy of the mystic is distraction. Ideas, images, desires demand our attention, split up the mind's wholeness, remove it from God. *Eyeless in Gaza* ends with Anthony's reflections on the themes of unity and diversity. They are not antipathetic, unity exists in diversity, but man's aspiration should be directed towards the support of unity. Then why diversity at all (Joad's question)? Why separation, why myriads of closed universes ? For twenty years the universe had been a non-sensical joke to Anthony. Now he had the intuition that " the point was in the paradox ", that the condition of life was separation,[1] which was equivalent to evil. Step by step, striving towards unity in peace, indefatigably pursuing love and compassion, reaching towards understanding with intellect and the grace of revelation : in the search for peace and unity lay an answer, amenable perhaps to no human logic, yet alone satisfying in its partial accomplishment.

Anthony was never able to answer Joad's questions in a way to satisfy a Joad or a Pickwick—or, for that matter, his personal friends. He felt he had had an illumination, that the principle of unity which was of such importance in his private life was the shadow thrown by a greater principle that involved all being. If it is difficult to give positive reasons why unity should be our most cherished principle, it is not so difficult to understand the objections to separation. Disunity and separa-tion from an embracing totality create suffering, which in turn intensifies separation. It is the urge-to-separateness which results in suffering, for

> The elements which make up man produce a capacity for pain.
> The cause of pain is the craving for individual life.
> Deliverance from craving does away with pain.
> The way of deliverance is the Eightfold Path.
> *(The Four Noble Truths of Buddhism)*

Racial wisdom, expressed through the structure of language,

[1] Cf Huxley's " there can be no humanity except in an inhuman world " (*Texts and Pretexts*).

confirms this view. Language " locks up truths which were once well known but have been forgotten ", in the words of Richard Trench. In Indo-European languages the root meaning " two " connotes badness. In *The Perennial Philosophy* Huxley gives several examples from different languages: " dyspepsia " (Greek prefix), " dishonourable " (Latin prefix), *bévue, Zweifel,* " dubious ", " two-timer " (American).

The weapons of division are memories and speculations which disrupt the unity of meditation. Mr. Propter knew how difficult it was to concentrate the mind on something outside itself. It wasn't a case of the spirit being willing and the body weak. The spirit was certainly willing but the person, mind plus body, was unwilling—and very strong. The contemplative must take the unanalysed sense of his own being and annihilate it in a sense of the being of God. He cannot do that until he has dispersed all distractions, the creatures of his unregenerate self. This was the conclusion reached by Maine de Biran, that the highest function of the personal will is freely to will itself out of existence. If a man fights against his Original Virtue, the Pure Ego or Atman, his phenomenal self finds allies in that area of Original Sin, lying in the subliminal mind and crystallising into the personal subconscious " with its accumulations of septic rubbish, its swarms of rats and black beetles and its occasional scorpions and vipers ", which receive such unremitting attention from the Freudians.

The Freudians are in fact behaving with the utmost human consistency when they devote so much of their energies to this area of the mind at the expense of the other. It is on the human level that man finds the good most elusive. Below it, on the animal level, good exists in the proper functioning of the organism in accordance with the laws of its own being. Above it, on the " eternal " level, it exists in the form of a knowledge of the world without desire or aversion. But on the human level we are obsessed with time, our personalities and their projections which we call policies, ideals and religions. We are forever craving and worrying. " Directly or indirectly, most of our physical ailments and disabilities are due to worry and craving ", said Mr Propter. " . . . We worry and crave ourselves out of the very possibility of transcending personality and knowing, intellectually at first and then by direct experience, the true nature of the world." If eternity is to experience itself within the temporal and spatial cage of a human being, the " soul " must renounce its frenzy of activity, must make room for the other timeless consciousness. " God is completely present only in the complete absence of what we call our humanity. No iron necessity condemns the individual to the futile torment of being merely human " (*After Many A Summer*). Dr Obispo, the cynic, acknowledged man's fall but did not believe he could ever transcend his hypocrisy. Typically human behaviour, he said, was for *homo* to conduct himself like *sub-homo* and then to be *sapiens* to prove that he was really *super-homo*.

Disgust with man on the human level has led many mystics to shrink from outward works, for fear of being distracted from their contemplation of God. · But this shrinking defeats its own purpose. Introversion implies extroversion; it must be rejected for the very reason that extroversion must not be admitted. " One must live continuously in the abyss of the divine essence and in the absolute nothingness of things ", wrote Benet of Canfield. If a man finds himself separated from the divine essence he must return, not by introversion, but by annihilation. The only alternative will be to behave consistently like a human being. The result of existing unregenerately as natural man is one of the themes of *Grey Eminence*. No amount of good intentions will save us from the very crimes and follies we wish to avoid if we are determined to live the " natural life ".

*The Genius and the Goddess* is Huxley's most concentrated effort to express in fictional form the consequences of living on the three levels upon which men have their being. God is the son of Immediate Experience, said Rivers. (The conversation was being conducted metaphorically, and the relationship is not to be taken too seriously.) God manifests himself in Nature and must be worshipped moment by moment with the whole being, not in memory and as a spirit. *The Doors of Perception* and its companion volume, *Heaven and Hell*, are largely concerned with the occasional contact with reality that we make in moments of vision. Reality (to choose one of the ninety-nine names by which God is known) dwells in each object, and when we melt away sophistication and see clearly and piercingly we experience a moment of union, or at least of awareness. When in our visions we see objects in all their naked intensity, it is because we have transcended our systems of conceptual thought. These objects (and the same is true of more familiar objects, only we have smeared them with our ignorance) are intensely themselves and are " manifestations of the essential givenness, the non-human otherness of the universe." Perception is (or ought to be) Revelation, for the Reality shines through every appearance. Everything is significant in itself; it is folly to refer back to idea or form. As even the most stupid person is compelled to realise, one comes close to transcendence when one loves. One loves a woman, not for any demonstrable qualities, but for her being, her is-ness. The same is true of anything else. Objects and events cease to be representatives of classes, they are unique and informed by the divine essence. God's own definition of Himself is: I am that I am. And nothing is divorced from God. When Katy Maartens found herself on the edge of the abyss, her mind invaded by emptiness, she instinctively renewed herself with life at its simplest: physical companionship, experience of animal warmth, strong sensation, satisfaction of hunger. At the moment of crisis (we habitually call it spiritual crisis, but it is that very limitation that leads us astray) she knew how to find self-preservation. She found God, without realising it, not through ritual or spirituality, but through the channel that offered itself: through the emotional-sensational medium, beyond good and evil.

The Dharma-Body of the Buddha (which is another way of saying Mind, Suchness, the Void, Godhead) is anything you like. Nothing in the universe is good or evil in itself. Only ends have moral values. Naked existence has infinite value and meaning. The child may sense this, mescalin can induce it. The essential condition is one of egolessness. (In *Heaven and Hell* Huxley points out that mescalin does not provide an infallible route to bliss.) But these sporadic glimpses reveal existence with intensity but never in fullness. They give access to contemplation but it is a contemplation incompatible with action, the will to action, even the thought of action. There are no general rules of action. Right action will follow from the right understanding of one's relationship with the divine. One will know how to act without the preparation of subtle abstractions.

Like Dr Obispo, the sceptical Persona, Eustace Barnack (*Time Must Have A Stop*), had sufficient wisdom to see through the pretensions of the over-spiritual. It was just an excuse to talk a lot of high-class boloney about religion—a religion that separated like nothing else on earth. (It boasted of its intention to divide between sheep and goats.) But, again, like Obispo, Eustace was content to let matters rest. Each got what he could out of life, according to his lights and tastes, and each was convinced that nothing more could be got out of life. But Eustace dies and we are privileged to follow him into the world of spirit that horrified Joad so much. Eustace became aware of a boundless absence. Then he knew the presence of another awareness. There came the knowledge of being known, a satisfied, joyful knowledge of being included within and interpenetrated by a shining presence. There was the anguish of being forced to know more than it was possible to know. The awareness that had been Eustace was dis-integrated into dust, atoms of mere nonentity, shameful, known by participation as the most hideous of absences. These atoms knew, by direct awareness, that they were opaque and separate, the most appalling of privations. The struggle began: the unhappy dust of nothingness resisted, refused to give up its right to a separate existence, was scorched by the radiance of the invading knowledge, utterly annihilated. Then memory intervened and the light began to lose some of its intensity. The memories were earlier glimpses of the light, the sudden illuminations which had punctuated a very human life. The choir singing Mozart's *Ave Verum Corpus* in the church at Nice—the knowledge of perfection, ecstatically blissful and sad. Lying in the long grass beside the cricket field at school. when suddenly everything looked different, shattered by an inward and invisible earthquake. Then the struggle started again, the light grew brighter and more beautiful and the opaque clot of Eustace, enraged, began to curse in four languages. The light faded out and there was no more participation in the knowledge which compelled him to recognise his own shamefulness. He refused to feel ashamed. But "in the brightness and the silence his thoughts were like lumps of excrement, like the noise of vomiting." Now a galaxy of distractions swarmed about him—pages of Proust, wax flowers, St Sebastian, his favourite limericks—tormenting him, revolting him—but better these fooleries, evidences of his own hatefulness, than the extinction of all knowledge. Again and again he turned from the light towards his own intolerable yet self-imposed pains. It was obvious that Eustace would require many more incarnations before he could accept union.

Meanwhile Sebastian, under the guidance of Bruno, was approaching the wisdom that his uncle Eustace was rejecting so furiously. Bruno tells him that the ostensible search for knowledge usually leads to a diminution of knowledge. (Witness the later careers of so many young geniuses.) Knowledge cannot increase without a modification of one's inherited and acquired being. In short, "he that is not getting better is getting worse, and he that is getting worse is in a position to know less and less about the nature of ultimate reality." One is faced with the choice between apotheosis and deification: apotheosis, as with Michelangelo, where the personality is exalted and intensified to the point where the person becomes olympian, and deification, as with Fra Angelico, where the personality is annihilated in charity. "Not I, but God in me."

In the epilogue to this novel we find Sebastian some years

later, now a successful playwright, reflecting and scribbling notes upon man's condition. Goodness, as the world knew it, was not enough. It was limited by an impenetrable ignorance of the end and purpose of existence. Man's progression was from animal eternity into time, the human world of memory and anticipation; and from time, if he chose, into spiritual eternity, absorption into the Divine Ground. And, like the animal life, life in the spirit is exclusively in the present, never past or future.[1]   Sebastian jotted down the minimum working hypothesis: there is a Ground, the unmanifested principle of all manifestation; the Ground is transcendent and immanent; it is possible for human beings to become identified with the Ground; to realise this is the final end and purpose of human existence; there is a Law or Dharma which must be followed if men are to achieve this end; and the more there is of *I*, the less there is of the Ground, the Dharma being a Law of mortification and self-transcending awareness.

Why, asks Huxley in the Introduction to *The Perennial Philosophy*, should the one Reality be incapable of apprehension without surrender to the discipline referred to by Sebastian? We do not know. It is one of the facts of existence that we must accept. After all, he says, water is made up of hydrogen and oxygen and nothing we can do will alter this fact. " It is only by making physical experiments that we can discover the intimate nature of matter and its potentialities. And it is only by making psychological and moral experiments that we can discover the intimate nature of mind and its potentialities." His use of the word " psychological " rather than " religious " is a key to the resistance that the majority of men feel towards mysticism. For them it is primarily a religious discipline, not a corpus of psychological knowledge, and as such it conflicts with their institutional

[1] A drug such as mescalin can help in the attainment of this condition. It should be used as a gratuitous grace, Huxley says in *Doors of Perception*. One is reminded of Lenina Crowne as she takes her soma, murmuring, " Was and will make me ill, I take a gramme and only am " (*Brave New World*). " Every soma-holiday is a bit of what our ancestors used to call eternity," said Dr Shaw.

approach to God. The appeal of mysticism for Huxley lies partly in its capacity for providing a basis for a religion free of unacceptable dogmas. "To a non-Christian," he writes in *Grey Eminence,* "this seems the supremely important, the eminently encouraging fact about mysticism . . . To certain pious Christians, on the other hand, mysticism is suspect precisely because of its undogmatic and unhistorical character." The failure of organised religion can partly be attributed to its emphasis on rite and sacrament, which amount to a distortion of primordial fact and reality. Huxley does not deny that ritualism and sacraments work; he calls them white magic, but they also lead to idolatry. In his Foreword to Krishnamurti's *The First and Last Freedom* he mentions the transforming power of symbols, but points out that they can be used for evil as well as for good, idolatrously and even insanely. The harm is done when symbols are raised to the rank of dogmas. When you quote the sacred books you do not repeat the truth, for the truth cannot be repeated. The parroting of patterned thought is " blind thinking ", by which you respond to a new challenge according to an old recipe. " A world in which ideas do not exist would be a happy world," writes Huxley. It is mortifying to realise that I am quoting Huxley and that he quotes Krishnamurti. Their truths can only remain true by being born again, minute by minute.

The importance of semantics becomes increasingly obvious. Our words numb us, insulate us from understanding and illumination. The theologian's vocabulary obscures the grace of God. These words—Guidance, Inspiration, Providence— protest too much, beg all the questions before they're asked. Only use words when you have to, says Rivers in *The Genius and the Goddess,* and even then don't take them too seriously. Idle chatter is one of the distracting demons, and portentous polysyllables are others. Just as mathematicians found it necessary to invent new symbol-systems, so it will be necessary to invent a Spiritual Calculus before we can talk coherently about the Divine Ground and the world conceived as its manifestation. Until that is done, mystical utterances will continue to be couched in paradoxical metaphors and linguistic eccentricities, and the normal unregenerate man will continue to dismiss them as fantasies midway between nonsense and insanity.

# Chapter 15

## THE DOUBLE CRISIS

### A. The Politics of An Unpolitical Man

THE young Huxley was an aesthete and as such tended to regard politics as beneath his notice. It was therefore natural that he should hold certain powerful prejudices which were not analysed into principles but were capable of dictating his attitude towards the raw material of politics. (After all, a political Independent is always a Tory.) People in the mass disgusted him. They acted like a herd and believed their opinions were more important than they really were—as important as those of an Oxford graduate, say. Reason compelled Dick Greenow to believe in democracy, internationalism and revolution; morality demanded justice for the oppressed. But neither reason nor morality could make him endure the contaminating human element with even the semblance of pleasure.

Leisure and culture were what mattered. Indeed, the aim of political effort was really no more than a making the world safe for leisure and culture. The arrangement was rather exquisite. Multitudes toiled in the fields so that Mr Scogan and Denis might discuss the customs of Polynesia in comfort. Someone had to pay for the good life, but it wasn't the good-lifers themselves. Indirectly it was " the loutish young fellows all dressed in the hideous ill-fitting black which makes a funeral of every English Sunday and holiday . . . drearily guffawing as they smoked their cigarettes." But they made way for Henry Wimbush and touched their caps (labour's homage to culture). Mingled with the repulsion was a pity for people who had been deprived of their traditional rural pleasures and had been unable to replace them with any creative activity. And somewhere, very remote from

179

Huxley, were those infernos which made his comfort possible, glimpsed and shuddered at in a poem bleakly entitled "Lines":

> All day the wheels turn;
> All the day long the roaring of wheels, the rasping
> Weave their imprisoning lattices of noise,
> And hammers, hammers in the substance of the world
> Carve out another cavernous world, a narrow
> Sepulchre, and seal it from the sky,
> Lord, with how great a stone!
>
> Only a little beyond the factory walls
> Silence is a flawless bowl of crystal,
> Brimming, brimming with who can say beforehand,
> Who can, returning, ever remember what
> Beautiful secret. Only a little beyond
> These hateful walls the birds among the branches
> Secretly come and go.

Intellectually, Huxley felt he owed the unfortunate at least his compassion. But like Mr Hutton in "The Gioconda Smile", who as an undergraduate had once spent three days at a mission in the East End, he was filled with "a profound and ineradicable disgust". This response, with its accompanying load of guilt, continually crops up in the fiction. Sebastian Barnack, in some ways a re-creation of Huxley's youth, as recalled in the 1940's, always felt uncomfortable in the proximity of the poor. He felt ashamed, supposed he should have emulated his father and become a left-wing politician, but politics seemed futile. In *Antic Hay* Mercaptan expresses his admiration for Bruin Opps, who said with perfect openness that the poor and the ill and the old made him feel sick. "How well and frankly you express what we all feel and lack the courage to say," says Mercaptan.

We catch occasional glimpses of Huxley's discomfort during the early period, as when Gumbril feels impelled to help the down-and-outs. The feeling has been strengthened by the time *Two or Three Graces* appears (1926). There is even an attempt at identification with the outsiders in one of the stories, "Half Holiday", where we view the rich and careless Huxleyan world through the eyes of an ill-dressed, stammering orphan from Rochdale. In "The Monocle" we meet another outsider, though this time it is a wealthy but spiritually insufficient manufacturer's son. Despite his privileged social position, Gregory is forced into a concern for the poor and unfortunate because, like them, he is excluded.

But there was nothing you could do. If Gregory surrendered his income to the unemployed it would be sufficient to maintain twenty-five of them—twenty-five out of two million ! Far better to keep the mind averted from such problems, like Francis Chelifer. He compiled a little catechism which put the organisation of society in a more pleasing perspective. One works to enable Jewish stockbrokers to buy Armstrong-Siddeleys and the latest jazz records and to spend the weekend in Brighton; one goes on working that one may one day do the same; progress is stockbrokers, more stockbrokers and still more stockbrokers; social reformers desire a state in which every individual will enjoy the greatest possible amount of leisure; in this state they will all do what the stockbrokers do now; the condition of a contented life is that one should not think; the function of newspapers, cinemas and radios is to make thought impossible; without unawareness and stupidity the world becomes too uncomfortable to be borne.

But Chelifer had to work for a living, though he managed to organise his existence very agreeably. For those who could manage to avoid a routine job it was obvious, as Mr. Cardan said, that there was a hierarchy of existences. You couldn't prove this, but you knew it instinctively. Pity for the poor was a praiseworthy emotion, but where would the human race be without the rich and leisured ? You must have a class of people, Mr Scogan pointed out, who are " not compelled to waste their time in the imbecile routines that go by the name of Honest Work." And Chelifer, who whimsically called himself a " true democrat ", said that it was his duty not to think. It was the thinker who cherished social dissatisfaction, and was liable to pull down the brilliant edifice of human achievement.

Freedom was an attractive chimera. People who hadn't

got it demanded it, but when by some strange freak of fortune they acquired it they were embarrassed. Only the talented few were capable of coming to terms with it. Slavery, providing it was called by some other name and was not too unbearably harsh, was the most pleasant condition for the majority of men. The youthful Huxley could see no hope for democracy. The doses already taken had started to poison civilisation. He foresaw a kind of premature senility. "With a mind almost atrophied by lack of use", he wrote in "Pleasures" (*On The Margin*), "unable to entertain itself and grown so wearily uninterested in the ready-made distractions offered from without that nothing but the grossest stimulants of an ever-increasing violence and crudity can move it, the democracy of the future will sicken of a chronic and mortal boredom" (1923).

## B.  A Plea For Aristocracy

Huxley's journey round the world, described in *Jesting Pilate*, served as a severe jolt to his political complacency. His first serious consideration of political matters appeared in *Proper Studies* (1927).

In the first of these two books he admitted that, when he was being honest, he didn't "care two pins about political principles." All he cared about was his personal safety and the right to work in peace, and he wasn't much concerned whether he was guaranteed these by the British constitution or an alien despotism. Philip Quarles in *Point Counter Point* blessed the bureaucrats who allowed him to live in freedom and comfort. Having heard the Viceroy's speech at the opening of the Indian Legislative Assembly, Huxley acclaimed its hypocrisy. There was a time, he said, when he would have preferred a more brutally "realistic" outburst in the manner of Mussolini, but he had outgrown such boyish admirations. "The more cant there is in politics", he wrote, "the better . . . Politicians who cant about humanitarian principles find themselves sooner or later compelled to put those principles into practice—and far more thoroughly than they had ever originally intended. Without political cant there would be no democracy."

It may seem strange that Huxley should have shown any concern for democracy. But he was writing from the surface of his mind, where a demand for respectability received a dutiful answer. His prejudices were "Fabian and mildly labourite" he told the reporters at San Francisco—which wasn't true, but represented his public, Pecksniffian attitude.

The visit to India barely touched his conception of political principle, scarcely formed as it was, but it did introduce him to the realities underlying political action. Why did Europeans cling to the East? Whatever the economic advantages (and it is now believed that they are much less than was once taken for granted), there was a very powerful psychological one: even the most mediocre European could enjoy the sense of power there. The commercial traveller who went East found himself a much greater man than he had ever been at home. The average Indian still accepted white pretensions at their face value. The Englishman lived in and ruled India on credit and was respected simply because there was a convention that he should be respected. But when the majority of Indians ceased to accept the white man at his own valuation, British rule would be reduced to impotence: The country was held, not by force but by respect, but a respect that was wearing thin and was not renewing itself. Later, however, he remarked that General Dyer's action at Amritsar, however shocking to those at home, had achieved its purpose. There was no general rebellion. With the respect running out there was a reversion to naked force. From this Huxley deduced an important principle. "Anybody who has the power and is prepared to go on using it indefinitely and without compunction, can force his will on the whole world." The great barrier was the periodical surge of compunction which stultified the will and inhibited action.

The next question was: What gave power? Power cannot be made out of nothing, as the French are finding today. Huxley's conclusion was that political talk and political action were so much froth on reality. Political power was the invariable concomitant of economic power, which came first. "Be rich, control your country's finance and industry, and you will find that you have political leadership thrown in as a casual perquisite." The Indian economy was controlled by the British. The All-India Congress went on talking and acting in terms of politics. "One might as well try to cure headaches by applying corn plasters to the toes." There was no science of politics because no laboratory experiment could be made. One is faced with political choice (which is likely to be, at base, an economic choice) and no-one ever knows whether the chosen alternative was actually superior to the one rejected. In *Do What You Will* Huxley made the same observation about history, or the politics of the past. "I can observe how a piece of phosphorus behaves when it is dry, and afterwards I can drop it in a pail of water and observe how it behaves when it is wet. But though I can observe (very incompletely and superficially, indeed) what happened as a result of Wellington's victory at Waterloo, I cannot alter the historical circumstances experimentally and observe what would have happened if Napoleon had won the battle. There can be no crucial experiments in history nor, for that matter, any completely accurate observation. History is not a science." Rivers said the same thing in *The Genius and the Goddess* but the Cyprus and Irish experiments described in *Brave New World* suggest that political experiment may be a possibility.

When preparing the essays that make up *Proper Studies* (" the proper study of mankind is man ") Huxley decided to adopt the eighteenth century method of deduction from the postulate of individual human nature to conclusions about institutions, but not the view of human nature, which had caused the deductions to be invalid. The important thing was to be certain that the premisses correspond with reality. Of all the political philosophers he leaned most heavily on Pareto, while the psychologists whom he found most stimulating were Cardinal Newman and Jung.

He took his stand on the very un-eighteenth century notion

that all men are not equal. His visit to America had demonstrated how dangerous the doctrine of equality, manifestly untrue in itself, could be when put into practice. In the New World he had found stupidity, suggestibility and the business ethic set up as supremely precious values. Intelligence, independence and disinterested activity—once admitted—were in process of becoming evil things which ought to be destroyed. Democratic propaganda had led people, not only in America, to cherish a sentimental belief that the poor and uncultivated, being nearer to the " state of nature " than the cultured and the rich, were for that reason more virtuous. As a result the rich made every effort to persuade the poor that in spirit, at least, they were just as poverty-striken.

The original assumptions of democratic theory were that reason is the same and entire in all men, and that all men are naturally equal. To these are attached the corollaries that men are naturally good, that they are wholly the product of their environment, and that they are indefinitely educable. Given these unproved assumptions, the logical deductions were that the state should be organised on democratic lines, that governors should be chosen by universal suffrage, and that education should be the same for all citizens. Huxley realised that when he praised political hypocrisy because it made democracy possible, he was being inconsistent. He suspected he was repeating a meaningless formula that had been drummed into him at an early age. A little later, while trying to adopt a more reasoned attitude towards democracy, he admitted that strong prejudice had made a religion out of democracy. The metaphysic of democracy had become a universally true theology, and it had become humanity's highest duty to put it into practice, everywhere and completely. In fact, modern democracy is a farce. The British parliamentary system is government by oligarchs for the people with the people's occasional advice. The product of universal education is the newspaper-reading, advertisement-believing, propaganda-swallowing, demagogue-led suburbanite and factory-worker.

In fact, most men are not interested in politics or law-making which do not directly affect their everyday lives. The participation of the ordinary man in government has not been very encouraging. Political democracy has led to inefficiency and weakness of rule, it has permitted the least desirable men to obtain power, and it has encouraged corruption. Huxley's solution was " a ruling aristocracy of mind ". Paradoxically, such a system would be far more humanitarian than a democratic one, because careers would have to be opened to talent. Right and privilege would depend on capacity, as they do in other spheres of human activity. Government should be by grown-ups and men of tested ability—perhaps an echo from Peacock's Dr Opimian, who noted that the honourable member for Muckborough had been sent to Parliament because he was the most conspicuous Grub among the Moneygrubs of his borough, and for no other reason. The aristocratic ideal is that everyone should be in his place. This is loosely true of most human spheres today but conspicuously untrue of government, where position is gained not by intellectual merit or practical ability but by blandishment and repeated suggestion. Finally, direction and administration should be separate, as they call for quite different and often opposed qualities in those who practise them. Under the contemporary democratic system the chief of staff is also an officer in the field and, furthermore, has to get himself elected by his men before he can command. But the men, according to Huxley, are incapable of making the right choice and the chief is incapable of performing two duties adequately.

## C. Facing Up To Nationalism

After the publication of *Proper Studies* which, despite its imposing metaphysical pretensions, was a rather superficial work, Huxley's political thinking matured rapidly. He still distrusted the facile practice of daily politics but he also learnt that the basis is something more than economic. In *Point Counter Point* he puts into Lord Edward Tantamount's mouth a fundamental criticism of politicians. " You don't even think of the important things. Talking about progress and votes and Bolshevism and every year allowing a million tons of phosphorus pentoxide to run away into the sea. It's idiotic, it's criminal, it's . . . it's fiddling while Rome is burning." Lord Edward is in many ways a political innocent but he had the sense to see that the normal preoccupatons of politicians are often totally unreal. Spandrell has a similar criticism to make of the communists. They are obsolete, committed as they are to their nineteenth-century materialism. They cannot rise out of their bog of space, time and mass—anything else is bourgeois illusion.

But new forces were making themselves felt. Everard Webley, like his creator, was opposed to democracy. He wanted the " best " to rule. But Huxley saw how dangerous the aristocrat theory could be in the wrong hands. Webley's "best" included himself, whoever else it did not include, and he was prepared to fight his way to power with the help of his green-uniformed British Freemen. His policy was, he claimed, to resist the dictatorship of the stupid. The dull, brutish mob, by sheer weight of numbers, was getting stronger and would soon overwhelm the few who retained initiative and intelligence, if it was not checked. The communists, with their cult of organised hatred, were gaining influence and converts. Anthony Beavis, who chose pacifism rather than Webley's brand of aristocratic-Fascism, realised that communism held attractions for three types of people: idealists with an exceptional gift for self-deception, those who actually rejoice in hatred, and the ambitious who would use any movement to get what they wanted. Among the first group, the majority, were to be found the weak-headed rich, usually the fourth generation to enjoy the family fortune. " In the long run brewing almost infallibly leads to impressionism or theosophy or communism ", Huxley wrote in " The Claxtons " (*Two or Three Graces*).

He held the Jews and the Old Testament responsible for that " pernicious anti-political doctrine ", the all-importance in

H

human life of economic success. The Bible-reading Protestants introduced the idea into Europe. The doctrine of the primacy of economic values has found its home in America, and Karl Marx only gave a new twist to an idea that was already widely accepted. But his theories had scarcely been enunciated before their chief element, the proletariat, began to disappear. Wherever industrialism is well developed the proletariat has become prosperous and is approximating more and more closely to the bourgeoisie. No longer the victim, it is actually becoming the victimiser. In America, under modern capitalism, the proletariat is in a position to feel its essential equality with its masters. Within a century Bernard Shaw's dream of equal incomes for all should be realised. Like many intellectuals, Huxley was writing of a future state in contemporary terms. (*Do What You Will* appeared in 1929). When he visited Mexico City he was struck by the hopeless poverty of the workers under slump conditions. This section of the proletariat certainly had a long way to go before it reached the bourgeois level. But Mexico was still in the early stages of industrialism.

It was absurd to suppose that the equalisation of incomes alone could solve mankind's dilemma. One might as well claim apocalyptic benefits from the universal installation of sanitary plumbing or the distribution of Ford cars to every member of the human species. But the economic obsession exists and it is necessary to take it into consideration. One of its results has been that success in our society is attained by those who live intensely with the intellectual and voluntary side of their being, and ignore the rest of themselves, particularly the contemplative. The democrat would have us all Babbitts or Vanderbilts (the Babbitts who have proved, by personal example, that heaven is within everyone's reach.) But their doctrine is based on a false assessment of human nature. They fly in the face of reality and in effect foster a new kind of romanticism. However hard they try to persuade the human race to prove their dictum that all men are equal, they cannot prevent one man from using his opportunities more fruitfully than another. Much as they preach human brotherhood, they cannot persuade most men to love their fellows. And out of their teachings have come two offspring, ostensibly opposed but similar in their divorce from actuality : the pure individualism of Shelley and Godwin, the pure collectivism of the Bolsheviks. Each stressed the over-riding importance of environment, each treated man as uniformly capable of grace. But Shelley excluded biology and economics and Lenin excluded man's spiritual life.

In his dissatisfaction with the quality of life permitted by democracy, it is clear that Huxley's missing quantity was religious experience. The communists banned it, treated it as though it didn't exist. Shelley had blown it up into a monster by his unremitting superhumanism. Yet no religious innovator, whom one might expect to possess the required vision and wisdom, had ever offered adequate political advice. There was too great a gulf between the two fields of religion and practical politics. Religion appealed to the individual heart while politics was a " science " of averages. Yet even in politics individual thought and action were the ultimate dictators of policy. Bad thinking about one thing leads to bad thinking about other things, including politics. Huxley opened his *Texts and Pretexts* with a statement to this effect, and repeated it in *Ends and Means* and *The Perennial Philosophy*. Philip Quarles had been well aware of the effect with which politicians used one word with two or more meanings. " Liberty ", bawls the leader, and his audience visualises himself sitting with a bottle and a wench, no laws, no wife, no policeman, no parson. The result is the same as when the priest purrs, " The Holy Spirit is upon you."

All these random ideas were gathered together and given some coherence in *Beyond the Mexique Bay,* ostensibly an account of travel in the Caribbean and Central America, and published in 1934. Briefly one might say that it acknowledges the rise of nationalism as the major contemporary political problem, and associates it with the missing factor : the religious impulse. Asking himself why the British trouble to hang on to British Honduras, he replies that it is because the national persona must not be insulted. Few Englishmen care a damn about Honduras, but it is Britannia's will that it should be coloured red on the map. The starved religious impulse has found a new totem.

The recent history of Central America is a tale of petty and futile wars between the five republics. According to the theorists of the left these wars were fought for economic reasons. This, Huxley said, is nonsense. If capitalists were only interested in the exploitation of their victims and in private profit-making, they would not waste their resources in fighting one another. Yet, although it is against their economic interest, the rulers of these states persisted in prolonging the bloodshed. Why ? " Because all capitalist rulers are bound by a theology of passion that prevents them from rationally calculating their profits and losses." But wars are fought by the masses and it is necessary to persuade them that warfare will be in their own interests — or to make them equally subject to the passion that sways their rulers. This is done by indoctrinating them from childhood with the nationalist theology. The task is made easier by the average man's need of an occasional orgy through which he can annihilate the boredom of day-to-day existence. But the unfortunate result is that the greatest *immediate* happiness of the greatest number often leads to the greatest *ultimate* unhappiness. Anthony Beavis felt that modern urban existence is too safe, too removed from the conflict with nature which formed a part of primitive man's experience. In consequence men want excitement, risks, surprises, and they seek them through war, sport and sex. The fundamental problem of international politics, Huxley felt, was psychological. A World Psychological Conference, not a World Economic Conference, should have been sitting.

Certain matters had to be settled before the scourge of nationalist war could be removed. How can you persuade people to accept prohibitions placidly ? What emotional compensations can be given them ? How much emotional excitement do they need to keep healthy and happy ? And could a benevolently intelligent ruler dispense altogether with collective hatred ? "In one of its aspects", Huxley wrote in *The Devils of Loudun,* "civilisation may be defined as a systematic withholding of certain occasions for barbarous behaviour. In recent years we have discovered that when, after a period of withholding, those occasions are once more offered, men and women, seemingly no worse than we are, have shown themselves ready and even eager to take them."

Huxley was showing concern for humanity (after all, he couldn't contract out !) but his disgust was unimpaired. The products of universal education he called the New Stupid. They hungered for certainty and being unable to find it in the traditional dogmas of religion they accepted the pseudo-religious dogmas of nationalism. The theory of nationalism is demonstrably untrue, but the subject of the theory is "real", tangible, visible. The positivist modern mind surrendered to it completely. The new dictators have restored to the New Stupid some of the substantial pleasures of the Old Stupid in the form of collective hatred and vanity. People have always wanted someone to kick. Authority doesn't object because the kicking keeps the kickers happy. "If you want social solidarity," says the Arch-Vicar in *Ape and Essence,* " you've got to have either an external enemy or an oppressed minority." When the law began to protect wives, children and "witches", the boot was transferred to Hottentot. Now that even Hottentots are beginning to acquire rights or, in countries which do not possess colonies, are not available, targets are provided at home, in the form of Jews, Reds, capitalists. The Arch-Vicar replaced Hottentots by Hots, the sexually heterodox. The common orgies of daily life are now of such poor quality, and the routine which formed their background has been so much disturbed, new and more exciting distractions have to be provided. " Our choice is between bread and bunting ", says the Narrator in *Ape and Essence.* " And bunting, I need hardly add, is what we have almost unanimously chosen." Modern rulers must find the exactly right dose of bread and circuses, routine and orgies, or run the risk of allowing society to be devitalised or overturned by over-stimulation. Huxley confessed that he didn't know the answers. The terrifying lack of unity which pervaded Europe rested on the lack of a shared mythology. If Europeans could share anything at that time it was likely to be hatred, and he even envisaged the unification of Europe on the basis of hatred for Asia. But woe betide humanity if that hatred passed beyond the platonic stage !

## D.  *The Pacifist Response*

The real change in Huxley's political thinking was motivated by his switch from hate to love as the necessary basic drive of human action. It was paralleled by his conversion to pacifism and his adherence to the Perennial Philosophy, with their emphasis on the person instead of on personified abstractions. Whatever was to be at the centre of man's mythology, it had to be loved; the emotion that had been dangerously expended on abstractions had to find a new and more satisfying object. The young Huxley had hated and despised the bourgeoisie and working classes. Even in *Beyond the Mexique Bay* he categorised the greater part of his fellowmen as the New Stupid. He hated them for their bad manners, their ignorance, their vulgarity, their hypocrisy, their baseless arrogance and their imperviousness to the best in culture. His new attitude taught him that all of these were merely attributes which encrusted the real person. Within each human individual, however repellent his outward mask, there was the saving grace. It was this that should be appealed to. The unpleasant characteristics might be sidestepped and ultimately transformed by internal action. In *Eyeless in Gaza* Anthony Beavis decided that love alone would solve man's social and political problems. The love of abstractions, whether they represented " fellowmen ", " neighbours " or people in general, was an impossibility, and the very idea was harmful. We have managed to restrict our love artificially by means of conventions. We utter the words and the emotion never stirs. The greater love must be as personal as the more intimate one of daily life, but its expression will normally be negative, a refusal to surrender to certain weaknesses of the spirit: lust, hypocrisy, sloth and cowardice. There is a strong prejudice against what is called negative action, yet Huxley believed that the resistance of temptation was man's chief duty. Love is more than a single emotional state. It is the final conquest of the vices man is heir to.

First of all, we must realise that the Sabbath was made for man. Christ made this perfectly clear, yet Christians have generally chosen to ignore it. Man now insists (in his conduct, if not in his pronouncements) that he was made for a number of abstractions: science, industry, nation, money, religion, school. An attack on abstractions formed an important part of the essays in the volume entitled *The Olive Tree* (1936). In the political field, for instance, groups of individuals become personified abstractions. " Britain ", despite John Bull, is a female in classical fancy dress, holding a large toasting fork and endowed with very definite thoughts and emotions. Yet the concrete reality of Britain consists of some fifty-odd million diverse individuals. When a nation becomes a person in this way, deification follows and is shared by the government, which ceases to be a mere convenience (as it should be). Loyalty to the personified nation (or class or party) justifies the loyal in indulging those passions which they are not allowed to display in their more intimate relations with their neighbours. For the moral code applies only to human relationships, and need not be followed in the service of a god. It is psychologically much easier to justify attacks on certain categories of people when they are given an abstract quality and cease to be regarded as individuals. Foreigners become symbols divorced from the life they share with us; Brown, Jones and Robinson become heretics, gentiles, Yids, niggers, etc. Politics can only become moral if conducted in terms of people. " All current political thought is a mixture, in varying proportions, between thought in terms of concrete realities and thought in terms of depersonified symbols and personified abstractions " (" Words and Behaviour "). In dictatorial countries the proportion of concrete to abstract and symbolic thought is lower than in democratic countries.

Considering the reasons why nationalism has gained such a grip on the modern mind, Huxley traces it partly to the remarkable growth of information about any and everything to the exclusion of knowledge about matters of primary importance. People's minds today are filled with odd bits of gossip not only about current political events but also about criminals, aristocrats, sportsmen and film stars. About the intimate intellectual and emotional processes of his fellowmen he knows very little. Such knowledge is gained by introspection; knowing oneself one knows others. In the past, when minds were moulded by the same religious and secular literature, men could understand each other much more closely than today, when all they share is a collection of irrelevant pieces of information and scientific titbits. Spiritual union has disappeared and prepared the way for the positivistic superstitions of nationalism and dictator-worship. It is another way of saying that the religious impulse has been applied to other, essentially non-religious objects. Historical circumstances have conspired to intensify the nationalist cult. Discredit has been thrown on internationalism, especially in those countries which have suffered defeat in war, and the two theories which underly the internationalist ethic, the Christian and the rational, have been correspondingly reduced in their appeal. In consequence, governments have deliberately fostered the anti-Christian and irrational attitudes which served their purposes so well. At the same time they have been helped by the crude psychology of the revolutionaries, who made the mistake of appealing solely to the rational part of man, neglecting his innate love of display and extravagance. The nationalist leaders did not make this mistake. Miller, the anthropologist in *Eyeless in Gaza,* maintained that the study of savages is the best preparation for political and social activity at home. " Savage societies are simply civilised societies on a small scale and with the lid off."

The author of *Ends and Means* tried to apply his pacifist

principles to the contemporary political mess. He noted first of all the modern regression in charity and a decline in regard for the truth. Men are now so used to horrors they have become indifferent to them. As a result, the horrors multiply. Organised lying is practised shamelessly and with devilish efficiency. There has been a great retreat from monotheism towards idolatry, and the new local divinities are nations, classes and even deified individuals. Another, more subtle change, has been a decline in the desire for wealth, so strong in the nineteenth century, and its replacement by a passionate desire for a strategic post in the governing hierarchy. Today it is possible for a man on quite a small income to have everything he wants. The true meaning of this is that the lust for power is more naked today than at any other time in recent history.

The tendency, among both nationalists and revolutionaries, has been towards the institution of a planned society. The natural fact of human conservatism has been largely ignored, and too rapid changes have only intensified the already existing elements of discord and unbalance. It is extremely difficult to keep the two levels of national and planetary interests in harmony. Economic planning, for instance, on a national basis disturbs international relationships, for the two loyalties are often incompatible. The same thing occurs within the nation, where particular interests are often opposed to those of the community as a whole. Although it is true that economic independence may reduce the probability of war (this being the only alternative to genuine international cooperation, which the national deities would not allow), little attempt is made to remove the economic causes of war, obvious though they are, because war is in the great tradition; it is exciting, it gives people vicarious satisfactions, it has become a part of our education, and success, however achieved, is regarded as the major personal good. Huxley then listed the economic changes which he considered necessary. The indispensable ones were changes in management of large-scale industry, which should be taken from the irresponsible individuals controlling it, and the various units of which should be coordinated. But this important development should not be undertaken rashly. Violent opposition should not be risked, because this only leads to an intensification of government control. Where possible, all advances should be made by methods already familiar. If this is not done, the contexts of reform will deteriorate. It is senseless to introduce economic planning if its collateral is an increase in the power of the executive. At the same time comprehensive national planning leads to conflict with other countries, which means a deterioration in the international context.

The new nationalisms owe part of their success to mankind's astonishing patience, its constant toleration of the intolerable. These are backed by habit and inertia, fear of the devil they don't know, and a general philosophical belief that *de facto* rule is almost invariably *de jure*. Everyone is subject to the *Zeitgeist,* which creeps upon us silently and unawares. Because political power is becoming more and more concentrated, people come to believe that it is only right and proper that it should. The " real " is accepted as the rational, the " historical " has the sanction of right. The Kansas farmers in *After Many A Summer* had abandoned any idea of subsistence farming and thought exclusively in terms of a cash crop, even when year after year no cash was forthcoming. One goes on doing wrong in the comfortable belief that one is doing one's duty—to the company, the shareholders, the family, the city, the state, the fatherland, the church.

The ordinary man is not interested in large-scale politics. He is only too pleased to be relieved of any obligations in that direction. Some of them find scope in self-governing groups in industry and in local government. But this leaves the field open to the merely ambitious, and once again Huxley points out that there are no fitness tests in politics, as there are in other fields. He urged the setting up of self-governing institutes for our rulers, akin to that of the Chartered

Accountants. He pointed out that the most gratifying form of praise and the most unbearable form of blame are those of our fellow professionals.

Mr Propter, in *After Many A Summer,* gave voice to many of these ideas and in his own person tries to set an example. For instance, he believes that the social and political solution lies in " peasants plus small machines and power." About a third of production would have to remain as it is now, organised on a mass basis. The immediate problem is to work out the technique of small-scale production. Propter makes himself as independent of the city as possible. He has his own small electric generator, and employs a few men on his land. Big business inevitably means more bosses and less democracy, he says. The struggle for social justice must be on a personal scale. When it is organised as a movement it produces as many evil results as good, and the progress is little, if any. The French Revolution produced Napoleon, Napoleon stimulated German nationalism, which led to the war of 1870, the war of 1914, and then Hitler. The cost of enfranchising the French peasants and spreading political democracy was a heavy one. No politician can ever understand the full range of reality, and organised movements demand politicians. They move in a world of illusion, among projections of their own human personalities. They are oblivious of the animal and eternal levels, where alone good is manifested. Man is his own termite. As the temples and palaces rise, the heart of every beam is being gnawed to dust. " Madness consists in not recognising the facts; in making wishes the father of thoughts; in conceiving things to be other than they really are; in trying to realise desired ends by means which countless previous experiments have shown to be inappropriate."

### E.   In The Light Of Eternity

We never know the results of our actions. No episode in history is entirely irrelevant to any other subsequent episode. When writing *Grey Eminence* Huxley was aware that the

Thirty Years' War, and therefore Father Joseph's combination of mystical experience and power politics, were parts of a chain leading to the explosion of 1939. There is only one completely unquestionable generalisation that can be made about politics, which is that it is quite impossible for statesmen to foresee, for more than a very short time, the results of any course of large-scale political action. In fact, although politicians always claim that they are finding lasting solutions, they are praised and remembered for single, isolated victories. Richelieu's career is an excellent example of this. His admirers envisaged a Bourbon golden age, the enormous expenses entailed in his campaign against the Huguenots were excused on the grounds that they would check rebellion for "two thousand years", and modern historians praise his vision and the success of his policy. Yet Richelieu did much to create the conditions which led to the French Revolution and, indirectly, the subsequent catastrophes of Europe. As usual, nationalist passion overrides objective judgment.

It is therefore true to say that political policies, including reforms, always result in partial or complete stultification. Neither universal education nor public ownership of the means of production have led to a greater degree of human happiness, despite the hopes of millions of well-intentioned people. It should be clear, after so much failure, that these experiments do not produce the radical and permanent transformation of personality that is essential if political action is ever to lead to beneficial results. The method of the mystics alone remains, but very few people are prepared to adopt it. In fact, the opportunities for mysticism grow steadily fewer. The technological progress to which we are committed makes war and nationalism inevitable, as we have seen, and when totalitarianism flourishes mysticism becomes correspondingly less practicable. "A world made safe for totalitarianism is a world, in all probability, made very unsafe for mysticism and theocentric religion." Huxley believes that greater technological and administrative efficiency at the command of the modern totalitarian state and its greater power of coercion make the salvation of the individual correspondingly more difficult. Logically this would seem to be the case. Yet it would also seem that the greater efficiency of police methods, compared with those of the past, should make crime correspondingly more unattractive and less likely to succeed. Yet crime flourishes today, and possibly on a bigger scale than at any time in the past. Can something be deduced from this analogy? It is not complete, because criminals use the same methods and technical apparatus as are pitted against them. Individuals cannot do that, least of all when seeking spiritual redemption. But it does suggest that new methods do not always lead to the results originally forecast. In fact, this is Huxley's own point, the major part of his case against Utopianism. It might also be asserted that the future of the individual is therefore less gloomy than present trends suggest—but this could only be stated as a blind faith, for no one could delineate the ways by which totalitarian aims could be negated. But instead of smothering mysticism they might provide the necessary challenge.

The application of mystical discipline to our problems is not a mere repetition of the familiar and discouraging " entry of the Church " into political affairs. This always fails. When ecclesiastics try, with the best intentions, to raise the moral level of politics they are always dragged down to the level of ordinary politicians. The institutional God becomes the God of Battles, the God of Battles becomes the God of Brothels. Reforming Protestantism becomes the sponsor of capitalist exploitation. Francis of Assisi upheld a Mystical Body that was also a political machine and a business concern. Mankind cannot be saved by his institutions. Organised religion only intensified the existing tangle when it offered its services. The true innovation would be, not the activity of another organisation under a different name, but the transformation at the root of all organisations, the solitary person.

Sebastian Barnack, grown older and wiser, tried to sum up the real needs of the political and social situation. We are all aware of the evil inherent in the lust for power, but few of us understand that there are as many evils in our headlong technological advance, despite the evidence. We believe we can be overweening with impunity, and we are punished for it. We console ourselves with the dream of a Utopia made possible by our inventions, and sacrifice present happiness at the altar of an uncertain future. And yet, with sublime inconsistency, we waste the resources which the future must have if it is to realise its Utopia, for the sake of present satisfaction. Instead of working with Nature we abuse her, and believe we can get away with it. We have made an intellectual progress from the Garden of Eden to Utopia, and have exchanged the divine right of kings for universal conscription. One can read the popular press in vain, one will rarely find any awareness of these obvious follies.

In *The Perennial Philosophy* Huxley remarked that the political monism so fashionable today makes it almost impossible for those who accept it to realise their unity with the Divine Ground and with one another. Unity on the inferior level of the State involves disunity on the higher levels. Collaboration with the State offers so many lesser privileges we fail to ask ourselves what we lose by accepting them. The great temptation of modern times is that of idolatrous worship: " lead us not into temptation " should be the guiding principle of our social organisation. The " intelligent interest in politics " that is expected of us is the bane of our lives. It is a rubbing of our noses in the dirt until they come to enjoy the smell. St. John of the Cross would have called it indulgence in idle curiosity and the cultivation of disquietude for disquietude's sake.

The question arises (and St. François de Sales was called upon to answer it), can a man in high office practise the virtue of obedience? This is a crucial question, for if the answer is in the negative our society is doomed. De Sales replied that men in high office have " greater and more excellent ways of doing so (practising obedience) than their inferiors ". Huxley adds that the " great man " can be good if he denies himself the personal advantages of power and does not attempt to assume spiritual authority. But if this is not done there is nothing that can forestall what he calls a " somatotonic revolution " (after Sheldon). This is already well advanced. Action, not contemplation, is regarded as the end. Happiness is sought in the external environment, not in the individual's state of mind. Self-expression has replaced restraint. Popular philosophy stresses the rightness of indiscriminate satisfaction of physical appetite. Toughness is valued beyond any other moral quality.

These trends will continue and intensify until we substitute " Goodness politics " for power politics, Huxley wrote in *Grey Eminence*. There is only one method of transforming personality that is known to be effective. The reign of violence will never come to an end until most human beings adopt this method and the Perennial Philosophy is recognised as the highest factor common to all the world religions. The idolatrous time-philosophies must be renounced and the political pseudo-religions must be rejected. " If these conditions are not fulfilled, no amount of political planning, no economic blue-prints however ingeniously drawn, can prevent the recrudescence of war and revolution " (*The Perennial Philosophy*).

## F.  Food and Decentralisation

The ordinary man will not feel that the adoption of a more contemplative attitude is very helpful, nor will he know how to set about it. In *Science, Liberty and Peace* (1950) Huxley set out some more concrete and practical proposals. These proposals have a striking resemblance to those put forward by that wicked old atheist Bertrand Russell, except that there are occasions when the latter would apply force. Working from the premisses laid down in *The Perennial Philosophy* Huxley urged readers to exercise self-denial. So long as newspapers and radio put out their propaganda, there is no alternative. Reading and listening to them are psychological addictions, and only voluntary effort can end them. Scientists have contributed directly and indirectly to the centralisation of power in the hands of the few by supplying more effective instruments of coercion and persuasion and by creating a situation in which everyone seeks the assistance of the state.

The desire for security is stronger than that for liberty— ordinary people take less interest in power politics than in their next meal—and this helps increase the power of the controlling body. But unless there is a considerable measure of decentralisation, liberty will be lost for ever. Enquiries have shown that mass-production and mass-distribution are justified in about one-third of the total production of goods. In regard to the remaining two-thirds local production by individuals or cooperating groups would not only be more economical but more humanly satisfying. We have a lot of leeway to make up. Administration has copied scientific procedure and, by force and persuasion, has introduced social regimentation. This is held to be respectable because it is the method of science, whose prestige is enormous. Habit has by now led even the more thoughtful to accept it as right and proper and, most important of all, supremely efficient. Efficiency has become the end, men and women the means. The machine sets an unattainable standard. It is usually forgotten that this standard is subhuman. The kind of world this trend could lead to is described in Kurt Vonnegut Jr's *Player Piano*.

Huxley then points out that scientists, who are the key men in the modern situation, could refuse to serve the needs of war. He refers to a suggestion made by Dr. Gene Weltfish that all scientists and technicians should be required to take an oath, similar to the Hippocratic, pledging themselves to the good of humanity and opposition to the forces of destruction. But action more positive and effective will be required (Huxley will remember the fate of the Peace Pledge) if scientists are to exercise their influence to its fullest extent. Such action would be either primarily political, but manifesting itself in the field of science, or primarily scientific and manifesting in politics. The first alternative involves political control, in the interests of humanity, of the activities of scientists. The second requires a conscious and deliberate policy, on the part of scientists, designed to serve fundamental human needs and subjecting applied science to the service of man, instead of the opposite. Such a policy would have to be worked out in detail by an international organisation of scientific workers.

Huxley returned to the subject in *Themes and Variations* (1950). Men must realise that social, political and economic reforms could accomplish only two things: improvement in the conditions of organic life, and the removal of certain temptations. None of the improvements made possible by the application of science would benefit mankind if the third, or psychological, revolution was allowed to take place. This revolution, by which the State exercised absolute power over the minds of its subjects, had been the basis of the society described in *Brave New World*. He had put it five or six centuries away but now believed that Orwell's forecast of a much earlier realisation was correct. Resistance to this revolution must be fought on two levels, and it was this that led Huxley to adopt the term Double Crisis. There is an upper level of political and economic crisis and a lower level of demographic and ecological crisis. The first level gets all the headlines, but the two are so intimately connected that any upheaval on one is bound to affect the other.

Changes in social and economic organisation are not enough. All the superstructures of government and prestige, banking and trade, will be blown skyhigh if world population is not reduced and more food made available. Food is the major problem: the first question that prime ministers and presidents, generals and commissars, technicians and scientists, should ask themselves and each other, should be: How are all men, women and children to get enough to eat? Not only will military violence fail to solve this problem, it will actually exacerbate it. Added to the other problems touched upon, resistance to central authority and the restraint and direction of applied science, is this other, and even greater, human concern, the production of sufficient food. There is still room for the physical expansion of production — the Arctic can be opened up, but the potential good would be equalled by the temptation. While I am writing this international tension is growing in the Antarctic. Scientists may discover how to get more food from the sea, although the harvest of fish is diminishing. Huxley mentions, almost desperately, various possibilities of squeezing more out of a shrinking planet: processed sea-weed, plankton, enclosure of land-locked bays, more fish-ponds, fresh-water algae, conversion of sawdust and vegetable waste. But how long could these makeshifts keep pace with a population that grows so relentlessly?

Huxley is reduced to advising expedients that fall lamentably short of his ideal. Every man of goodwill welcomes an increase in international trade; it is supposed to unite the peoples of the world through mutual interest. Huxley sees that in fact the opposite often happens. At the present time the nations are not " fit ", he says, to have extensive commercial relations with each other. It would be better to reduce them to a minimum until such time as national passions have lost their intensity. A period of insulation and cooling might help the situation on one level, but it would unfortunately cause it to deteriorate on the other.

Technological problems should be given priority over political problems. The former, based upon observation and experiment, are capable of solution; the latter admit of no certainty. Man must become aware of his own danger. If he is his own termite, as Propter said, he is also his own Martian. He is invading the planet in hordes, and no other problem is of comparable importance—in fact, no other problem will have any reality if this invasion is not checked. At least three plans are required to prevent " this rake's progress towards human and planetary bankruptcy." The damage done to cultivated land must be repaired, destructive methods of farming and forestry must be rejected, and new sources of supply must be discovered. Unfortunately, at the present time the destinies of the world are in the hands of " self-made demoniacs—of men who are possessed by, and who manifest, the evil they have chosen to see in others " (*The Devils of Loudun*). They will not be able to cure themselves. It is up to the sane to drive them out and then to keep their own sanity by clinging to an awareness of unity with the Divine Ground and their fellow-men.

## Chapter 16

THE word Utopia has undergone a change in meaning. To Sir Thomas More and even to Wells it meant a world made perfect for men. To Huxley, the vast majority of all contemporary writers about the future, and to Bulwer Lytton back in the last century it serves as a warning of the world, very imperfect from the standpoint of man's higher nature, that will evolve if man does not change his ways.

There are hints all through Huxley's early work of a curiosity about the bed man was making for himself. The youthful author of *Leda* was impressed by the advancing mechanisation he saw all around him, and looked forward apprehensively to a world as uncomfortable and stony as a proposition in geometry. " Glorious unnature " will triumph. Man will laugh at this consummation, but his laughter will be uneasy, " like a flight of broken steps " (" Beauty ", *Leda*). What of the citizens of this perfect Rational State? Mr. Scogan tells us in *Crome Yellow*. There will be three main species: the Directing Intelligences, the Men of Faith, and the Herd. The Intelligences will govern through the Men of Faith, the madmen, not old-fashioned creatures of brute circumstance, but men who, believing their acts and feelings to be spontaneous, will nevertheless expend their passion on the propagation of a reasonable idea. They will have been conditioned, and will preach " with a generous mania the coldly reasonable projects of the Directors ". Generation will become impersonal. Scogan, who loathed nature, warmed to the idea of vast state incubators. In this new world (if it was the same one) Dick Greenow reserved a special place for women. Having suffered from their organising passion, which was given full scope during the first war, he proposed that they should act as society's bureaucrats, releasing men for creation and thought and educating the children.

Everyone seemed agreed on the role of the Herd. Francis Chelifer felt that the millennial state of the future would be millennial because for the first time slavery would be really scientific and efficient—and, he might have added, tolerable, for that was the great secret. The eugenist's job should be to produce a working man eight times as strong as the contemporary one, with only a sixteenth of his mental capacity. The inefficiency of early industry resulted in a demand for semi-educated machine-minders. But when the machines were perfected this error might be eliminated. Man had spent centuries climbing out of a tribal condition, in which he blindly obeyed a social code impressed on him since birth. Now the way was open to a new type of tribalism, world-wide and American, composed of innumerable individuals all thinking and acting in exactly the same way. In the ideal democratic state no "irrelevant Holy Ghost-possessed exception should trouble the flat serenity of the rule." Of course, nearly everyone would die of spleen. Only a few very intelligent people can bear the almost intolerable burden of leisure and prosperity. The majority will wither away or cut their throats, or perhaps return gleefully to barbarism and cut each other's throats, especially those of the intelligent. Huxley returned to this concern with the agony of boredom in his essay on Baudelaire in *Do What You Will*. Efficiency was the measure of all things. Both passion and the inhibition of passion interfere with efficiency. Therefore modern man seeks substitutes for feeling and hastens from distraction to distraction. Modern amusements killed, by the fierceness of their impact, large numbers of Melanesians. We will die more slowly as our boredom becomes an intolerable agony.

There is a growing conflict in our society between man as a human being and man in his role of citizen. We produce specialists whose dissatisfaction at not being allowed to be complete men makes them extremely bad citizens. They fit into neither world. One remembers Shearwater sweating his guts out and living for long periods on a purely automatic level in his praiseworthy effort to discover how much sweat he lost in a day's cycling. If man could really change his basic personality he would not suffer, but human faculties do not seem to have been improved or radically altered during the last few thousand years. At most they have been developed. Of course, a new biological invention might show the way to salvation! In " A Note on Eugenics " (*Proper Studies*) Huxley declared that the possibility of a change in individual human nature might be safely set aside. Even if such a thing could happen we could not imagine its results. This was before Bokanovsky's great biological discovery had been put into practice.

If man outlaws some of the elements of his constitution, they will take their revenge. Western society, with its mad ideals and lunatic philosophy, could not persist much longer in its current state. Either a violent conclusion or a radical transformation was at hand. Social degeneration, caused by the multiplication of inferior human types, would soon lead to the elimination of superior breeds. The submen were strong because they were being technically trained. When the birth-rate declines it is most rapid among the more accomplished and gifted members of the population. This fear has remained with Huxley, for in *Themes and Variations* he referred to Sir Cyril Burt's forecast that at the end of the present century there will be, in Great Britain, half as many children of scholarship ability as there are at present, and twice as many defectives. And even if the population of the future is to be recruited solely from the socially successful, which appears to be the only practicable alternative, another problem would arise. Such people would live in a chronic state of civil war, torn by rivalry and conflicting ambition, unwilling to perform the necessary menial tasks—as happened in the Cyprus Experiment described in *Brave New World*.

In *Do What You Will* Huxley forecast a nihilist revolution, the fruit of boredom and reduced intelligence. The more materially prosperous we become, the more likely it is to happen. No-one will believe in the betterment of humanity, or in anything else, and the only motivating force will be universal hate. " A society constructed by and for men can't work if all its components are emotionally submen ", Tilney said in " Chawdron " (*Brief Candles*). " When the majority of hearts have turned to hog-wash, something catastrophic must happen." Life will avenge itself—it was Lawrence's doctrine of a revolution which would smash money and the possessive spirit, rising up unbidden, the inevitable response to intolerable frustrations.

In *Music At Night* Huxley is obviously preparing for his excursion into the future. Continuous general progress was only possible on two conditions: " that the heritable qualities of the progressing population shall be improved (or at any rate changed in a specific direction) by deliberate breeding; and that the amount of population shall be reduced " (" Notes on Liberty "). He foresaw a Bolshevik-Fordian Earthly Paradise which would be acceptable to communist and capitalist alike. Leisure would be as highly organised as toil; the condition of entry into this society would be that men should be, not as little children, but as little machines. The ideal man would be the thoughtless consumer. The less self-sufficient a man is, the better consumer he will be of commodities and transport. Hence the need for organised waste. As an American contractor once said, " The man who builds a skyscraper to last for more than forty years is a traitor to the building trade "—and, by extension, to humanity.

It is amusing to read in *Do What You Will* of Huxley's distaste for speculation about the future. " My own feeling, whenever I see a book about the Future, is one of boredom and exasperation. What on earth is the point of troubling one's head with speculations about what men may, but almost certainly will not, be like in A.D. 20,000? . . . Let us think about the present, not the future. If we don't, there will soon be no future to think about " (" Spinoza's Worm "). Three years later *Brave New World* appeared. Perhaps he changed his mind about the " point ". Perhaps he felt that one kind of future might be ruled out if we *did* think about it sufficiently. Certainly this type of speculation was in the air. In fact, as P. G. Wodehouse wrote to W. Townend soon after the publication of *Brave New World,* " it's a ruddy epidemic".

## " Brave New World "

The society described in this novel had taken good care to guard against the dangers outlined in the previous section. The sacred principle of organisation was to be stability, and anything likely to sap stability was brought under control by conditioning or, whenever possible, by removal of the circumstances responsible.   (For instance, emotions were conditioned, poverty removed.)    " No civilisation without social stability," said the World Controller.    " No social stability without individual stability."    The planetary motto was " Community, Identity, Stability " and these qualities were insured, not by political means or moral sanctions, as had been ineffectually attempted by previous societies, but by a biological process which produced scores of identical twins : this was bokanovskification, consisting of a series of arrests in the development of the embryo, followed by budding.  It was rightly regarded as a major instrument of social stability, a distinct improvement on nature's casual methods.

Neo-Pavlovian Conditioning Rooms inculcated a hatred of nature and a love of field sports into the lower groups, who served as a ready-made proletariat, loving its enslavement. The economy of the state was based on continual consumption.  Games, for instance, which used to be played with a stick and a ball and had no appreciable effect on economy, now required elaborate apparatus.  " Ending is better than mending " became a popular proverb.  The ethics of this culture were taught by hypnopaedic methods, or sleep-teaching, " the greatest moralising and socialising force of all time". Every effort was made to stifle feeling, strong emotions were regarded with horror.  Thinking was equally tabu. Everyone was too busy enjoying himself to have time for thought, which in the past, allied with emotion, had led to discontent, rebelliousness and dissatisfaction. If by some unlucky chance distractions should pall or their continuity should be broken, there was always the happiness-drug, soma. They boasted that everyone was happy now; the link between individual happiness and social stability was emphasised. But individual happiness really consisted in the elimination of individuality, its swamping in the social body. Freedom was no longer desired, or even understood. In the past freedom had been regarded as a condition of happiness. Now it had been by-passed.

For some years Huxley had been considering the possibility of a drug being used which would give the illusion of well-being without unpleasant consequences. However agreeable to the individual it might be, it would also be of immense political utility, for good or for ill. In "Wanted, A New Pleasure" (*Music At Night*) he had said that such a drug, a more efficient and less harmful substitute for alcohol and cocaine, would actually solve our problems by making paradise accessible whenever required. After the publication of *Brave New World* he returned to this idea in *The Olive Tree*. Writing of the propaganda of the future, he said that the chemist might be brought in to assist the writer with the help of chloral and scopolamine. Under the influence of these drugs a person becomes highly suggestible, and even a permanent modification of habitual modes of thought and feeling might be effected. In Vedic mythology Indra had become one with the drug, and was the mediator between the human and the divine. Later Huxley carried out a personal test with mescalin, the American Indian peyotl, which induced a state of alienation from the self. The purpose and character of these various drugs were different, but in one thing they were alike—the power to modify human consciousness. The drug may be used as a short cut to the visionary world or as an instrument for creating a loving solidarity.

Self-denial, one of the old virtues, stood in the way of a successful industrial civilisation. It was replaced by self-indulgence up to the limits imposed by hygiene and economics. In this way, for the first time in history, the demands of industry and of personal happiness coincided. In the great re-casting of values that had taken place, happiness was given precedence over truth. The paradox was that science, which had made this civilisation possible, had to be carefully controlled and only applied to immediate problems. To allow science to be used as a weapon in a never-ending search for truth would be to pass the death-sentence on stability.

However scientific the basis of the civilisation, religion could not be set aside. As Huxley had remarked so often in his other writings, the religious impulse existed and could not be eliminated. And in any case, science was degenerating into pseudo-science, and had lost its former creative power. It had become a watchdog, a Defender of the Status Quo. Any new advance that might be made was purely local, the refinement of known processes. Complementary to science in its role as social refrigerator was the worship of Our Ford, whose spirit used to descend, accompanied by palpable footsteps, upon his devotees who had achieved consummation in a Solidarity Service. Unorthodoxy was the unforgivable crime. No brilliance could forgive it—in fact, the greater the talent the more dangerous the unorthodoxy it served. Murder killed the individual, which was nothing. Unorthodoxy threatened society itself. No-one was allowed to consider the purpose of existence—nor, of course, would any properly conditioned person think of doing so. Once there was a loss of faith in happiness as the Sovereign Good, society would be shaken to its foundations. There was no tragedy in the Brave New World because tragedy was the fruit of social instability. "People are happy," said the Controller. "They get what they want, and they never want what they can't get. They're well off; they're safe; they're never ill; they're not afraid of death; they're blissfully ignorant of passion and old age; they're plagued with no mothers or fathers; they've got no wives, or children, or lovers to feel strongly about; they're so conditioned that they practically can't help behaving as they ought to behave. And if anything should go wrong, there's soma."

This world, however brave and new, was not quite one hundred per cent. efficient. Sometimes there was an accident in conditioning and the resultant individual was not completely satisfied with his lot and, worse, upset others. There was also an Indian Reservation which had not been considered worth the expense of integrating into the grand scheme, and here lived the savages in all their traditional squalor and pre-scientific bestiality. One of them was brought to London as an exhibit. Instead of surrendering to the charm of civilisation, he revolted against it, retired into the country to live in remorse and self-punishment, and finally committed suicide. In a Foreword to a new edition, published in 1946, Huxley wrote that he regarded it as a fault that he had left the Savage only the two alternatives, between " an insane life in Utopia, or the life of a primitive in an Indian village." At the time of writing *Brave New World* he found the choice amusing— for the author in those days was a " Pyrrhonic aesthete." Today he believes that sanity is possible. This is a measure of his own development, for the objective situation in 1946 seemed even less encouraging than it had been in 1932. There is no mention in the novel of nuclear fission, which today is regarded as the greatest threat to man's future. But his concern was not with the advance of science but with its effect on human beings. Advances in biology, physiology and psychology seemed much more relevant for this purpose.

## " Ape and Essence "

While writing or just after writing *Brave New World* Huxley again announced, this time in *Texts and Pretexts,* that " personally, I must confess, I am more interested in what the world is now than in what it will be, or what it might be, if improbable conditions were fulfilled." In fact, he felt that prophecies about the future are mainly interesting for the light they throw on the age in which they are uttered. *Brave New World* expressed fear—it is nonsense to suppose that a cultured individual such as Huxley wrote of such a world in

the spirit of wish-fulfilment. " Our notions of the future ",
he wrote in " Crébillon the Younger " (*The Olive Tree*), "have
something of that significance which Freud attributes to our
dreams." It is true that the libido may be expressing its
desires but they are distinctly uncomfortable for the rational
ego. The conscious, volitional part of Huxley sets to work in
*Ends and Means* and produces " a kind of practical cookery
book of reform ". There are also warnings, but the chief
warning was the bad dream of *Brave New World*.

Interest in the future, at one time a dilettante recreation,
has developed into a faith. A majority of twentieth century
Europeans and Americans have no other faith. They *know*
that the Future will bring with it a world of undiluted satisfaction. The astonishing thing is that it will be a state they
themselves will never know. In this respect it has less obvious
attractions than the old Christian Paradise. The only tangible
possession, the Present, is willingly sacrified on behalf of this
unknowable Future. As Huxley writes in *The Perennial
Philosophy*, the modern ethic appears to be, " Die (and kill),
for tomorrow someone else will eat, drink and be merry". But
man's forecasts are rarely accurate in detail. The purpose of
*Ape and Essence* was to show that dying and killing would
probably not lead to Utopia but to a condition even more
loathesome than the Indian Reservation.

It would constitute a surrender to the ape in man. William
Tallis's film script gives glimpses of normal human occupations, but the actors are all apes, very self-satisfied apes —
bosomy young female baboons singing into microphones, stout
baboon housewives frying sausages, baboon babies dialling a
radio programme, middle-aged baboon financiers reading the
stock-market news. This is by way of prologue. Then we
are shown the re-discovery of America in February 2108, an
America blasted by atomic war. We always get what we ask
for. There are many ways of destroying civilisation and at this
moment we are experimenting with all of them. We can do
it by explosion, by radio-active gases, bacteria and viruses,
diseases of food plants, cutting off the water supply and the

" psychological treatment ". By 2108 all these methods have been used. In *An Encyclopaedia of Pacifism* Huxley had described the likely panic results of aerial bombardment. These had not occurred in the Second World War, but there was still time.

Fear ultimately cast out humanity. Fear had become the very basis and foundation of modern life: fear of technology, of science, of our fatal institutions, of our Great Men, of the War we don't want to plan unceasingly. And then there was truth without charity. Knowing the menace of this, the World Controller in *Brave New World* had chosen to abandon the search for truth. But we have done the opposite, we have made an idol of truth, and truth without the wise guidance of love is Moloch.

And so we find the post-Bomb world digging for its clothes and feeding its fires with the contents of public libraries, yet utterly unregenerate. When they capture Dr. Poole the botanist, he explains that he is an expert on plants. " War plants?" asks the Chief, hopefully. They fashion recorders and flutes from shinbones and play the old sex-charged song hits of an earlier day. Sexual patterns have changed but tastes are still rooted in lusts and self-indulgences. Literary education has become wonderfully simple. Everyone is taught to read one word, NO, the prohibition which must be imposed because it is by now obvious that men are incapable of restraint, even in their own interests.

The big NO is on sex. One on each breast, one on each buttock, one covering the pudenda. " Morality'd be very queer ", Philip Quarles had said in *Point Counter Point,* " if we loved seasonally, not all the year round. Moral and immoral would change from one month to another. Primitive societies are apt to be more seasonal than cultivated ones." Morality *had* become very queer, and society had become very primitive. The gamma rays had changed the sex-pattern, sex had become seasonal, females enjoyed a short rutting season of five weeks. But, because sex was wicked, the allowable period of intercourse had been reduced to a fortnight only, during which time it was indulged in intensively and with full ecclesiastical rites. Woman, the temptress, the producer of monsters (for large numbers of children were deformed as a result of chromosome mutation), was the vessel of the Unholy Spirit. She was the enemy of the race, calling down punishment on all those who succumbed to Belial in her. The priesthood was delivered from temptation by a simple operation. It was clear that Belial had used woman as His major instrument in the moral destruction of the race. The tenets of the new faith were expressed in the Shorter Catechism: the chief end of man was the propitiation of Belial, Belial had elected all now living to everlasting perdition, Belial had corrupted man in all parts of his being, and man's duty towards his neighbour was to do his best to prevent others doing to him what he would like to do to them.

It was not only atomic war but also atomic industry that had helped produce the catastrophe. The very substance of the species had been disintegrated. The characteristic product of progressive technology was a hare-lipped Mongolian idiot. Is there any wonder that the Arch-Vicar of Belial regarded his faith as an entirely rational one? Man had set himself against Nature, the Ego against the Order of Things. Man had done everything he could to destroy himself. What used to be called " self-interest " was disregarded. At whose inspiration was this done? Obviously, the Devil's. Even the Christian Church had dimly realised what was happening. From the second century onwards no orthodox Christian had believed that a man could be possessed by God but he was only too willing to believe that he could be possessed by the Devil. Diabolic possession was not a poetic concept but a fact. Man's bumptiousness had caused his downfall. At the very moment when he upset the balance of Nature he congratulated himself on conquering her ! His much vaunted Progress gave him the instruments with which he could destroy himself; his theory of Nationalism, which amounted to the worship of gods with the mentality of juvenile delinquents, was surely an undeniable proof of Belial's existence. Belial had in fact produced this new society by purely natural means, using human beings and their science, without recourse to anything miraculous or supernatural. Belial knew that machinery would subordinate flesh to iron, that mind would become the slave of wheels. He knew that feeding meant breeding, that science could grow more food and that more food would lead to over-population, that men would erode their soil and waste their minerals. He knew that men would prefer dabbling in power politics to ensuring a sufficient supply of food. He knew, above all, that nothing bored man more than an understanding of his own predicament. And when Dr. Poole, reading his report on Soil Erosion and Plant Pathology in Southern California, tried to tell the Chief how man's thoughtless exploitation of his environment was certain to lead to the ruin of his civilisation and even the extinction of his species, the Chief cut in angrily, " Couldn't you make it a bit snappier?"

## The Prospect Before Us

It seems probable that Huxley regards *Brave New World* as the more important of his two visions of the future. There is a tinge of bad temper about *Ape and Essence,* the exaspera-tion of a schoolmaster whose pupils will not attend. It was written in a mood of pessimism that may have been transient, whereas *Brave New World* has the marks of a much more considered point of view. In *Themes and Variations* (1950) it is to the earlier book that he refers when he considers the third revolution. Although the human race deserves *Ape and Essence,* is even planning it, a degree of caution and common-sense may frustrate it. In which case the earlier forecast will be realised, only much more quickly than seemed probable in 1932. Huxley concluded that Orwell's date of 1984 was more realistic.

We may therefore take as his last words on the subject the opinions expressed in the 1946 edition of *Brave New World,* though *Ape and Essence* was yet to appear. In the Foreword he foresaw an intensified degree of totalitarianism throughout the world, whatever names might be applied to the actual political systems. Taking the hint from Hiroshima as our seventeenth century forefathers did from Magdeburg, we may expect a future of limited and only partially ruinous warfare. Humanity will be made to fit a new social system based on the use of atomic energy. The only thing that could arrest the trend towards greater centralisation and government control is a large-scale popular movement based on self-help, and there are no signs of it. The " problem of happiness " will come increasingly before our notice. Permanent security is now possible—the problem will be to make people love their servitude. This will be done through an improved technique of suggestion—infant conditioning and the use of drugs—and an advance in the science of human differences, enabling managers to assign individuals to their place in the hierarchy without undue bruising; a more efficient substitute for alcohol and heroin, and a foolproof system of eugenics.

Sanity is possible but not likely. Huxley has been told he is a sad symptom of the failure of the intellectual class in time of crisis. His reply is, Look around and see the "hilarious symptoms of success ". Today he would offer the Savage a third alternative, in which economics would be decentralist and Henry-Georgian, politics Kropotkinesque and cooperative, science and technology would be used in the service of man and religion would be the conscious and intelligent pursuit of man's Final End. Philosophically the Greatest Happiness principle would be secondary to the Final End principle. But the chances of the Savage choosing this alternative is very remote. The academic " realists " base their realism on a denial of the facts (which is, incidentally, a definition of insanity). This is just a part of Belial's huge joke, expressed in a wonderful syllogism: pessimism is a betrayal of the race; looking at the contemporary situation steadily and whole inculcates pessimism; therefore facing up to facts is a betrayal. Huxley stands convicted, and the rest of us can go our ways, comfortable in blinkers, and secure in the good books of our Borstal gods.